HEMINGWAY
GOES TO WAR

'I think there is a steady renewal of immortality through storms, attacks, landings on beaches where landing is opposed, flying when there are problems and many other things which are all awful and horrible and hateful to those who are not suited to them. . . . These things make a catharsis, which is not a pathological thing, nor seeking after thrills but it is an ennobling thing to those who are suited to them and have the luck so that they survive them.'

Ernest Hemingway

HEMINGWAY GOES TO WAR

CHARLES WHITING

SUTTON PUBLISHING

First published in the United Kingdom as *Papa Goes to War* by
The Crowood Press in 1990.

First published in this edition in 1999 by
Sutton Publishing Limited · Phoenix Mill
Thrupp · Stroud · Gloucestershire · GL5 2BU

British Library Cataloguing in Publication Data

ISBN 0 7509 2250 8

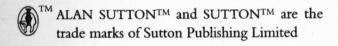
Typeset in 11.5/14 pt Bembo Mono.
Typesetting and origination by
Sutton Publishing Limited.
Printed in Great Britain by
The Guernsey Press Company
Guernsey, Channel Islands.

CONTENTS

ACKNOWLEDGEMENTS

How good it is to have pals and acquaintances who are both intelligent and helpful! I certainly made good use of mine in the preparation of this book. Without them, it would have been hardly possible. In particular, I should like to thank the following:

New York: Hy Schorr, Tom Dickinson, Iz Goldstein and Professor and Mrs L. Morris.
Paris: Eric Taylor and Sheila Furgener.
Luxembourg: Jean Milmeister and the Attwells.
Aachen: Wolfgang Trees.
London: Mr Cyril Ray, Mike Tollhurst, my son Julian and Martine de Geus of the 'Dorch'.

Charles Whiting
Bleialf, Germany/York, England, January 1999

INTRODUCTION

I thought he was silly with this machismo thing. I can remember saying to him that if I had his talent and lovely home in Cuba, what the hell would I be doing in this mud? . . . You see, he was playing soldier. The general was very concerned because Hemingway wanted to go out on infantry patrol and this meant other soldiers had to be told to guard him and risk themselves to protect him. The general couldn't tolerate an injury coming to Hemingway.

(Major Maskin, Divisional Psychiatrist of the 4th Infantry Division)

It is said that writers of the imagination feed off the experiences they have before they reach their majority. After that, their experiences, with certain exceptions, are never again as intense, searing, significant. For most writers, there is only *one* great love affair, *one* great traumatic experience, *one* earth-moving event like a war, and these experiences usually take place when the writer is in his late teens. Thereafter, they provide the material, the inner subsistence, the motivation for all which will be written in the long years to come.

Ernest Hemingway, the greatest fiction writer of his time in the United States, was an exception. At the age of 44, at a moment of great crisis in his personal and professional life (his third marriage was breaking up and he hadn't produced a book for nearly half a decade), he had a second chance. In the spring of 1944, he was allowed to go to war again; and war was his special subject, one that always got his creative juices flowing.

This second chance would offer him a new love, and a whole range of dramatic experiences spread over five countries at the height of the most terrible war mankind has ever known. It was a unique opportunity, one granted to none of his other fellow creative writers.

Surprisingly enough, for him, he went reluctantly at first. He told his third wife, Martha Gellhorn Hemingway, who, in essence, shamed him into going to Europe, that she'd get him killed there. Well, he wasn't and soon he'd be writing to one of his three sons, 'I have never been happier nor had a more useful life ever'.

Hemingway went to Europe officially as a war correspondent. In fact, in his own mind, he saw himself as more of a participant, who wrote out some of his 'combat' experiences for the benefit of his employers, *Collier's* magazine.

According to his own account and the 'legend', he flew with the RAF on ops. He landed on the beaches under fire on D-Day. He did two spells in the line with an infantry regiment in Germany after helping to liberate Paris at the head of his 'Irregulars'. And finally, before he returned to the States, he went 'on patrols' with his brother in Luxembourg at the height of the Battle of the Bulge. At various times Hemingway was seen carrying a tommy gun, hand grenades and a forty-five pistol. Once he took a 'very snotty SS Kraut' prisoner. The German was impertinent. He told Hemingway that it was against the Geneva Convention to threaten to kill prisoners if they did not reveal information. As Hemingway wrote to his publisher Charles Scribner: 'What a mistake you made, brother, I told him, and shot three times in the belly fast and then, when he went down on his knees, shot him on the topside so his brains came out of his mouth or I guess it was his nose.' All in all, according to his mood and degree of sobriety, the author killed between 21 and 122 'Krauts'. . . .

Hemingway would have 'a good war': short, exciting spells at the front, followed by long stays in luxury hotels to the rear. It would be an experience he would savour almost to the end of his life, sixteen years later. He would remain in touch with the comrades he made then, from general to private, for years afterwards. He would even join a post-war divisional association and weep openly when he was handed the regimental history of the regiment with which he had 'served'. For the rest of his life he would speak in the tough argot of the frontline soldier, replete with four-letter words.

During the war Hemingway had planned to write a great post-war trilogy. It would be based on his 'combat' experiences at sea, on land and in the air. Nothing came of it. All we know of his wartime adventures from the author personally is based on the six thin despatches he cabled *Collier's*, his letters, and parts of his poor novel, *Across the River and Into the Trees* (1950).

But around that limited information, a tremendous legend has grown in the intervening years. Hemingway striding into the Ritz Hotel in Paris, at the head of his ragged young Irregulars, and liberating the bar with a demand for 'about seventy-two martinis'. . . . Hemingway helping the infantry attack on the bunkers of the Siegfried Lane, out on a limb in 'Schloss Hemingstein', hand grenades on the table in front of him, waiting for the Krauts to attack. . . . Hemingway up there with his 'favourite division' in the 'Death Factory' of the Huertgen Forest, watching the Kraut dog feeding off the half-roasted dead Kraut.

What a bold macho legend it all makes! Hemingway on the beach of 'Bloody Omaha' on the morning of D-Day, 6 June 1944. 'Listen to me,' he yells, 'they've got us zeroed in with those mortars. They'll get us in another minute or two. We've got to get out of here. See that hill. . . . They've got a couple of machine guns planted at the corner of that hill. *Don't* run that way. Keep straight ahead. Now get out of here. Keep down low

– *and don't stop running!*' That was good old 'Papa' Hemingway for you. He always kept a cool head in action and knew exactly how to get out of a jam. . . .

In the early nineteenth century, when Johann von Goethe wrote his own reminiscences, he called them *Dichtung und Wahrheit*. The title can be variously translated as *Poetry and Truth* or *Invention and Truth*. The wise old German knew that creative writers observed little distinction between real life and the fantasy of their fictional worlds; they just kept 'inventing and re-inventing' their own lives. For Hemingway, there had always been a compulsion to turn his own life into fiction ever since he had become famous early in his career. Perhaps it had something to do with the fact that writing had never been considered manly in America. It was better to be a bruiser and a brawler, an all-action man, than a Caspar Milquetoast of a writer. After all, five out of the eight American authors who have won the Nobel Prize for Literature have been alcoholics! Hemingway, during his ten months in Europe in the Second World War, continued to foster the 'Legend'. As one of his close companions of that time has said of him, 'He [Hemingway] lost track of what was fantasy and was real. I think at the time he probably believed these stories.'

But what did he really do in Europe between May 1944 and March 1945? What is the *Dichtung* and what is the *Wahrheit*? That is what *Hemingway Goes To War* is about. . . .

Book One

ENGLAND, SPRING 1944

'I'm sorry to be so dull, but I am bad at generalisation. I think any writer – especially a war correspondent – is dull in conversation. It's only the phonies who are personally colourful.'

Ernest Hemingway to British reporters, May 1944

'He was a genius. . . . It is sad that the man's hand-made falsehoods – worthless junk demeaning to the writer's reputation – survive him.'

Martha Gellhorn Hemingway on her husband, 1981

DEAR OLD LONDON TOWN

Just before midday on Wednesday 17 May 1944, a misty and overcast day, a rather brittle-looking ash-blonde in her mid-forties posed at the top of the steps of the *Clipper* which had brought her and her fellow passengers on the long, dangerous haul from New York to England. Below the cameraman tensed.

Prior to the war she had been the toast of the West End stage before going to America and becoming an equally great success on Broadway. Noel Coward adored her. It was said that if he had not been homosexual he would have married her. Olivier thought she was a 'blazing great star'. Yul Brunner, another actor with whom she later starred, had a somewhat shrewder assessment of her character. He said of her: 'She loved life, she loved people, she loved the theatre – *and she loved applause*!'

Now Gertrude Lawrence prepared to perform for the 'gentlemen of the press'. Back in 1939 when, like so many other British stars, she had not returned to her native country, she had been accused of having 'gone with the wind-up' – a pun on that celebrated movie of the year when the war broke out, *Gone With The Wind*. Now, after an absence of seven years, she was finally coming back to do her 'bit with ENSA'.

As befitted a star of the West End and Broadway, she made a suitably dramatic exit from the big four-engined plane, carrying what was left of two dozen fresh eggs. The picture of her holding eggs rather than a bouquet of red roses would have the desired effect on the British reading public.

She had brought them three thousand miles across the Atlantic for her beloved secretary Evie Williams, who had remained behind in England which had been starved of 'real eggs' for years. Here the wartime quip was that it was 'one egg, *per* person, *per* week, *Per-haps!*' Unfortunately during the trip across some of the eggs had been broken and stained her skirt, which had elicited bawdy comments about 'Gertie's' sex life from some of her fellow VIP passengers.

But despite the embarrassing stains on her skirt, Gertrude Lawrence came down the ladder in the style expected from a famous star. In one arm she held the attention-grabbing eggs and in the other the plane's other famous 'personality'. He would, she knew, draw the attention of the photographers from the London papers waiting to interview her.

He was a huge man, seemingly taller than he really was, with a barrel chest. His tanned face was mottled and marred here and there with unsightly blotches that were half-hidden by a greying beard. Hypochondriac and almost pathological liar that he was, he had told his fellow passengers that the patches were skin cancer due to over-exposure to the sun and that he wore the beard (which made him look much older) to hide them on his doctor's recommendation. The huge man was exactly Gertie's age, but the reporters thought he could have passed for her father as they both posed there, grinning inanely as the cameras clicked.

All the same, Gertrude Lawrence, all capped teeth and fluttering false eyelashes, avoided getting too close to the other personality. At the *Clipper*'s stopover in Shannon in neutral Ireland, he and a couple of the younger VIPs had indulged in a liquid breakfast of Irish whiskey. Now the huge man's breath smelled of drink, which was nothing new really. For he habitually went to bed with a bottle of champagne at his bedside table and took his first drink of spirits before breakfast.

As soon as the newspapermen were finished with her, Gertrude Lawrence said goodbye and hurried off to be re-united with her American husband, who was now serving with the US Navy in Bristol. He was just another of the million-and-a-half American servicemen currently waiting in Britain for the invasion soon to come.

The others, all naval officers in mufti (they all wore civilian clothes out of deference to neutral Ireland where they had landed that morning) now took our their 'short snorts'. These were one-dollar bills upon which the other passengers scribbled their signatures to certify the holder had crossed the dangerous Atlantic during wartime. The big man watched, amused. Then it was the British customs and parting, at least for a short while.

Before they went their various ways, however, the big civilian proposed to young Lieutenant van Dusen, who was the aide to the most senior officer present, Rear-Admiral Leland Lovette, that they should meet again once they all had settled in. He was going to stay at the Dorchester Hotel in 'dear old London town'. Perhaps the young naval officer would come along to the hotel, bringing with him his sack of buckwheat flour, with which he had just surprised the British customs officials? They had wondered why anyone would lug the stuff three thousand miles across the Atlantic; Britain wasn't *that* short of food!

They would have drinks, the civilian suggested, and then the Lieutenant (who was completely awed by the big man and had swallowed all the tall tales he had told him during the flight) could cook them all an American-style pancake breakfast with his precious buckwheat flour.

Hastily the officer, who was flattered, agreed. After all, the civilian was a really 'big name' back in the States. He promised he would do just that. He would, too. Rather less than a month later, they would indeed celebrate an American-style pancake breakfast in the civilian's room in the famous London hotel. But it would be a breakfast marred by tragedy and horror and totally unlike the one envisaged by these happy young men now saying their goodbyes.

But that was in the future. Now the huge man picked up his valpack, musette bag and, most important of all, two large flasks which had been filled to the top with potent cocktails when he had left New York, and set about finding his way to the Dorchester Hotel. Ernest Hemingway, the future Nobel Prize winner and perhaps the most famous American writer of his generation, had arrived in the land of his forefathers for the very first time. 'Papa' had come to the war at last!

For a man who had always seemed to glory in action, violence and war, both as a writer and a man, Ernest Hemingway's 'war service' (if that is what one could call it) had been strangely limited up to now.

In 1918 he had volunteered as a teenager to serve as an ambulance driver on the Italian front and had been wounded in action. Thereafter, he had reported from the war fronts in Turkey and Greece. Twenty years later he had gone to the front in Spain as a war correspondent during the Spanish Civil War and, if we are to believe his own accounts, he was constantly close to the scene of battle.

But by 1944, when America had been at war for three years, Hemingway's sole contribution to his country's war effort had consisted of what he called 'sub-hunting' off the coast of Cuba, where he had his home. (In contrast, Dashiel Hammett, the author of *The Thin Man* and *The Maltese Falcon*, had volunteered for the US Army as a private at the age of 48.) Most of Hemingway's Cuban friends, however, thought these sub-hunting expeditions in his boat *Pilar* were just an excuse to obtain rationed petrol so that he could go off drinking and fishing with his hangers-on and cronies.

Later he would often boast that between 1941 and early 1944, he was engaged in 'secret work for the Government'. But as one friend, Mayito Menocal, recalled years later: 'That was a stunt. . . . They didn't do a goddam thing – *nothing*! Just cruise around and have a good time. . . . . He built this up into a war act. We used to kid him about that.' But by late 1943, thanks to Ultra, the US Navy, with or without Hemingway's help, had elimated the German U-boat threat around Cuban waters. The writer's excuse for his unpatriotic inactivity had vanished. He needed another war.*

Not that Ernest Hemingway really needed to go to war. Despite his prowess with the boxing gloves and great physical strength – the night before he had left New York to come to England, during a drunken party with fellow writers John Steinbeck and John O'Hara, he had cracked and split a blackthorn walking stick across his skull for a fifty-dollar bet – he was a prematurely aged and sick 44-year-old. Grossly overweight, face blotched and patched with heavy drinking, he was afflicted with half a dozen diseases and sicknesses usually associated with chronic alcoholism.

Hemingway was a prodigious tippler. On one day in June 1940, for instance, he noted in his diary boastfully, but truthfully: 'Started out on absinthe, drank a bottle of good red wine with dinner, shifted to vodka in town before the *pelota* game and then battened it down with whiskys and soda until 3 a.m.' When he and his many cronies went out on their 'sub-hunting expeditions', he always took a bottle of chilled champagne to bed with him and had finished it before 'duty' called next morning. And in this same year of 1944, Colonel 'Buck' Lanham, who would become his friend and with whom he served at the front, would note of Hemingway, 'a massive drinker. Bottle at bedside . . . drank all day.'

---

* Whatever the doubtful value of his activities off Cuba, FBI Director Hoover thought: 'Hemingway is the last man in my estimation to be used in any such capacity', as memoed in 1942. 'His judgement is not of the best and if his sobriety is the same as it was some years ago, that is certainly questionable.'

The result was predictable. His blood pressure was very high, as was his cholesterol count. His liver was inflamed and he suffered some inflammation around the aorta. He probably had incipient diabetes, and for a man who prided himself on his vigour in bed, he was (as we shall see) suffering from a severe sexual disability. No wonder then, at 44, he was a confirmed hypochondriac, always detailing his various bleedings from penis and anus, daily marking up his blood pressure on the walls of his bathroom and routinely taking pills for all sorts of illnesses, real and imagined.

No, Ernest Hemingway certainly did not really need the stresses and strains, the hardships and dangers of war. But by early 1944, circumstances were forcing him to give up his drunken, idle existence in Cuba and make the attempt to come to Europe to see the war. His German U-boat excuse had collapsed. He had not produced a book since *For Whom the Bell Tolls*, although he claimed he had been writing for three years ever since he had finished that novel. But most importantly, his third wife, Martha Gellhorn Hemingway, was forcing his hand. . . .

Martha Gellhorn was unlike Hemingway's first two wives. She had refused to order her life to accommodate Hemingway's wishes, but had continued her career as a correspondent and short story writer. Ever since she had ceased being his mistress to become his wife, she had puzzled and angered him because she had consistently refused to 'tag along and like it', as his previous two wives, Hadley and Pauline, had done.

Now, in March 1944, after an absence of six months from Cuba, Martha flew home to inform him that he had to do something. She intended to go to England as a war correspondent for the US magazine *Collier's*; what was he going to do?

Two months before, Hemingway had written Martha that he had no special interest in going to Europe. Now under pressure from his wife, who got on his nerves almost constantly, he decided to do something. In the middle of one of their angry quarrels, he told her maliciously he would cover the coming invasion of Europe for *Collier's*!

It was a dirty trick on her. By press corps rules, magazines were allowed to have only one correspondent at the front. This meant that Hemingway, the noted writer on war, would receive the official accreditation to cover the coming fighting in France; she wouldn't.

Thus it was that, while Hemingway had flown across the Atlantic on this May Wednesday, three weeks before D-Day, Martha Gellhorn, who had forced his hand in the first place, was following him to England in a slow cargo boat, laden with dynamite!

It would be quite some while before she finally rejoined her husband at the Dorchester Hotel in 'dear old London town,' as Hemingway would insist on calling the British capital, although he had never been there before in his whole life. By then, Ernest Hemingway would have already decided who the fourth Mrs Hemingway was going to be.

On this fateful day in May 1944, when Hemingway took up his temporary residence in the capital, there were two great centres of US military influence in London. There was the one located around Piccadilly Circus, its famous Eros statue long boarded up and covered in sandbags. This was the place patronised by the American rank-and-file out to enjoy one last desperate fling before that bloody drama commenced on the other side of the English Channel.

Here were the 'good time' girls, talented amateurs and hard-boiled professional whores drawn from all over the country, attracted to the capital by the magic of American money. 'Piccadilly commandoes', the GIs called them, just as they named their sisters-in-arms prepared to sell their favours in the open air the 'Hyde Park Rangers'.

Despite the army-sounding titles, these ladies of the night were not military, simply *mercenary*, with a going rate of five pounds, about twice the weekly pay of the average unskilled British working man of that time. When the GIs began to bargain with the whores for their favours, the usual opening ploy with them was, 'Honey, I don't want to *buy* it . . . just *rent* it for a while!' It never worked.

Many years later one American infantry sergeant recalled that crazy night world around Piccadilly thus: 'There were girls everywhere. They walked along Shaftesbury Avenue past Rainbow Corner [where the US servicemen's canteen was located], pausing only when there was a policeman watching. Down at the Lyons' Corner House on Coventry Street, they came up to soldiers waiting in doorways and whispered the age-old question. At the Underground entrance they were the thickest and as the evening grew dark, they shone torches on their ankles as they walked and bumped into soldiers, murmuring, "Hello Yank . . . hello soldier . . . hello dearie!"'

This was the American part of London, claimed by those Americans who would soon fight, and perhaps die violently, in the great battle to come. . . . The other centre of American influence in the British capital belonged to the chairborne warrior and the civilian dressed in a fancy officer's uniform to which he was mostly not entitled. These Americans would rarely see any of the fighting to come. For these were the 'feather merchants', 'the canteen commandoes', as the frontline GI called them bitterly. Most of them would survive to a comfortable old age – and die in bed!

Novelist John Steinbeck, whose blackthorn walking stick Hemingway had broken over his balding skull on that last night in New York, had visited London as a war correspondent in 1943. He wrote of these chairborne warriors long afterwards: 'We [the correspondents] knew, for instance, that a certain very famous general officer constantly changed press agents because he felt he didn't get enough headlines. We knew the commander who broke a Signal Corps sergeant for photographing his wrong profile. . . . There were consistent sick leaves which were gigantic hangovers, spectacular liaisons between Army brass and WAACs [US female soldiers], medical discharges for stupidity, brutality, cowardice and even sex deviation.'

These Americans, who would fight the war from a desk, behind a movie camera and with a movie scriptwriter's yellow block, were grouped around Grosvenor Square, the centre of 'American-Occupied England'. The Square had been built in 1725 when one of its first residents had been Lord North, the King's minister who lost North America for Britain to the 'colonials'. What would that pompous, somewhat foolish gentleman have thought if he could have viewed the power of those former colonials on his very doorstep now?

This second sphere of American influence was centred on the United States Embassy at Number One, Grosvenor Square. Back in 1939 and 1940, the Ambassador to the Court of St James who had resided there had been Joseph Kennedy, the father of the future President of the United States, John Kennedy. He had been violently anti-British and was convinced that Britain would lose the war against Nazi Germany. Now he had been removed to be replaced by the pro-British Ambassador John Winant. (It would be an irony of fate that Ambassador Kennedy's eldest son, whom he was grooming to become the future President of the United States, would be killed this spring flying from England attempting to knock out V-I sites in France.)

Soon after America's entry into the war, Ambassador Winant was joined in the Square by the 'Special Observers', who lived at Numbers 19 and 20. In June 1942, the future Allied Supreme Commander set up his headquarters at that same 20 Grosvenor Square, and as the Americans began to stream into Britain, it became a matter of prestige for every outfit from the American Red Cross to the American OSS (the US espionage organisation which became the forerunner of the CIA) to establish a foothold in the neighbourhood.

Typically, General George Patton was the only senior American officer to turn down quarters in the area. After inspecting a flat offered him, he snapped to an aide that the bedroom, with its enormous mirror on the ceiling directly above the huge bed, was an 'Anglican bordello'! He wanted nothing to do with the place.

As for Eisenhower's headquarters in Grosvenor Square, it was 'so goddam high-level, you have to carry an oxygen tent to live up there!' So Patton abandoned London altogether to retreat to his rural Third Army Headquarters at Peover Hall, Cheshire, where he swiftly succeeded in making one of the local 'county' ladies his latest mistress. Sex was all right, it seemed, as long as it was carried out discreetly, well away from the prying eyes and wagging tongues of higher headquarters in London.

Patton's boss, Eisenhower, couldn't leave London. His first accommodation in a London hotel had not been up to his taste. The extravagant decor had proved too much for him (he described the bedroom as being 'done out like a whore's parlour'). So he had moved into one of the capital's greatest hotels, the Dorchester. There he established himself in Suites 104 and 105 on the first floor overlooking the bricked-up front door. (The sandbags which had protected the entrance at the beginning of the war had now long been replaced by bricks.)

It was the 'supreme accolade' (as the hotel management described it) to be bestowed on the hotel which had been built in 1931; and it was in this same place that 'Papa' Hemingway established his first 'command post' in Europe. . . .

Even after five years of war it was no hardship to live at the 'Dorch'. Admittedly there were ruins in the streets outside and the downstairs gymnasium cubicles and the ladies' Turkish baths had been turned into makeshift air-raid shelters. Food was short, too, in tightly-rationed Britain. But master chef Jean-Baptiste Virlogeux could still turn out menus with three entrées and four main courses, plus possibly *le biscuit glacé des Samaritaines, Les Frivolités* as a dessert. And there was always dancing (formal dress or uniform obligatory naturally) to the music of Maurice Winnick and the Dorchester Hotel Band afterwards.

The Dorch was crowded not only with the top brass such as Eisenhower and Lord Portal, the Chief of British Air Staff. It was also full of famous pre-war society hostesses such as Lady Cunard, Lady Sybil Colefax and Mrs Ronnie Greville, who all believed the rumour that the hotel was one of the safest in London and the place's shelters were bombproof. They weren't. In reality, they were only a couple of feet beneath Park Lane and slightly less secure than the average Anderson shelter most people had erected in their suburban gardens.

Ironically enough in these grand surroundings, with so many titled ladies present who would soon be falling over themselves in their attempts to invite the famous American author to tea, Hemingway's first visitor at the Dorch was an overweight, shambling ex-newspaperman in the uniform of a private, first class, of the US Army.

The soldier was Hemingway's kid brother Leicester, whom he had not seen for two years. Leicester, who was Hemingway's favourite sibling (when Leicester was a baby, Hemingway had changed his nappies), was invited into the palatial bar where Ernest offered him a whisky before saying in a quiet calm voice: 'Got something to show you. Promise not to tell anyone? *Anyone*, you understand?'

Intrigued, Leicester, whom Ernest nicknamed Baron, promised, whereupon his older brother took a photostat of a letter with a Department of State letterhead out of his pocket.

It was from Spruille Braden, the US Ambassador to Cuba, and stated that the bearer Ernest Hemingway had performed 'hazardous and valuable operations in the prosecution of the sea war against Nazi Germany that were of a highly confidential nature'.

Baron was duly impressed, for he had always hero-worshipped Ernest, and asked for further details.

Sotto voce, Ernest explained about the *Pilar* and how for the last two years he and a makeshift crew had been hunting 'Kraut subs' in the waters off Cuba. Once he had been so close to a German U-boat that 'we could hear them talking out by Cay Sal and both east and west of the city, down the coast. I found myself remembering plenty of Kraut and they used slang even, talking with each other. The one we located for certain was bombed by a plane the day after we were called in. The pilot said he was certain that he got it, but it didn't satisfy the *Pilar*'s crew.' Baron ate it all up, including the reason for Ernest's new beard. 'That's how I got this unprintable skin cancer crud. Too much sunburn on some places. Doctor advised skipping the shave for several weeks . . . so make cracks at your peril. Let's have another drink.'

They did, and Baron departed believing the first of the wartime myths that Hemingway would now weave about himself. Over the next ten months there would be many more. . . .

The next day Hemingway asked his brother to take him on a tour of the capital. Together they walked down the edge of Hyde Park, past the Palace, through the Mall and so on, with Hemingway stopping from time to time to admire the buildings. 'This is a rich country,' he concluded to Baron. 'Look at that, Baron. Even after the big bombing raids, these buildings stand up well. And the clubs and homes. Such quiet taste. The dough they have, they know enough not to show. I even like the stores.' With that he decided to walk round to Hardy's where he had been buying fishing tackle (by post) for years. That was about the last admiring statement Hemingway would make about his 'host country', as the American called Britain officially.

As soon as he had established himself at the Dorch, Hemingway started to make his contacts with those Americans who were centred on the Grosvenor Square area. Here he went for his briefings on the progress of the war, information on the whereabouts of his wife Martha, to meet drinking cronies and even for Army food at the 'Will Run' – the gigantic US officers' mess set up in the ballroom of the Grosvenor House Hotel, Park Lane, where 500 British civilians could serve up to 1,000 American officers in one sitting.

During the seven or so weeks Hemingway spent in wartime England, he had few contacts with British people other than with hotel servants, waiters, batmen and drivers and the like, and the few contacts he did make outside this group, he mostly disliked.

Within a week of his arriving in 'dear old London town,' Hemingway had seemingly attached himself to that group of American officers who called themselves cynically, 'the Johnnies-come-lately'. They were those who felt, with Patton, that Eisenhower was the 'best general the British have' and harboured a strong antipathy towards their British hosts and allies.

Ralph Ingersoll, former editor of the US publication *PM* and now a major on the staff in London, expressed the attitude of these Johnnies-come-lately, thus: 'The British always first tried being charming. If successful, they Anglicized [sic] the individual to a point where in any Anglo-American argument he would, at worst, be neutral and, at best (and more frequently) an active exponent of the British point of view.' As for outright anglophobes, well, according to Ingersoll, an anglophobe himself, they were got rid of by half a dozen ingenious methods.

Surprisingly enough, Hemingway had once been very proud of his almost pure British heritage. The Hemingways were of old New England stock which had come to the United States in the seventeenth century, while the Hadleys, his mother's family, were from Yorkshire – the grandmother was from

Doncaster and the grandfather (after whom the writer was named Ernest Hadley Hemingway) was from Sheffield. During his early years Hemingway had admired the 'stiff upper lip' Kiplingesque image, which is reflected in some of his early stories, and which was exemplified by one of his greatest friends, the Anglo-Irish British Army regular soldier Dorman-Smith, known from his appearance as 'Chink'.

But when fame came to him, Hemingway had started to go sour on the British. The British critics did not take too kindly to him. They thought his work was brash, brutal and violent. He took a dislike to his English publisher, the tall, elegant son of a Derbyshire blacksmith, Jonathan Cape. He felt that Cape, unlike his American publisher Charles Scribner, did not hold him in the highest regard and did not promote his books effectively enough (although his last one *For Whom the Bell Tolls* had already sold 100,000 copies in the UK, where printing paper was strictly rationed). He came to feel that the English were effete, snobbish and affected.

This growing anglophobia was not helped by the fact that in 1942 his friend Chink, whom he had first met in a military hospital back in 1918 in Milan when they had both been recuperating from their wounds, fell from grace. By then Chink was a General and Chief-of-Staff to General Auchinlek, desperately trying to save Egypt from Rommel's advancing panzers. But Churchill, who had come out to the Western Desert at this moment of supreme crisis, soon lost faith in both of them. He sacked both Auchinlek, 'the Auk' as he was known to the troops, and his Chief-of-Staff.

As a bitter Hemingway described the situation in a letter he wrote to his friend General Lanham after the war: 'He [Chink] was to have the 8th Army, but Churchill put in Monty (that prince among men). . . . They had Rommel beaten when he could not take Alexandria and they were just recuperating [sic] and getting ready to run him out on a cheap basis when in comes

Monty with his 14/1 of I won't move concept of war.' As a result Hemingway disliked Churchill and detested Montgomery – 'that prick Monty', as the latter would become known. Now he would always adopt that patronising attitude to the British Field Marshal taken by those US generals with whom he would associate; and this negative approach would be extended to the senior RAF officers he would soon meet, and those members of the British upper class that sought his company while he stayed in the capital. For there were many in London eager to patronise and lionise the author of *For Whom the Bell Tolls*.

The film of the book – *Ernest Hemingway's For Whom the Bell Tolls*, as it was billed in the British cinemas – was currently running in London, starring his friend Gary Cooper and Ingrid Bergman. As a result he would be invited by society hostesses. But, as he told Mary Welsh (one day to be his fourth wife), 'the upper-uppest-classes of London are the worst. Immoral!' To which Mary, who was not particularly moral herself, replied 'You poor innocent country boy!'

In the end, in his role as war correspondent, Hemingway would write only one article about Britain during his seven weeks' stay at one of the most crucial periods in the island's history. It would be about the RAF bombing attacks on the German V-I sites in Northern France. Otherwise he wrote nothing (and seemingly cared nothing) about the sufferings of the British people during the war.

During the Spanish Civil War he had been politically active in a naive sort of way, working hard for the Republican cause in both Spain and his own country. But during the Second World War he had drunk, idled away his time and played games on his boat in Cuba, seemingly unaware of the global conflict raging elsewhere. In Britain's case, he knew nothing of the 1940 blitzes, the Battle of Britain in that same year or the harsh standard of living forced on the nation by the German U-boat blockade of 1941–42. During those years his main concern was how he was going to pay his income tax, or so it seemed. Nor was he aware of the bitter road back to victory after years of the blackest defeats.

On their first date together, Mary Welsh, who did spend most of the war in embattled Britain, discovered that this newly accredited war correspondent of *Collier's* magazine was 'signally uninformed about the general organisation of the RAF [to which he was attached] and about the British and American bombing offensive against Europe. I filled in some gaps in his background knowledge and suggested some remedial reading.'

But Ernest Hemingway had no time for remedial reading. Nor was he in the mood for it. As he saw it, he 'had had no wife since September 1943'. Now he was travelling again and that always seemed to stimulate his sexual appetite, though at this particular moment there were certain embarrassing problems in that area. He wanted action, amusement and, of course, alcohol. That was very important.

He found these things in the artists and would-be artists and their hangers-on in uniform. It was the same sort of crowd that he had mixed with in the 1920s and '30s when Europe had still been at peace. These were American expatriates of artistic leanings, finding their pleasures within their own tight circle, separated from the 'natives' all about them by their money and their very Americanism. For however sophisticated they appeared to be, and however much they disliked the provincialism of the country they had left behind them, they remained essentially and unmistakably American.

Basically, during his sojourn in Europe in the last year of the Second World War, Hemingway remained the American expatriate he had always been in that continent, save that now he wore a uniform.

MISS MARY

That spring the high spot of the week for the handful of American *Time-Life* staffers, who worked in a rabbit warren of offices in Dean Street, was Friday lunch in a nearby Soho restaurant. The White Tower restaurant, formerly the Eiffel Tower, located at the corner of Soho's Percy and Charlotte Streets, might have seemed shabby and not very inviting in appearance, but the owner John Stais was all charm. He was eager to please these comparatively rich, lively Americans who worked for two of the world's greatest magazines, and he did know his way around the black market!

Since 1942, British restaurants had been limited to a five-shilling meal (or in the case of luxury establishments, such as the Savoy, seven shillings and sixpence), plus a cover charge of three shillings and sixpence. The meal, which was unrationed, could consist of one main course only. If you had fish, for example, you couldn't have meat, and vice versa. In 'free' wartime Britain, there were none of the luxurious meals still available in 'occupied' Paris or Brussels just across the Channel.

Still the restaurateurs flourished. Bills could still be doctored and with a bottle of very rough, imported *Rouge d'Algérie* selling at thirty shillings, which was now coming into Britain in great quantities ever since French North Africa had been liberated in November 1942, Soho's restaurant owners were making money. None more so than the obliging John Stais, who knew how to obtain non-rationed delicacies such as rabbit, duck and oysters. Stais was very wise, too, in that he didn't attempt to bar lowly GIs from the White Tower, which was patronised by civilian and service bigwigs, including Alexander Fleming, the discoverer of penicillin.

He knew the GIs who patronised his restaurant were personalities themselves, with plenty of money in their pockets which didn't come from their Army pay. These GI patrons were mostly from the American Office of War Information located in Wardour Street, in particular, from Major George Stevens' 'SPECOU', the Special Coverage Unit of the US Army Signal Corps.

Stevens, a Hollywood director who had started his career in tinsel town with Laurel and Hardy and who had made such movies as *Gunga Din* in the 1930s, now commanded a unit whose task it would be (on the specific orders of Supreme Commander General Eisenhower himself) to give high-quality motion picture coverage of the forthcoming D-Day campaign to free Europe from German occupation. These 'Hollywood Irregulars', as they called themselves jokingly, included among their ranks officers, such as veteran movie director Henry Hathaway or the newer, younger directors like William Wyler. But they also numbered private soldiers, who had been well known in Hollywood before the war.

There was Private Irwin Shaw, born in New York in 1913, who had written the famous anti-war play *Bury the Dead* in 1936, followed by the successful *Gentle People* the next year. There was Private William Saroyan, the playwright, who saluted only certain officers. When asked why, he answered puckishly, 'I salute the *looks* on their faces'. There was also 'Baron', Leicester Hemingway, now worried that his older brother was not able to pick up a woman, like they all had, because of his enormous beard. He need not have worried. . . .

Hostess to these Hollywood Irregulars and far higher ranking personalities at these long, drawn-out liquid Friday lunches at

the White House which signalled the end of the working week
for most of them, was a small American newspaper woman aged
thirty-six. She was Mary Welsh. She had a sharp, hard-looking
face, short curly honey-brown hair, heavy strong legs and a very
good bust. Ever since the age of twelve, when her mother had
tried to get her to wear a brassiere (and failed to do so) she had
been very proud of her breasts. She felt they were too good to
be confined by a bra. Let them jiggle. Men liked that kind of
thing, and Mary Welsh always liked to attract men.

By 1944 Mary Welsh had been in London off and on since
1936. In that year the young divorcee (she had married for the
first time at college, but the marriage had been a failure) had
accepted an invitation to try for a job on the staff of Lord
Beaverbrook's *Daily Express* in London.

The little Canadian tycoon, known as the 'Beaver' behind his
back, had told her he would give her 'tea and ten minutes' to sell
herself to him. That had been sufficient time for her to charm the
gnome-like newspaper magnate, who had a weakness for pretty
women. He had given her, according to her own account, 'a short
dry kiss' on the forehead to speed her on her way and she had the
job, over the protests of the *Daily Express*'s editor-in-chief.

This bold approach to her new boss was typical of Mary
Welsh. Malicious tongues maintained that she used her sexual
charms to obtain favours and information from high-ranking
officials and later, when the war commenced, from similarly
placed officers. Hemingway, in one of his rages, apparently
snorted at her: '*I* haven't fucked generals to get *my*
information!' Now, in this spring of 1944, she had been on the
London staff of *Time Magazine* (after transferring from the *Daily
Express*) for four years and was now remarried. Her second
husband was the Australian newspaper correspondent Noel
Monks, a broad-shouldered, ruddy-faced journalist, who
worked for the *Daily Mail*.

But Noel Monks was away in the Middle East reporting the war for his paper from there, and she was footloose and fancy-free in the sexually-charged London of that spring, where everyone she knew seemed to have a mistress or a lover.

She was also free to indulge herself in her old passion of collecting names and personalities in that leisurely part of London insulated by money from the stresses of war. Or, if the people she associated with didn't have money, then they had position which they could use to escape the everyday common lot of the hard-pressed, undernourished civilians. And there were the young airmen, run ragged and living off their nerves. Names were meat and drink to Mary Welsh.

On 5 April 1944, for example, Mary Welsh gave a small cocktail party to celebrate her thirty-sixth birthday. Her Soho black market contacts supplied her with Scotch at five to six pounds a bottle which was all to the good, for nearly sixty guests crowded into her small room at Number 32, Grosvenor Street. As was usual at her functions, there was a bevy of American generals present, carefully selecting only pretty girls for their attentions.

But there was a big catch there, too. No less a person than lantern-jawed, bespectacled General Omar Bradley, who would soon command three US armies in Europe, numbering millions of men. He was standing in front of her electric fire, chatting amiably with Private Saroyan of the Hollywood Irregulars, drink in hand. It would be another seven months before they met again in another capital, and on that day, General Bradley's world would be about to fall apart.

By that April, Mary Welsh was having an affair with another personality who had just arrived from the Middle East to play his role as caption-and-dialogue writer for the Hollywood Irregulars, Irwin Shaw. He had been romantically involved with Mary, who was five years older than he, almost from the start of his stay in London. But in later years he would seem to have less than fond memories of her.

In his post-war novel *The Young Lions*, Shaw portrayed her in the character of Louise McKimber who 'seemed to know every bigwig in the British Isles. She had a deft tricky way with men and was always being invited to weekends at famous country houses where garrulous military men of high rank seemed to spill a great many dangerous secrets to her.' His hero in the novel, Michael Whitacre, perhaps a portrait of Shaw himself, 'never could decide whether he loved Louise or was annoyed with her'.

Soon, in real life, Irwin Shaw would not have the time to make that particular decision, for Mary Welsh would leave him for a far greater personality – Ernest Hemingway.

One bright May day that spring, Mary Welsh decided to dress up in her 'glad rags' for a lunch with her lover Shaw. She had had one of her absent husband's pin-striped suits converted into a nifty, top-fashion outfit for herself, which she completed with dark glasses. The outfit impressed Private Shaw, who commented, 'fresh from Hollywood'. Together the two of them walked the mile from her office to the White Tower in the sunshine and were given a table on the second floor where half a dozen friends were already seated.

Mr Stais's restaurant was, surprisingly for England and the average American's love of steam heat, too hot for Mary. She removed her new jacket to reveal those splendid breasts, unfettered by any bra. Shaw showed his approval: 'God bless the machine that knit that sweater!' he commented happily.

Other friends displayed their admiration too. As they passed downstairs after lunch, they mumbled, 'nice sweater . . .', '. . . the warmth does bring *things* out, doesn't it . . .', '. . . Mary, I'd like to see *more* of you'. Flushed with pleasure at their comments, Mary Welsh ate her food and bathed in their admiration. And she knew, too, that there was another personality in that shabby dining room who had noted her presence and was slipping her admiring glances.

It was Ernest Hemingway, eating by himself and looking 'much too warm and uncomfortable' in his heavy woollen RAF uniform. Mary Welsh, of course, knew immediately who he was. After all, there had been three movies made of his books and his latest, *For Whom the Bell Tolls*, was currently a box-office success in the capital. Besides, she had already met the great man's wife Martha Gellhorn a few months before at a party, where 'Miss G. had devoted her entire attention to a couple of Polish pilots'. Already, it seemed, she was mentally setting her sights at Hemingway, although he was already married. But then, so was she.

Unlike Mary, Irwin Shaw knew Hemingway, not by reputation, but personally. They had met when Hemingway had just returned from Madrid during the Spanish Civil War and Shaw had just produced his *Bury the Dead*. Hemingway had quipped to the young Shaw, 'We *make* the dead and you *bury* them!' This, Hemingway believed, had put Shaw firmly in his place. Shaw was a mere scribbler; Hemingway was the doer, the warrior. Shaw had not liked the quip one bit.

Now, his meal finished, Hemingway lumbered across and Shaw introduced him to Mary. From Shaw's possessive manner it was clear to Hemingway that he was having an affair with the woman. That brought out his latent anti-semitism, the dislike of Jews which had been directed at people like Harold Loeb in Paris in the 1920s, who was fond of *goy* blondes. Ignoring Shaw, he asked Mary if she would have lunch with him at the White Tower one day in the near future, then he left.

This typical Hemingway muscling in annoyed Shaw. Hemingway was playing on his reputation and talking down to him. Besides he could sense Hemingway's anti-semitism. He had been brought up with it and he knew it permeated the whole US Army. Indeed, he would make the feeling one of the central themes of his novel, *The Young Lions*. Later he would take his revenge in that novel. He would portray Hemingway as a 'short, fat correspondent' from *Collier's*, with a 'very serious round face, mottled heavily with much drinking'.

Six years later, when the two of them met as civilians in New York's '21 Club', Hemingway flew off the handle. Shaw had had the temerity to write about Hemingway's own special subject, war. Besides, he hated Shaw for having slept with Mary. He felt that the younger writer had portrayed her as a whore and him as a drunken fool in his novel. He threatened to punch Shaw on the jaw and made a snide ironic reference to the latter's Jewish background by calling him a 'Brooklyn Tolstoy'.

But that was in the future. On this bright May day, Shaw said to Mary, 'Well, it's been nice knowing you.'

'You off somewhere?' asked a surprised Mary, who thought Hemingway's eyes were beautiful and felt that the writer had an 'air of solitude' about him. Shaw looked at her. 'A monopoly has just been born, you dummy,' he snorted in that tough New York way of his. 'The Soho answer to De Beers diamonds.'

'You're off your rocker!' Mary retorted.

But Irwin Shaw was not off his rocker, he was right. Ernest Hemingway had set his sights on this woman. She had the closely cropped hair that he always greatly admired in his females. But there was a catch. Not only was Hemingway still married to Martha Gellhorn, currently making her slow way to Britain in that cargo boat laden with dynamite, but he was also impotent!

Mary Welsh's second meeting with her new personality was not a success. John Stais of the White Tower decided, on account of the warmness of that May, to put tables outside his restaurant on the pavement in the continental fashion. There he placed his regular, Mary, and her new friend as a special favour. But the squat, black London taxis turning the corner into Charlotte Street made conversation difficult and the waiters inside only occasionally remembered their customers sitting outside.

However, Mary did find out that Hemingway was lyrical about his first encounters with the RAF, though he could understand little of their accents over the intercom or the strange slang they used, replete with incomprehensible words such as 'gen', 'wizard prang', 'gone for a Burton', and the like (although he would come to use the word 'gen' for information for the rest of his life).

He also told Mary that he had met her second husband Noel during the Spanish Civil War and felt that the Australian, a former champion swimmer, was a 'great guy' . . . 'classy'.

But Mary Welsh decided that their first date was a failure and hurried off 'to brighter encounters not expecting to see Mr H. again'. Yet once again she would be proved wrong.

Their next meeting took place in the presence of a future leader of the Labour Party. By now, Mary Welsh and her friend Connie Ernst had moved into the same hotel as Hemingway, but not for any romantic reasons. Mary had left her flat at 32 Grosvenor Street because German raiders had returned to London.

One week after her birthday party, 125 German bombers had attempted to attack the capital. Only thirty reached London and of those, fourteen were shot down. But Mary, whose nerve had gone during the original blitzes of 1940–41, decided that she and her friend, who also worked in the US Office of War Information in Wardour Street, would be safer in the Dorchester, which supposedly had a bomb-proof roof of lovely thick concrete. It hadn't, but Mary still felt better there.

One night before dinner, Mary found herself once again with Hemingway who told her rather sadly, that 'my mother never forgave me for *not* getting killed in the First World War, so that she could be a Gold Star Mother'. He meant that his mother would be able to replace the blue star in her window, indicating that her son was in the armed forces, to a gold one, meaning her son had been killed in action.

Mary Welsh, knowing nothing of Hemingway's life-long hatred of his mother, Grace Hadley Hemingway, did not comment. She thought the statement a 'sad joke', but she did feel the same kind of antagonism to his being a big writer that she would notice on strangers' faces in his presence in years to come.

Just before Mary left to meet her date, Hemingway said something about dropping in later but she said she had to go to bed early as she had a hard day's work ahead of her on the morrow. She got back early and found Connie lying on the big bed with her friend Michael Foot, then the editor of the *Evening Standard*. Bespectacled, pop-eyed (perhaps indicating a thyroid complaint), Foot was ultra left-wing. Talkative and argumentative, he still enjoyed the favour of that pillar of the Conservative Party and friend of Churchill, Lord Beaverbrook, that same Beaver who had given Mary her first job in the United Kingdom. The three of them were relaxing on the big bed, with the lights off and the blackout curtains undrawn in order to allow the warm night air in, when there was a knock on the door. It was Hemingway asking to come in. He was allowed to do so and immediately embarked on a long account of his childhood in Oak Park, Illinois, where he had been forced to dress up as a little girl, complete with ringlets, so that his hated mother could pretend that he and his sister Marcelline (whom he also hated) were twins.

What Mary Welsh and the future leader of the Labour Party made of this strange discourse in the May twilight, neither of them ever recorded. But Mary Welsh did record her reaction to the writer's next and even stranger comment.

Suddenly, and completely out of the blue, Hemingway said 'I don't know you, Mary, but I want to marry you. You are very alive. You're beautiful like a May fly . . . I want to marry you now and I hope to marry you sometime. Sometime you may want to marry me.'

After a moment, Mary Welsh overcame her surprise. 'Don't be silly,' she said, 'if you're not joking. We're both married and we don't even know each other.'

Hemingway was not put off. 'This war may keep us apart for a while,' he persisted, adding one of those military terms which were now entering his vocabulary. 'We must begin our Combined Operations.'

'You are very premature,' she said.

Hemingway stood up. 'Just please remember I want to marry you,' he said. 'Now and tomorrow and next month and next year,' and with that he went, leaving Mary Welsh exhausted.

That May, Hemingway was certainly no starry-eyed Lothario. He was 44 years of age, much married with a third wife and three children, two of them still at school. Yet here he was proposing marriage to a married woman, whom he had met a mere three times, using language which might have come straight from some Hollywood B-movie. *'Just please remember I want to marry you. Now and tomorrow and next month and next year. . . .'* What can be made of it?

By mid-1944, Ernest Hemingway seemed to have lost all contact with reality and the strange marriage proposal in front of two total strangers was symptomatic of this. The drink, the fame, the three years of lazing in the sun in Cuba, surrounded by admiring, even fawning cronies had taken their toll. From now onwards until the day he committed suicide sixteen years hence, Hemingway would live in a world of his own making, virtually totally divorced of reality.

In wartime London, the great majority of the capital's citizens had better and more urgent things to do than lionise a great American writer. In the past year, other well-known American writers such as John Steinbeck and John Marquand, whose novels had also been turned into popular Hollywood films, had passed through the city without raising a ripple of excitement in the local populace. However, there were still many who were eager to give Hemingway a party and particularly those associated with the Hollywood Irregulars (though this did not include Irwin Shaw) who wanted to celebrate the presence of the author of *For Whom the Bell Tolls* in London.

Robert Capa, the *Life* photographer who had known Hemingway in Spain, was first off the mark. In theory, the small volatile Hungarian Jew was in Britain illegally. He had come from an assignment in Africa to London without a visa. Moreover, although a Jew, he was technically an 'enemy alien' being a citizen of a country which was fighting the war on Germany's side, and should have been interned. But such considerations did not worry Capa and his girlfriend 'Pinkie', an Englishwoman whose real name was Elaine Parker, but whom Capa named Pinkie on account of her 'goldish-pink' hair, and the fact that she 'tasted of strawberries' when kissed.

In May 1944 the two of them were living together in a penthouse, two floors above the 'fascist Spanish Ambassador' to the Court of St James in Belgrave Square, while Capa waited for the Invasion. As he maintained all that spring, it was as impossible for a combat cameraman 'to miss an invasion as it would be for a guy just released after five years at Sing-Sing to pass up a date with Lana Turner!'

During the waiting period, Capa and Pinkie decided they'd throw a huge party for Papa Hemingway with the ten bottles of Scotch and eight bottles of gin Pinkie had stored away in a cupboard during the ten months Capa had been away in Africa. To that Capa added brandy and champagne at thirty dollars a bottle (about six pounds). Then he and Pinkie set to work making a punch. 'I bought a fish bowl, a case of champagne, some brandy and half a dozen fresh peaches. I soaked the peaches in the brandy, poured the champagne over them and everything was ready. The party could commence.'

As Capa noted after the war: 'The attraction of free booze, combined with Mr Hemingway, proved irresistible. Everyone was in London for the invasion and they all showed up at the party.'

It was a boozy party very much after Hemingway's heart. Hemingway kissed Pinkie and made her blush by telling her 'Miss Pinkie, my daughter, you are a treasure. You are the kind we seek. You are something beyond words.' To this Capa objected: 'Get your own girl.'

He chatted with Baron and was introduced to a colleague of Mary Welsh's, war correspondent Bill Walton, newly trained as a paratrooper, who was to jump on D-Day with General 'Slim Jim' Gavin's 82nd US Airborne Division, currently moving down from Leicester. They would meet again later under totally different circumstances when Hemingway would regale the young journalist with full details of his sexual prowess with Mary. Walton wouldn't be impressed. He knew that Mary Welsh's life had always been full of lovers.

Hemingway then sparred a little with his kid brother, inviting Baron to punch him in the stomach. This was followed by the same invitation to the rest to do the same, including Dr Peter Gorer, a 37-year-old biologist and geneticist, who was engaged on research at the Lister Institute. Somehow he had been invited to the wild party with his German-Jewish wife Gertrude whom he had married two years before. She was a refugee and spoke little English. She was also dying of tuberculosis and would be dead within a year.

Gorer took up the challenge and suffered a sore fist for his pains. Then the two of them fell to chatting, with the tall, hawk-nosed doctor listening as Hemingway did most of the talking. Again Hemingway brought out his precious photostat from Spruille Braden, thanking him for his 'anti-submarine operations', and told the doctor that during these operations he had contracted skin cancer due to over-exposure to the sun.

Dr Gorer, who, prior to the war had been investigating the genetics of individuality working with antigens in mice, found Hemingway's story highly dubious. But he was a diffident, withdrawn man, almost shy in company, and he said nothing.

So they talked and drank. Bottle after bottle disappeared. At four in the morning, the fish bowl was empty, and they were squeezing out the peaches. The guests slowly began to trickle away. Capa ate the last of the peaches. Hemingway decided that it was time for him to get back to the Dorch, but when Dr Gorer assured him he wouldn't get a taxi in London at that hour, he accepted the Doctor's offer of a lift home in his car.

Dr Gorer had been drinking since ten the previous evening, but he reasoned that the streets would be deserted and he'd make it. He did for half a mile. But the drink, the slight fog, the blacked-out streets illuminated only by the twin slits of light coming from the car's blacked-out headlights, told in the end. With a crash, the tinkling of broken glass, and rending of metal, Gorer rammed his car head-on into a static water tank placed in Lowndes Square by the National Fire Service to be used in an emergency. Help appeared from nowhere. All three of them, Hemingway, the Doctor and his wife, were escorted to St George's Hospital at Hyde Park Corner, where the American, the worst injured, was diagnosed as having a severe concussion, swollen knees, and a badly cut face. For two and a half hours, the doctors worked on Hemingway, urged on by Gorer who told them of the importance of their patient. He received fifty-seven stitches and was fixed up with a huge turban of a bandage for his injured head that did little to assuage the blinding headache that would now torture him for weeks to come.

It seemed that the injured correspondent, who was yet to make any attempt to write about the war he had come some five thousand miles to record, was out of the Invasion before it had even started. But his doctors, who had strictly forbidden him to touch alcohol, had not reckoned with Hemingway's remarkable powers of resilience. As accident-prone as he was throughout his life, he always seemed to manage to spring back, even when his doctors predicted the most dire of results from his injuries.

Now in the four days he was going to spend in the London Clinic recovering, he held open house for anyone who cared to visit him. A young British Para of the SAS was introduced. He asked Hemingway's advice on jumping into Occupied France. Hemingway, who had never jumped out of a plane in his life, replied heartily, maliciously parodying Rupert Brooke: 'Just keep your bowels open and remember – there's some corner of a foreign field that is forever England!'

Two other members of a secret organisation, Lieutenants North and Burke of the OSS, who had crossed the Atlantic with Hemingway, also turned up at hospital to visit the sick man, bringing with them a half-bottle of Scotch, only to find Hemingway was generously supplied with booze already. Indeed, the author took their half-bottle and gave them a full bottle in return.

Mary Welsh made an appearance, taking with her a bunch of tulips and daffodils, wrapped in newspaper (tissue paper had long vanished in rationed England). He told her that he would be back in the Dorch in a day or two and thanked her for the flowers.

'Flowers are good for everybody,' she said.

'You're good for me,' he answered.

One visitor to that big, bare, dusty room in which he lay was not so welcome and she certainly did not bring flowers, wrapped in newspaper or otherwise. She had just arrived in London from Liverpool, still boiling with anger and resentment at the long dangerous voyage in the dynamite ship which her husband had inflicted upon her. Now Hemingway's third wife, Martha Gellhorn, was in no mood to sympathise with her injured husband, as he lay there, with a profusion of bottles underneath the bed next to the white enamel chamberpot.

Indeed, instead of expressing compassion, she merely laughed at the huge turban of bandages adorning his head. As she later snorted: 'If he really had a concussion, he could hardly have been drinking with his pals or even receiving them! . . . He did not look ill anyway.'

Now Hemingway taunted her, stating that although he had been in England two weeks already, he hadn't yet had an American woman soldier (a WAC) 'shot out from under him'. It was a common enough statement made by American chairborne warriors that May, who would explain to anyone prepared to listen that a WAC was merely a 'double-breasted GI with a built-in fox hole!'

But Martha was in no mood for male chauvinism of that kind. She told Hemingway angrily that she had had plenty of time on the dynamite ship to think of his 'ceaseless, crazy bullying' of her in Cuba and his disgraceful 'play-acting' aboard his 'anti-submarine vessel', the *Pilar*. She announced that she was through with him. Thereupon she stalked out and cancelled the room next to his in the Dorchester. Instead, she took another room on a higher floor. Hemingway's third marriage was about over.

On the morning of 29 May he was discharged from the London Clinic, head still swathed in the bandage turban and his knees badly swollen. All the same, he could indulge in a little horseplay. He asked Lieutenants North and Burke to put on Navy field dress and wear their pistols to accompany him to Barclay's Bank where he had opened an account. This would impress the somewhat pompous manager. They didn't, but the pompous manager obliged with some money which they spent in a pub called Frisco's, run by an American black Hemingway had known in Paris back in the 1920s. Here he turned to the organisation of what he called 'Hemingstein's Bearded Junior Commandoes', drilling his 'troops' in a language which he identified for them as Turkish. (Here again is that 'Hemingstein', a supposedly Jewish variation of his name which revealed his latent anti-semitism.)

But the time for high jinks and silly boorish games was nearly over – D-Day was almost on the country. In their cages throughout Southern England there were 200,000 men – American, British, Canadian and half a dozen other nationalities – behind barbed wire, guarded by sentries from their own armies. These were the young men of the initial wave and waiting to follow them there was a further two million. Big notices attached to the barbed wire around their camps urged the local civilians: *Do not talk to the troops.* It was almost as if they were condemned men and the civilians were expected to have nothing to do with them.

For exactly four years Britain had been waiting, working, suffering and sometimes dying for this moment. Now the mood was sombre. Despite the fine weather, there was a feeling of emptiness, both spiritual and emotional. The wait had been too long, and those who were going to do the fighting very soon were gripped by a terrible feeling of uncertainty. 'Hemingstein's Bearded Junior Commandos' had no place in this real world of those young men who would soon fight – and perhaps die. The time for games was over.

On that Wednesday, when he had arrived in England with Gertrude Lawrence, Hemingway had told the waiting newspapermen that he didn't want to discuss the war. 'I'll leave that to Eisenhower,' he said. 'He knows, I don't. I'm sorry to be so dull, but I'm bad at generalisation. I think any writer – especially a war correspondent – is dull in conversation. It's only the phonies who are personally colourful.'

Now Hemingway was at last going to the war as 'a war correspondent' (of sorts). Would he turn out to be one of those colourful phonies?

HEMINGWAY'S LONGEST DAY

Early on the morning of Friday 2 June 1944, Hemingway, in company with several hundred correspondents accredited to SHAEF, received his call to arms. In London they were loaded into fleets of buses and commenced their long journey through the capital's dreary, bombed streets towards the south coast. The streets were still mostly empty, save for a few women, but then the menfolk had long vanished into khaki. No one took much notice of the buses. Why should they? Perhaps it was just another of those military convoys which had been passing this way for weeks now, heading for the cages.

After what seemed an interminable journey on hard wooden seats they reached their first halt. One correspondent moaned there was no need for identification discs. After sitting on the seat for what seemed hours, he had four broad stripes across his rump which would remain as a lasting identity disc!

Here each correspondent was given a sealed letter. In it there was the name of the ship (and there would be five thousand or more of them in the assault force) in which he would sail for France. Hemingway drew a veteran.

It was a fast-attack transport, the *Dorothea L. Dix*. Originally owned by the American Export Lines, it had been called the *SS Exemplar*, but after being commandeered by the US Navy in 1942, it was renamed after the feminist crusader Dorothea Lyne Dix, founder of about thirty-two asylums for the mentally ill in the United States before her death in 1887. Perhaps some of

Hemingway's many enemies might have felt (if they had known) that it was a highly suitable ship to transport the writer to war.

The *Dorothea L. Dix*, currently anchored in Portland, had already taken part in two assault landings. Back in November 1942 she had unloaded the troops of Patton's attack force off French Morocco, where the first American soldiers to die in combat in the West would be killed (ironically enough) at the hands of the French, their erstwhile allies. One year later, the *Dorothea L. Dix* had participated in the assault on Sicily, where she had come in for severe dive-bombing attacks by the *Luftwaffe*. Later the ship's gun crews had claimed seven 'kills'.

Thereafter, the ship had crossed the Atlantic a couple of times, ferrying troops and equipment back and forth before taking her anchorage in Portland. Here, under the command of Commander William Leahy, USN, an Irish-American, she had suffered a hit-and-run raid by German planes on 27 May. The fast Focke-Wulfes had come roaring in at 300 mph dropping bombs and mines in the harbour. But, though one crew member was injured by a bomb fragment, no damage was sustained by the ship. Now, on this Friday morning, Commander Leahy was preparing to receive troops of General Gerow's US V Corps, consisting in the assault wave of one regiment each from the 1st and 29th Divisions.

Both were formations consisting of somewhat reluctant heroes. The 1st US Division – 'the Big Red One', as it was called after its divisional patch – was America's premier invasion division. It had fired the first shots of the United States war in Europe in both world wars. But its men, who had taken a bad beating at the hands of Rommel in Africa at the Battle of the Kasserine Pass in early 1943 and then had seen thirty days of very hard fighting in Sicily in July of that year, were not particularly pleased to have been honoured with leading America into its invasion of France.

Major Frank Colacicco of the Big Red One felt that 'We'd done our war, we should go home. We kept reading in the papers about the huge increase in US strength.' Corporal Sam Fuller, later to be well known as a director of very violent films in Hollywood, who had already won the Bronze Star in Sicily and who would win the Silver Star on D-Day, also thought that 'the men [of the 1st Division] had had their fill of combat and they rightly assumed . . . that somebody else should carry the ball this time. . . . There would be no chance of walking off that beach. . . . Their luck would not stretch that far.'

The soldiers of the 29th Division's 116th Infantry Regiment, who would also take part in the initial assault, were less than sanguine too. The Division had been in England for two years, training. Indeed, they had been stationed in the United Kingdom so long that many of them felt they would never go overseas and maintained (in a pun on that popular song of the time *A Bluebird Over the White Cliffs of Dover*) that they would remain behind after the invading force had gone in, 'to wipe the bluebird shit off the white cliffs of Dover!' Now the joke had backfired and they certainly would not be staying behind to do a cleaning job on the cliffs.

On the night of Monday 5 June, Hemingway limped aboard the big grey-painted transport, which was already packed with these tense, nervous, reluctant heroes. He still had a severe headache and it was drizzling. All the same, he headed for the big bluff skipper, Commander William Leahy, and asked him a direct question. Was this simply a diversion to fool the Germans, while the main attack force landed elsewhere in France?

Commander Leahy, whose first assault crossing this would be (he had just taken over command of the *Dorothea L. Dix* on 10 March 1944), said this was not a diversion. They were really going ashore. This was the real thing!

Hemingway was pleased. He limped about the ship over the wet glistening decks, pushing his way through the infantry laden down with equipment like pack animals, each one of them with the chalked number of his landing serial stuck on the front of his helmet, inspecting various pieces of equipment, including the huge landing nets rigged midships down the sides of the *Dix*. He was worried about them. Would he be able to clamber down them in a choppy sea (and out in the Channel the waves were definitely high and stormy) with his accident-damaged knees? He need not have worried. Commander Leahy was not going to allow one of America's greatest contemporary writers to suffer a second accident while under his command. He had already made provisions.

By two o'clock on the morning of 6 June, after Eisenhower in nearby Portsmouth had agonised whether or not to postpone the whole operation due to the terrible weather in the Channel, the great armada was under way. The ships of 'Force O', which had sailed from Portland, Poole, and Weymouth, were destined to make landfall on four beaches stretching some five miles along the shore of Normandy. This was part of the Omaha (as it was code-worded) section of the coastline – 'Bloody Omaha' as it would soon go down in the annals of American military history – on the right flank of the British landing sites at Colleville-sur-Mer, and the left flank of the other US Force, 'Force U', heading for Utah beach.

Well before zero hour on that fateful Tuesday on which the future of Europe was going to be decided, Commander Leahy had his vessel in position on the eastern flank of Omaha, lying off the coast at Port-en-Bassin. Now Leahy sprang a surprise on Hemingway. When the order came to change ships, the author was tied into a bosun's chair instead of having to go down the nets and was swung across to another transport, the British ship, the *Empire Anvil* (the Royal Navy and Merchant Navy supplied seventy-five per cent of the Invasion shipping). Leahy had strict orders that nothing should happen to Hemingway. Above all, higher authorities had decreed that Hemingway should not land in France on D-Day!

'The day *we* took Fox Green beach was the sixth of June, and the wind was blowing hard out of the north-west. As we moved in toward land in the grey early light, the 36-foot coffin-shaped steel boats took solid green sheets of water that fell on the helmeted heads of the troops packed shoulder to shoulder in the stiff, awkward, uncomfortable, lonely companionship of men going to battle.' Thus wrote Ernest Hemingway in his article published in *Collier's* under the title 'Voyage to Victory' on 22 July 1944.

As the landing barge crested yet another wave, and the line of cruisers and the two battlewagons, raised from the bottom of Pearl Harbor after the 'day of infamy' on 7 December 1941, which had brought America into the war, slammed their shells into the German defences, the skipper of the little boat, crammed with troops, seemed to be in trouble. He was a 'handsome, hollow-cheeked boy with a lot of style and a sort of easy petulance'. Now this 'boy', otherwise Lieutenant (junior grade) Robert Anderson, USN, asked: 'Mr Hemingway, will you please see if you can see what that flag is over there, with your glasses?'

'Mister' Hemingway, the old campaigner who knew all the tricks of war, obliged. He removed his 'old miniature Zeiss glasses' out of the protective woollen sock (he wouldn't be fool enough to hang them around his neck dramatically and get them fouled up with sticky seawater) and focused them. 'It's green,' he announced after a moment.

There was a sigh of relief. 'Then we *are* in the mine-swept channel,' 'Andy' (otherwise Lieutenant Anderson), announced. Mister Hemingway had saved them from disaster. It wouldn't be the last time.

Now they started to come closer to the embattled shore, where already six waves of assault infantry had gone in before them to be slaughtered on that bloody beach. At that moment General Cota, plus half a dozen assorted full colonels, were acting like infantry-squad leaders in order to get their men moving.

Again Anderson was running into trouble. Hemingway, however, was a tower of strength. He had 'studied this map [of the beach] and memorised most of it, but it is one thing to have it in your memory and another thing to see it actually on paper and be able to check and be sure.' 'Have you got a small chart, Andy?' he shouted over the thunder and drumroll of the mighty barrage. 'Never had one,' the young Virginian roared back, as they were approaching the coast of France, which looked increasingly hostile. What was to be done? Again Hemingway stepped in. 'There's the church tower that looks like Colleville,' he roared.

And he was right, of course. This was Fox Green beach, their objective.

As they neared the beach, Hemingway was first to alert the officer: 'There's something wrong as hell. See the tanks? They're all along the edge of the beach. They haven't gone in at all.' There certainly was something wrong on Omaha beach, although Hemingway did not know what it was. The two assault regiments of the 1st and 29th American Infantry Divisions were well on their way to losing one-third of their number in killed and wounded that morning. As Major Frank Colacicco, who had felt before the Invasion that his 3rd Battalion of the Big Red One's 18th Regiment had done enough already, now saw as his landing craft approached Omaha that 'the beach was loaded with men, tanks and DUKW's. . . . It was like a theatre. We could see it all, we knew that something was knocking the tanks out, but we kept asking "Why don't they clear the beach? Why aren't our people getting off?".'

If the professional officers did not know what to do, Hemingway did. As German machine-gun fire was throwing water all around the boat and an anti-tank shell tossed up a jet of water over them, Hemingway gave the young naval officer his seasoned advice: 'Let's coast along,' he suggested, 'and find a good place to put them ashore. If we stay outside of the machine-gun fire, I don't think they'll shoot us with anything big because we're just an LCV(P), and they've got better targets than us.'

Andy accepted it and their landing craft burst away from the impending danger and moved alongside another vessel which had been holed by a German 88mm shell (how Hemingway would have known that it was an 88mm shell which had done the damage was anyone's guess). 'Blood was dripping from the shiny edges of the hole into the sea with each roll of the LCI. Her rails and hull had been befouled by seasick men and her dead were laid forward of her pilot-house.' For a while Andy conversed with one of the officers of the stalled craft and then Hemingway's craft pulled away. Apparently the other officer had told Andy that they had to wait.

Hemingway, the man of action, was not in favour of waiting. He told Andy: 'Let's get in where we can keep track of it. Take the glasses and look at that beach but don't tell them forward what you see.'

Their craft moved on, while a nearby Allied destroyer blasted the beach with its 5-inch guns. They passed a sinking landing craft full of wounded, which had been caught by a burst of German machine-gun fire. Now crawling forward at low speed, they began to cross *Rommels Spargel* ('Rommel's asparagus', as the German defenders called the underwater obstructions consisting of metal stakes with mines attached to them). Most of them they could not see, but the ones they could, 'we fended off by hand'.

Now, finally, they reached that deadly, hotly contested beach. 'As we lowered the ramp . . . I saw three tanks coming along the beach, barely moving, they were advancing so slowly. The Germans let them cross the open space where the valley opened onto the beach and it was absolutely flat with a perfect field of fire. Then I saw a little fountain of water jut up, just over and beyond the lead tank. Then smoke broke out of the leading tank on the side away from us and I saw two men dive out of the turret and land on their hands and knees on the stones of the beach. They were close enough so that I could see their faces, but no more men came out as the tank started to blaze up and burn fiercely.'

After that they busied themselves taking on board wounded before starting to feel their way back through Rommel's asparagus, while yet another Sherman on the beach was hit and started to burn. Now, however, Allied destroyers were moving ever closer to the burning shore and 'were blowing every pillbox out of the ground with their 5-inch guns'. Hemingway reported to the readers of *Collier's* that he actually saw 'a piece of German about three foot long with an arm on it sail high up into the air in the fountaining of one shellburst. It reminded me of a scene in Petrouchka.'

After dealing with the wounded, their vessel now finally made landfall. 'We ran in to a good spot we had picked on the beach and put our troops and TNT and their bazookas and their lieutenant ashore and that was that.'

That it was and Hemingway's part in the 'longest day' was over. Or was it?

In his dispatch for *Collier's*, he ended his account entitled 'Voyage to Victory' (someone evidently liked the alliteration of the title although victory was another eleven months away) with: 'Real war is never like paper war. But if you want to know how it was in an LCV(P) on D-Day when we took Fox Green and Easy Red Beach on the 6th of June 1944, then this is as near as I can come to it.'

Overlooking the total lack of modesty, which was typical of Hemingway, the intent was quite clear. '*When we took Fox Green . . .*' makes it absolutely obvious that Hemingway wanted his readers to believe that he had taken part in the actual assault. Seven years later in a letter he wrote to his publisher Charles Scribner (included in an attack on James Jones for having had the temerity to write about *his* war in his best-selling *From Here to Eternity*), Hemingway already obviously believed that he had indeed been a participant in that great invasion: '[We had to] stay in the landing circle until we went in for the assault on Fox Green Beach of Omaha Beach.' This puts him in the forefront of the assault instead of being (as he put it in another letter written in 1948) to the rear, 'hitting the beach in the *seventh* [author's italic] wave on D-Day'.

Despite his comment on his arrival in England on that Wednesday that 'it's only the phonies who are personally colourful', Hemingway, within three short weeks, was already attempting to make himself an interesting man of action and leader, instead of a mere observer armed with a pen and not a rifle. It was already obvious that Hemingway was now going to use the final year of the Second World War as yet another vehicle to add to that collection of myths about himself which had commenced nearly a quarter of a century before in the First World War.

Then, in July 1918, he had written home to his family: 'I'm the first American wounded in Italy' (although he wasn't and he knew it). He maintained further that he had received 227 wounds, both from shrapnel and from machine-gun bullets, which had ripped his legs apart while he was trying to rescue a wounded Italian soldier. In fact, in his first cable home that July, the 19-year-old Red Cross ambulance driver had stated: 'WOUNDED IN THE LEG BY TRENCH MORTAR. WILL RECEIVE VALOR MEDAL. WILL WALK AGAIN IN TEN DAYS.' It was the beginning of the big lie.

A quarter of a century later he was still at it, and, worse still, believing his own lies! Now he was actually encouraging others to spread those lies for him. In the mid-1960s, shortly after Hemingway's death, an article appeared in one of the men's magazines that were popular at that time (before *Playboy*, *Penthouse* and the like killed the market). The magazine was *True* and the article in question was entitled 'Hemingway's Longest Day'. Obviously the title was meant to cash in on the popularity of Cornelius Ryan's book of that name and the subsequent star-studded movie based on it.

In the article, dated 1 February 1963, the author maintained he had landed on the beaches a few days after D-Day when he came across some unnamed veterans of Omaha beach. He asked them about their commanding officer. They answered 'Our CO? Hell, we've had a dozen in the last four days. They keep gettin' killed.'

'Tell him about that wild man that dumped us on the beach,' one of the veterans prompted their spokesman.

'Who?' he replied. 'Ernest Hemingway? Aw, he'd never believe that. I don't think it's true myself – and I was there.'

The veteran went on to explain that 'this Hemingway guy' had assumed command of a combat team pinned down on Omaha. He ordered them to dig in and sit tight, while the tanks came up to deal with the murderous fire coming from a German pillbox on the height above them. About noon, 'he left us and started to crawl back over the beach toward the water. We figured he was going to get somebody to do something about that big German gun up on the hill after that.' The 'veteran' continued with, 'Never did see him again. He must have got it before he could get back.' Then he asked the author, 'You think that was really Ernest Hemingway?'

'Could be,' the author answered. 'Could well be. . . .'

A few weeks later the author of the article, set between pin-ups, ads for self-improvement, and chest expanders, caught up with 'Papa', who was holed up in the Ritz Bar in Paris. 'I told him what the GIs from Omaha beach had said about the guy with the Hindu towel around his head. He just kind of laughed with his eyes and ordered another bottle.'

The author of this gripping yarn, told in the tough, terse style of such magazines, was no other than that former naval lieutenant William van Dusen – he of the buckwheat flour and the liquid breakfast at Shannon.

But who had been that unnamed veteran who had told him his tale of Papa's bravery on the beach at 'Bloody Omaha'? The answer is – Papa himself!

That very same evening, Hemingway was already back at the Dorch in the company of van Dusen and Baron. There the British press was waiting for him. 'Come over Baron,' Hemingway said waving a drink. 'I want you to meet these gentlemen from the London press. Friends, my kid brother, Leicester, like the Square. But he's shaping up and rounding off, a little more all the time.' Hemingway indicated his brother's stomach which caused a laugh, while Leicester refilled the journalists' glasses and brought in some more club soda.

'Goddammit, my head still hurts,' Hemingway said, drawing attention to his 'wound'. 'What any wound needs is a good stiff drink. . . . Make a note of it, Baron. Future historians will one day realise that alcohol has been one of the most profound contributions to the prosecution of any war known to man.'

Glasses were raised and the press asked their first question. 'Does your own family know you are safely back from the beachhead?'

'Write to our mother, Baron,' Hemingway directed, as though in answer. 'Tell her we're safe and had an easy time, like we always do.' He winked knowingly to the reporters and they understood; he hadn't had an easy time at all. 'Gentleman, I've got too much to do right now getting ready to go back where the fighting is heavy at this moment.'

Then he launched into his account of the battle. 'There was a lieutenant near to me. "Come on, boy," I said, "they'll zero in here in a minute." He shook his head. So I said, "You mother unprintable, unmentionable, undoable, let's get up the beach to where we can shoot back," and I kicked him squarely in the butt as I got going forward. That got action.'

The press must have loved it. Certainly, Leicester Hemingway and van Dusen did, for in due course both of them would dutifully detail Papa's derring-do on D-Day on 'Bloody Omaha' in their own writings. The legend was being added to dramatically and rapidly.

In the event, it seems that Hemingway, going in with the 'seventh wave' as he called it, must have been in a landing barge carrying combat engineers and *not* assault infantry – the men who would do the actual fighting on Omaha.

What other explanation is there for the fact that he described the men in his barge as carrying TNT? Assault infantry and their accompanying engineers would have carried the 'bangalore torpedo', an explosive charge fixed to long poles to be used in the attack on pillboxes, to blast through wire and to set off minefields. Later, waves of engineers would be equipped with TNT to blow up pillboxes so that they could not be reoccupied by the Germans in case of a counter-attack. More importantly, these army engineers would be used to blow lanes clear through the beach obstacles, preparing the way for the rapid and early landings of the rest of the 1st and 29th Divisions, four regiments of soldiers, some 12,000 men in all. It is hardly possible, too, that Hemingway could have seen 'a piece of German about three foot long with an arm on it sail high up in air in the fountaining of one shellburst'. This description was reminiscent of the *grand guignol* style with which he had reported the Spanish Civil War from Madrid. The German defences at Fox Green were located on the high ground, with the gently curved strand in between being protected by mines and barbed wire. How could Hemingway possibly have made out the fact that this was a piece of some unfortunate German from his position in the water at a distance of some half-mile – even with those old Zeiss glasses of his?

In fact, by the time Hemingway had arrived on the scene, the Americans themselves were moving along this cliff-top at Fox Green, slowly but steadily progressing east towards Port-en-Bassin, where they were to link up with the British. In his article for *Collier's*, Hemingway made this clear himself when he wrote: 'The infantry had now worked up the valley on our left and had gone on over that ridge.'

This clearing of the German-held ridge took place about nine-thirty that morning and meant that Hemingway was watching events which were taking place some four or five hours *after* the initial landing. So what are we to make of Hemingway's written account of his D-Day adventures?

Well, it is clear that he was there. It is also clear that he did not land on the beaches. By the time his landing barge arrived off Omaha (in virtually every account of that day, the kind of vessel in which Hemingway sailed was grounded on the sand banks *off* the shore and did not make landfall), the defenders of the 352nd German Infantry Division were in retreat. It is then decidedly possible that Hemingway made up the stories of the two shelled Sherman tanks and the 'three foot' length of dead German sailing through the air. These yarns would make his copy more dramatic, interesting, and naturally add to that myth of Hemingway as the man of action. Right throughout that article, 'Voyage to Victory', it is obvious that Hemingway saw himself (and wished his readers to see him in the same manner) not as a mere observer, but as a participant – and leader! It would be the role he would select for himself for the rest of his time in Europe.

On the morning of 7 June 1944, Martha Gellhorn returned to England with the hospital ship, carrying its cargo of misery. On disembarking she bumped into William van Dusen, the aide to Admiral Lovette, in charge of public relations for the US Navy. She had been concerned about her husband's safety. Now van Dusen, who had already heard Hemingway's account of D-Day and would store it away for future use, told her that her husband was back safely at the Dorch.

Martha said she was delighted at her husband's safe return and asked van Dusen, who could move about freely due to his job, if he would deliver a note from her to Ernest. He agreed. In it she wrote that she was very happy that nothing had happened to him on D-Day, but that she would be leaving shortly for a 'hopeless Cook's tour' of that forgotten front in Italy. Then came the sting in the tail: 'I came to see the war,' she wrote, 'not to live in the Dorchester.' Her husband was not prepared to leave the comfort and comparative safety of the Dorch just yet, despite his remarks to the British reporters about 'getting ready to go back where the fighting is heavy at this moment'. It would be more than another month before he finally ventured across the Channel for good.

Now, on this fateful Tuesday which had changed the world, he drank and rested after the reporters had gone, mulling the events of the morning for his forthcoming article for *Collier's*.

In due course, the future novelist Roald Dahl, then a fighter-pilot with the RAF, who had been instrumental in obtaining Hemingway his permission to come to the UK, would come across the great man finishing that article. He asked to see it and found it very bad.

To hide his true opinion of it, he said: 'But Ernest, you've left out that marvellous bit you told me about the expression on the man's face as he tried to get out of a burning tank.'

'My God,' Hemingway exploded indignantly, 'you don't think I'd give *that* to *Collier's*, do you?'

The statement was indicative of the way Hemingway would use the events of that Tuesday. They would further the

Hemingway myth and, in due course, furnish the raw material of the great book he would write on the war when it was all over.

The fate of nations, the future of Europe, the despair, the misery, the suffering of the ordinary decent young men who were fighting and dying on and off those beaches that evening – all these things were of no concern to him. For him the war was to be exploited, in the same way that a greedy gold-miner might hack away, secretly and jealously, at a newly discovered rich seam of ore.

Then it was midnight at the Dorch, and over the Channel on those desolate shattered beaches, the last of the 4,200 young Britons and the 4,600 equally young Americans who had been killed or grievously wounded this epic day, passed on.

D–Day was over.

BUZZ BOMBS, BOOZE AND BUCKWHEAT PANCAKES

Tuesday 13 June, one week after D-Day, dawned cold and with a threat of rain in the air. At 5 a.m. the blackouts were still up everywhere in the county of Kent, for the sun was not due to rise till 5.43. All the same, there were plenty of people about – civilians, Civil Defence workers and soldiers – for the Germans had been unusually active during the night.

After a lull of several months, which had been only disturbed now and again by 'tip-and-run' raiders attacking the Kent coast, the great German coastal batteries around Calais had fired twenty-two heavy shells into Folkestone and a further eight had landed as far inland as Maidstone and the nearby village of Otham. The result had been that the air raid sirens had shrilled their warnings all over Kent twice, once at ten to four and then, after the 'all clear' at 4 a.m., almost immediately once again. Something strange was going on, but what it was only a select few on duty that early morning knew.

In the event, it was a greengrocer and a jobbing builder, both part-time Observer Corps observers, on duty on top of a Martello tower near Dymchurch, who were to be the first to spot what was the start of a new and terrible kind of warfare. Stuck out on their lonely post – code-named 'M2' – surrounded by the bleak fens of Romney Marsh, the two middle-aged civilians in their blue battledress heard a sound in the sky they had never heard before. It was like a 'Model-T Ford going up a hill'. Then they saw the source. It was the size of a small fighter-plane with stubby wings and it trailed behind it a fiery-red flame. At five miles' distance they identified the strange object, all the same, from the identification tables which had been given to them the previous April. Hurriedly, one of them picked up the phone which linked them with the countrywide Observer Corps network. 'Mike-Two,' the observer yelled excitedly as the object came ever closer with its strange put-put sound, 'Diver! . . . diver! . . . diver! . . . one four, north-west one at one!'

A few minutes later, at 4.18 a.m., the first of these strange new weapons crashed down at Swanscombe. A handful of seconds afterwards, the second came down at Cuckfield in Sussex, its one ton of high explosive blasting several unfortunate cows into eternity. The third followed at 5.07 a.m. at Crouch End near Sevenoaks and the fourth wrecked the railway bridge at Bethnal Green in London, killing six people and injuring nine others. The long-waited Battle of the Flying Bombs had commenced.

For a few days now, Hemingway had been rousing himself sufficiently from the lingering results of his accident and his ardent pursuit of Mary Welsh (which was now proceeding at a swifter pace, as Irwin Shaw was on his way to France), in order to fulfil the assignment which had brought him to England in the first place: the coverage of the RAF's role in the new campaign in France. At first it had been thought he might take part in some of the RAF's night bombing missions over occupied territory, but now a new German 'wonder weapon' had caught the public's attention, both in the UK and in the USA. Hemingway felt he might be able to achieve an exclusive scoop by reporting on the RAF's fight against the 'V-1s', 'buzz-bombs', or 'doodlebugs', as they were variously being called. The nicknames minimised the terrible menace of a pilotless plane which could fly at 400 mph, the limit for most Allied fighters, to deliver a warhead of one ton of explosive.

The British officer who was delegated by the Air Ministry's Department of Public Relations to take charge of Hemingway during his trips to various RAF airfields in the south of England was Flight-Lieutenant John Pudney, then aged 45. He was a gently spoken former newspaperman with the *News Chronicle*, and a minor poet whose *For Johnny*, written in 1941, had made his name. With its simple but nostalgic 'Do not despair for Johnny-head-in-air; he sleeps as sound as Johnny underground', it is one of the most evocative of all the poems of the Second World War. Pudney had been in the RAF since 1940 and, although he had never fired a single shot during training, he had had many hazardous escapes during the years he had flown sorties on various RAF missions. These would give rise to his claim to have been the only wartime officer who had 'never fired a shot – *except in anger!*'

A week before, Pudney had flown over the invasion beaches under fire. Soon he would be joining General Leclerc's Free French armoured dash for Paris, which would rouse Hemingway's ire – 'that prick Leclerc', he would call 2nd French Armoured Division's commander – where he could claim proudly that he had been the first Allied officer to visit the painter Picasso in his studio.

Pudney did not take to his charge. 'To me,' he confessed afterwards, 'he was a fellow obsessed with playing the part of Ernest Hemingway and hamming it to boot: a sentimental nineteenth-century actor called upon to act the part of a twentieth-century tough guy. Set beside . . . a crowd of young men who walked so modestly and stylishly with Death, he seemed a bizarre cardboard figure.'

Indeed, the future Air Marshal Sir Peter Wykeham, with whom Hemingway would fly and who thought that Hemingway was 'the sort of a man who spends his whole life proving that he is not scared', felt that Pudney was 'like a gentle man who's accidentally found himself leading a rampaging bull.

He got into more and more drunken parties, fights and wrangles, being thrown into fountains, ejected from hotels and locked in people's rooms.'

In that third week of June 1944, the two very different writers, the gentle retiring poet and the man of action (although both of them, Hemingway and Pudney, would end their lives as alcoholics), set off for a tour of the RAF forward bases under the command of the future Air Marshal Sir Basil Embry, head of the 2nd Tactical Air Force. He interviewed pilots who had shot down some of the first V-1s and went to the local pubs with them in the Salisbury Plain area. He was even reported to have prayed at Salisbury Cathedral, where he called upon blessings for the souls of his English ancestors. Anyway, that is what the papers said.

On Thursday 15 June he was having a drink, propped up against the bar of the RAF Officers' Mess at the RAF field at Dunsford near Guildford, when there was that now familiar put-put of an approaching V-1 which had crossed the coast some forty miles away.

Excitedly, the assembled officers rushed to the windows, which were all protected by a criss-cross of sticky paper tape to prevent them blowing out completely if a bomb dropped, and there it was. The dark shape with its stubby wings, trailing its red flame behind it, chugging by the airfield, heading for some objective known only to those who had launched it minutes before somewhere in Northern France.

Abruptly, the engine cut out. Once again there was that familiar chilling silence. Suddenly the V-1 dived. A crash. A thud. A dark plume of smoke started to rise from a spot not too far away.

The opportunity was too good to miss. Madly, the correspondents, including Hemingway with his damaged knees, piled out of the Mess and headed straight for the site of the explosion. Now, before the police or the military could arrive on the scene, the correspondents searched through the tangled hot wreckage for souvenirs, like excited schoolboys. Hemingway was not excluded. He picked up several pieces of twisted metal and secreted them about his person before returning to the Mess for yet another drink.

The local police were not long in finding out where several valuable pieces of the bomb had disappeared to (they were urgently needed by Air Ministry scientists probing the secrets of the devilish device). They appeared at the office of the station commander Wing Commander G.J.C. Paul, and told him it was strictly forbidden to take souvenirs. Where were the people who had done so? 'Hemingway had just arrived at the bar of the Officers' Mess and had taken up his favourite position,' the station commander recalled long afterwards, 'when the police came in.' As was required of them, when entering a mess, they took off their helmets and belts politely enough, but they were still intent on carrying out their duties. They headed straight for Hemingway.

'As he had either been recognised or accurately described by witnesses, he received first attention. The police took a dim view of the whole proceedings and made no bones about it.' According to the station commander, 'Hemingway was quick to appreciate the situation and, looking like a small boy who had been caught with his hand in the cookie jar, went in the company of the police to his room to give up the pieces, as in due course did all the other culprits.'

Up to now the V-1s fired by Colonel Wachtel's flak regiment on the other side of the Channel had landed outside the capital or in London's humbler boroughs to the south and east. None had crashed down into the centre of the British Empire's power, the City of Westminster. For here were located the Houses of Parliament, 10 Downing Street, and all the major government departments.

In the early hours of Sunday 18 June, however, the first enemy flying bomb crashed down on the City of Westminster at Hungerford Bridge, where the railway lines were carried across the Thomas between Charing Cross and Waterloo Stations. At ten to nine that morning another landed on Carey Mansions in Westminster's Rutherford Street, and William Sansom, wartime fireman and Westminster's future historian, noted that although 'ten people were killed and fifty-two seriously injured, the incident presented no serious problems'.

It was about now that Hemingway started to wake up in the Dorchester. The bombs landing so close had disturbed his sleep. He wasn't a good sleeper at the best of times unless he took pills, which he did frequently. This morning there was going to be a party in his room. Admiral Lovette, the Navy's PR chief, was going to provide the bourbon and Bill van Dusen (of the buckwheat flour) was going to cook that long-awaited 'American-style' pancake breakfast. The two OSS Lieutenants North and Burke, now officially enrolled in 'Hemingstein's Bearded Junior Commandos', were also going to attend. Everyone was going to have a swell time.

Over on the other side of the Channel, Colonel Wachtel had other ideas for that pleasant Sunday morning, as some 500-odd yards from the Dorchester the worshippers started to assemble for Sunday morning matins at the Guards Chapel.

The service on Sunday at the Guards Chapel in Wellington Barracks was quite a fashionable occasion even in the shabby, rationed London of the fifth year of the war. The Guards Armoured Division, which contained the cream of the Brigade of Guards' officers, was already marshalling ready to cross over the Channel and take part in the Battle of Normandy. But there were still plenty of establishment figures left in the capital who on a Sunday liked to visit the Guards Chapel in order to 'see and be seen'. On this particular morning, no less a divine than the Chaplain General to the Forces would be preaching there.

In due course, the matins commenced and some in the packed congregation noticed the Chaplain General's voice shook a little when he spoke of 'our beloved chapel'. Later, he would confide to a friend that he had sensed 'a strange unfamiliar sadness and doom overshadowing the sacred precincts'. But that was later.

At the Dorch they were well into Lieutenant van Dusen's buckwheat pancakes. Hemingway's reaction to them is not recorded; he was concentrating on the Admiral's free bourbon. But North of the OSS found them a little leathery. His fellow OSS officer, Burke, on the other hand, declared they were 'delicious'.

The talk veered round to the V-1s which were 'sailing up the river [the Thames] with some regularity that morning'. Hemingway, always trying to prove his bravery, even when it wasn't necessary, offered his favourite theory that no one was ever in danger unless he was being shot at personally.

It was exactly at that moment that 'Buddy' North, as Hemingway was now calling him (using his college nickname) looked out of the open window and remarked that one of the infernal German devices seemed to be heading straight for the room they were currently occupying.

But Buddy was mistaken. That particular V-1, after travelling 130 miles, was heading elsewhere. For a few seconds, according to a British WREN (member of the Royal Naval women's section) who saw it too, it seemed to hover – 'a high black shape over Queen Anne's Mansions in Queen Anne's Gate'. Then its engine cut out and it fell out of the morning sky, heading straight for the packed Guards Chapel.

Standing in that packed congregation singing 'All the earth doth worship Thee: the Father everlasting', ATS subaltern Miss Sheppard-Jones did not even have time to duck. 'There was a noise so loud it was as if all the waters and the winds in the world had come together in mighty conflict and the Guards Chapel collapsed upon us in a bellow of bricks and mortar. . . . One moment I was singing the *Te Deum* and the next I lay in dust and blackness, aware of one thing only – that I had to go on breathing.'

Over at the Dorchester, they saw the V-1 crash to earth. The two young OSS officers forgot their pancakes. They left them cooling in the thick syrup and raced across Green Park, full-out, to offer their services; and their services were certainly badly needed, for 119 men and women, mainly in the services, had been killed outright and 102 seriously injured, with another 32 slightly hurt. There was death, destruction and misery on all sides.

Lying trapped in the ruins, the young ATS Officer Sheppard-Jones heard 'screaming, screaming, screaming, like an animal caught in a trap. . . . My eyes rested with horror on a blood-stained body . . . the body of a young soldier whose eyes turned unseeingly to the sky. . . . I tried to convince myself that this was truly a nightmare, one from which I was bound to wake up.' But it wasn't. The young female officer was maimed for life. 'I still felt no pain but I did begin to have an inkling that I was badly injured. I turned my freed head towards a Guardsman who was helping with the rescue work and hysterically I cried, "How do I look? Tell me, how do I look?" "Wonderful, madam," the Guardsman replied. "You look wonderful to me!".'

Later, after she had been freed from the smoking rubble, Miss Sheppard-Jones learned the dire truth of her condition at St Mary's Hospital. 'My spine was fractured and my spinal column damaged. . . . I was paralysed from the waist downwards.' That morning walk to the Sunday services at the Guards Chapel had been the last she would ever take. Miss Sheppard-Jones would join the hundreds, perhaps thousands, who were maimed for life by this terrible new weapon.

And in the Dorch, after the initial shock of a flying bomb exploding so near, Hemingway and the rest, minus the two young naval officers, returned to their pancakes and Admiral Lovette's bourbon.

This apparent indifference to the suffering of the British civilians all around him was typical of Hemingway during his seven weeks' stay in the country. Naturally, he shared some of the arrogance of American soldiers who had believed they had crossed the Atlantic to 'American-occupied England' to bale 'Ol' Jolly' out of the mess it had gotten itself in. They had come from a country which was booming and prosperous and which knew no shortages, to one that was ravaged by five years of war and privation. The 'natives' were skinny and grey and didn't look too good. In general, they were a little stand-offish, save for their womenfolk who were 'easy lays' and could be 'had' for a pair of nylons and a couple of Hershey bars. In consequence, many of the GIs who were in the United Kingdom tended to look down upon their hosts. Ernest Hemingway, his views reinforced by the prejudices he had brought with him about the English, was no exception. But in his case, there was another dimension which seemed to deaden him to the sufferings all about. His lack of sensitivity and compassion was derived, too, from his egotism and his drinking. He could see little beyond his own sufferings – his general ill health, the concussion, the blinding headaches and double vision, all attributable to his alcoholism.

Also, because he was a non-combatant, dealing primarily with men in uniform who were all potentially combatants (although most of them never did hear a shot fired in anger), he was developing a kind of self-centred swaggering boastfulness and toughness. This allowed of sentimentality, it must be admitted, but then sentimentality of the maudlin kind is common in drunks, but not of sympathy or compassion.

By the time Hemingway had arrived in the UK, nearly 60,000 British men, women and children, all civilians, had been killed in the raids (more than the total US Army's casualties on all fronts up to that time), and another 20,000 would be killed in the V-1 and V-2 attacks before it was all over. But in the two wartime dispatches that Hemingway sent *Collier's* from London, his letters written from there in the same period, and in his diary jottings, there is no single mention of what was happening to the civilians all around him. It was as if Hemingway was living in a vacuum.

Of course, Hemingway was a very lonely man preoccupied by his own private problems. Despite the fact that he could always attract hangers-on, admirers, even toadies, because he was a writer and personality and always seemed surrounded by a crowd, he felt himself very alone. Mary Welsh had spotted that at their very first meeting when she had seen him eating alone at his table in the White Tower and 'sensed an air of solitude about him, loneliness perhaps'.

As Hemingway saw it, he was without a woman, far from his children – two were in the States and another was in Africa training to be a paratrooper, and would soon drop into occupied France with the OSS. The family circle had broken up and even among these new 'friends' of his, he was always much older than they, distanced from them inwardly by his age, experience and artistic ability. After all, wasn't he calling himself 'Papa' more and more these days to emphasise the difference in age and experience, although he was only 44?

Then there was the problem of his writing, which, as a professional writer of a quarter of a century's standing, must have preoccupied him constantly, cutting out the concerns and worries of others, who did not possess his gifts. Except for an introduction to a collection of essays on fighting men through the ages, *Men at Arms*, published in 1942, he had not written anything since he had finished *For Whom the Bell Tolls* in 1940.

Of course, he boasted to anyone who asked that he had been writing every day for the last three years. He would make a similar boast ten years later when he finally realised he was burnt out. Naturally he *did* write, but the stuff he produced was either no good or seemed to be a parody of some second-class writer parodying Hemingway.

Already Dahl, who would make a name for himself after the war as a first-class writer of children's and ghost stories, had noted just how bad that first dispatch to *Collier's* was. Dahl, who found Hemingway to 'be shy and rather jumpy', felt that even 'as a war correspondent in Hitler's war, I would rate him as very poor'. Dahl thought that the reason Hemingway was turning out such poor stuff was because he was saving his best material for the big book he would produce after the war. But that wasn't the case at all. He simply wasn't up to the task of being a war correspondent any more, although he had done the same job after the Great War in Turkey and Greece.

Naturally, Hemingway always had made a distinction between journalism and serious writing, but in the second and last of his two pieces written from Britain: 'London Fights the Robots', published in *Collier's* on 19 August 1944, Hemingway couldn't even produce decent journalism. From the very start of his short article, dealing with the RAF's attempts to stop the V-1s, he made elementary mistakes, such as confusing in the very first line the type of plane being used: 'The Tempest is a great gaunt airplane', whereas, in fact, he meant the Typhoon. Then he would wander off garrulously to horse racing, the fact that the British call college 'university', and the actress Tallulah Bankhead. After making the point – at length – that his article was being written under the eyes of the British censors, he compared writing on air warfare with boxing. 'It is sort of as though in the old days you had found Harry Greb having a breakfast of double orders of ham and eggs and hashed brown potatoes in bed at nine o'clock in the morning on the day he was to fight Mickey Walker. Greb, placed on the scales, weighed exactly 12 pounds over the 162 he was to make at two o'clock that afternoon. Now suppose you have seen the weight rubbed and pounded off of him and got rid of by several other means and him carried on the scales too weak to walk and almost too weak to curse you . . .' and so on and so on for another irrelevant paragraph. One wonders what his poor readers stateside, eager to find out about this new and deadly phase of warfare, made of it all!

In fact, if anything at all emerged from this confused account of his first period with the 2nd Tactical Air Force, it was simply that Hemingway had flown with the Royal Air Force and that once again he had been in the forefront of the action.

In essence, the article was not about the RAF, but about Hemingway. He maintained he could not understand the RAF slang, that he didn't like the kind of missions they flew, and that he should have left the whole thing and gone back 'to writing books in stiff covers'.

'Why,' he expounded in the article, 'I understand that there is a feeling freely expressed in some quarters that Ernie is yellow. With a chance to go on absolutely wizard ops, he is up in his room at that pub, doing what do you think?

'"What?" in a horrified tone.

'"Writing!"

'"My God! The old boy's had it."' Thus Hemingway ended his account, with he himself foremost in the picture. Naturally.

Of course, everyone with any sense whatsoever knew that the statement 'Ernie is yellow' was utterly laughable. It had to be meant as a joke. His bravery was surely beyond question. Wasn't he a war hero, the first American to be wounded in Italy in the First World War, who had hunted big game, fought in the boxing ring, even against professionals, and so on, and so on? Indeed, the only thing in that silly second-rate article that had a ring of truth was his statement that 'Ernie' was up in his room writing. For in June 1944 Hemingway was more concerned with living than writing. *Collier's* was simply the means to justify his stay in wartime Britain. Just as he had wasted the previous three years as a writer, penning material which he would never publish, living off his reputation, now he was producing mediocre journalism which featured Ernest Hemingway, the great novelist. If someone else other than Hemingway had written such garrulous, inaccurate, egocentric stuff, it would surely never even have been published! Of course, Hemingway justified his lack of production during these war years with a lot of boastful talk of a great trilogy on the global conflict, which would emerge from his experiences during his 'anti-sub' campaign off the Cuban coast, his present adventures with the RAF and those soon to follow. In the event, nothing came of his experiences in Europe in the Second World War save that one bitter confused novel which he was now going to promise to Mary Welsh. . . .

Some time that same week, Hemingway took his new love out to lunch at a French restaurant in Jeremy Street, 'where they cooked unrationed vegetables quite well'. Since that night at the Dorch where the author had made his startling forthright statement that he wished to marry Mary, he had not mentioned the subject again. Now, after a couple of drinks and a bottle of wine with the food, Hemingway announced grandly, 'I'll dedicate a book to you'.

Mary wondered if he always said things like this to win a girl's devotion. If so, he couldn't have had many girls, for he had written so few books.

'With love?' she prompted.

'I've never done that,' he answered, on the defensive at once, 'but yes,' he conceded, 'with love.'

Six years later he produced that sole book on his wartime experiences and he did dedicate it to Mary, 'with love'.

Mary would be disappointed with it. She would declare that she thought it 'his poorest book'.

Perhaps in that June of 1944 Hemingway was exhibiting a large degree of prescience when he announced (through the mouths of the unknown air crew featured in 'London Fights the Robots'), 'My God . . . the old boy's had it!'

PAPA GOES TO WAR – AT LAST

In the early summer of 1944, the 140th Wing of Sir Basil Embry's Second Tactical Air Force was a rather special formation. The wing was equipped with sleek, plywood-built Mosquitos. They were the only all-wood aircraft still in service with any air force throughout the world and many of these planes were built by cottage industry, being assembled by small groups of civilians in outhouses, barns and sheds, instead of the huge conventional factory.

Despite that, the Mosquito, armed with four 20mm cannons, could deliver a 1,000 pound bomb load, flying at 300 mph, with a crew of only two. In contrast, the heavily armoured American Flying Fortress, flying at half the Mosquito's speed, needed a crew of eight to deliver a mere 2,000 pounds of bombs.

But it was not merely the strange origin of its wooden planes and the Mosquito's bomb-carrying capacity that made the 140th Wing something special. It was the kind of daring, unusual operations which the Wing had begun to fly in February 1944 and which it would continue to fly right up to the end of the war.

That February, in a mission code-named 'Operation Jericho', the 140th Wing, commanded then by big, bluff Charles Pickard, had flown across the Channel at wave-top height (to avoid the German radar network) to attack the French prison at Amiens. Here a large number of French resistance workers languished in German captivity, waiting to be shipped off to the concentration camps of the Reich, and death.

Now, on 18 February 1944, eighteen Mosquitos, under Pickard's command, had gone in in three waves of six. The task of the first six was to break down the prison's walls and destroy the German guardhouse. The second formation was to place bombs against the walls of the gaol, while the third was to be held in reserve.

Virtually everything went as planned. Although 102 prisoners were killed in the raid, many of them being shot down by the German guards as they attempted to make a bolt for it, over 150 members of the resistance organisation made it, including their key underground members, all of whom were under sentence of death. But 'Operation Jericho' cost the life of the attack-leader Charles Pickard, who was recommended for the Victoria Cross on account of his exploits that day – he never received it. He was replaced as head of the 140th Wing by another officer, a veteran of five years of combat in France, Britain and the Middle East – Wing Commander Peter Wykeham Barnes – an officer who would later lead similar raids on Gestapo headquarters in Denmark.

In the early summer of 1944, however, the 140th Wing had been transferred from these daring, pin-point special operations to the more immediate task of supporting the Invasion army in Normandy. Flying from a forward airfield at Thorney Island, not far from the great Royal Navy base at Portsmouth, Wykeham Barnes's Mosquitos were in action all around the clock. Night and day they flew constant sorties across the Channel against the German lines of communication in France, trying to prevent the enemy from bringing up supplies and reinforcements.

It was to Thorney Island that John Pudney, still worn from the brawls and drinking sessions of the last week, escorted his charge Ernest Hemingway on 28 June. Still adorned with his grizzled beard, Hemingway seemed an incongruous sight in his 'extremely inferior RAF battledress, very hairy and ill-fitting', as Pudney noted. To the latter, Papa looked rather like a 'blue-grey bear'.

By now, Pudney was completely disillusioned with Hemingway. Although he was a heavy drinker himself, he intensely disliked the American's boastfulness and tendency to brawl when he was drunk. Now, almost as soon as he arrived at Thorney Island, Hemingway succeeded in putting his foot in it. As Pudney related to Nigel Hamilton, the author of the definitive biography of Field Marshal Montgomery, just before Pudney's death of throat cancer in 1977: 'To John's disgust, Hemingway held court at the bar, pontificating before three junior pilots and claiming that their senior officers were cowards.' What Hemingway didn't know was that all RAF senior officers who were 'bigots' (who knew the secrets of D-Day), had been grounded so that they couldn't fall into German hands and reveal what they knew. Nor did he know that all the senior officers of the 2nd Tactical Air Force had been in constant action since 1939, including the 2nd TAF's commander, Basil Embry, who had won *four* Distinguished Flying Crosses for bravery and who, after being shot down and captured in France, had escaped and made his way back to the UK to fight yet once again.

Pudney, who was still an admirer of Hemingway's writings, now felt absolutely furious over his 'buffoon-like performance'. 'I was *ashamed* of him,' he told Hamilton. That Hemingway should boast at the bar about his own bravery and exploits, in front of innocent but brave pilots, and condemn the senior officer who was much decorated and certainly the most courageous flier John knew – the reference was probably to Basil Embry – was to John 'a typical case of the egoism, vanity and shameful bragging of a certain kind of writer'.

Peter Wykeham Barnes, who had commanded the 140th since February, took Hemingway in his stride. He was a big, bluff man (bigger than Hemingway), with slicked-back hair, who had been in action with fighters for four and a half years – 'non-stop', as he usually put it. Although he was impressed by

Hemingway the writer (he had read all of his books), he was less impressed by Hemingway the would-be warrior.

Afterwards he remembered: 'He [Hemingway] had a great deal to say on mental stress and strain, on courage and fear, traditional Hemingway topics, and though he was as intelligent as one might expect, he tended to take a tougher and brawnier line than that acceptable to us worn-out old veterans.'

Wykeham Barnes told Hemingway he didn't agree with the harsh attitude of the 8th US Air Force stationed in the UK with any of their fliers who had become 'flak happy' and lost their nerve. In the RAF their records were, admittedly, stamped in red ink 'LMF' (Lacking in Moral Fibre), but men of this type were posted away to a completely new unit and even a new arm of the service, such as the British Army. He quoted the 'case of a Fortress captain who was busted down to private and put to work, the next day, cleaning the Fortress he had captained'.

But Hemingway 'kept up the tough line and we told him that he'd have to get some service in; that the bravest men were the newest in action and so on. It was all very good-humoured.'

On the afternoon of 29 June, Hemingway convinced the big RAF man to take him up for a trial flight in the 'Mossy', as the aircrew called the Mosquito. In the fast fighter-bomber, instead of sitting one behind the other, the pilot and the navigator sat side to side. This was tough for the two big men. They were very crowded and as they tried to settle in, it resembled, Hemingway said later, the attempt of a grizzly bear to enter an Austin.

The purpose of this first flight with the Group Captain was, as Wykeham Barnes recalled, 'to give him [Hemingway] some experience in riding in the navigator's seat and he urged me to roll the Mosquito and throw it around quite considerably'.

The big Group Captain obliged. It wasn't altogether a pleasant experience for Hemingway. Perhaps it was this trial flight out across the Channel from Portsmouth, still crowded with vessels bound for the Invasion beaches, which prompted Hemingway to alter the RAF motto, *Per ardum ad astra*, to *Ad astra ad nauseam*!

But, however disastrous that first flight in a Mosquito might have been for Hemingway's sensitive stomach, he did not decline when Wykeham Barnes invited him to take off with him that night. There could be little danger during the flight because the Group Captain 'had been told I must not take Ernest over enemy territory and indeed I could not go far, at night and low level, without a proper navigator. So we meant to run around the English Channel and see if we could pick up anything interesting.'

Hemingway did not know just how much the authorities were taking care of his life, as they had done on D-Day. He really thought he was flying a combat mission with the RAF, and the Group Captain would always remain one of his heroes, despite what he had said previously about the cowardice of the 2nd TAF's senior officers. As he wrote to Lillian Ross of the *New Yorker* in 1948, 'I have heroes still: Peter Wickham [sic] Barnes of the RAF who used to take out Gestapo HQs in daylight precision bombeing [sic] with Mosquitoes.'

They set off at midnight. It was a pitch-black night with no moon. But despite the poor conditions the Group Captain soon spotted the tell-tale, fiery-red exhaust trails of the V-1s to his front. Three days before on the 26th, Colonel Wachtel, on the other side of the Channel, had fired an experimental salvo of some dozen missiles at Southampton, which the Germans guessed was the British supply port for the invasion forces in Normandy. Two of these missiles had missed Southampton altogether and had crashed home on Portsmouth. The first, with its point of impact in Locksway Road, caused nineteen minor casualties and sixteen more serious ones. Now Wykeham Barnes assumed, as did the British authorities below, that the Germans were deliberately aiming their missiles at the great naval base. So he zoomed in to see what he could do to protect what was his home base.

'Towards the end of its flight,' he recorded long afterwards, 'the V-1 was going better than 400 miles an hour, a good 30 mph faster than my Mosquito's top speed. Intercepting one at night was very difficult indeed. The first one we tried for, getting above and ahead and diving as it passed under us, was too near the Portsmouth guns and before we could get in a shot, we were having a bad time from the full-scale AA barrage. I fired one short burst at the V-1 and then pulled away before we reached the barrage balloons. Ernest seemed to love the fireworks bursting all around us and urged me to press on and make sure of the V-1.'

Wykeham Barnes, the old hand, was more cautious. He didn't want to be shot down by his own flak. Neither did he want to be in close range if the V-1 was hit by a shell from below. More than one foolhardy young pilot had lost his life that way since the V-1 offensive had started.

Ten minutes later they spotted another burst of cherry-red, angry flame breaking the inky darkness. A flying bomb! Later the Group Captain confessed, 'I was already in a state familiar to those who tangled with Ernest – I was acting against my better judgement. My wing had no responsibility for destroying V-1s. I knew I could not catch one except by a fluke. I knew there were proper night fighters after them and I was getting in the way and I knew I was supposed to keep Ernest out of trouble. If you did blow one up, particularly at night, it was touch and go for yourself also.' All the same, Wykeham Barnes went in for the attack.

'We dived even more steeply on the second V-1 and got nearer to it. I really had to dive the old airplane to her limit, even to hold on for a while. I reckoned it was in range and gave it two long bursts. I thought I saw a flash a bit off-centre of its fuselage and then we were in the Portsmouth barrage again.

I pulled away in a confusion of searchlights and intensive flak. As we winged over, there was a huge flash behind us and the aeroplane danced around like a leaf in a whirlwind. Someone got the V-1 but not us. We patrolled some more and then landed. Ernest seemed to have loved every moment.'

Thereafter, the two men talked and talked almost till dawn. By that time, the 'Groupie', as Wykeham Barnes was called by his admiring pilots, was all in. He said goodnight and fell into his bunk in his tent. Within minutes he was fast asleep.

Next day, he met Hemingway about midday, heading for the bar of the Officers' Mess. The writer looked terrible and Wykeham Barnes asked him if he hadn't slept well. Hemingway said he hadn't slept at all. He had sat at his typewriter in his own tent all the time since they had parted just before dawn. 'He said he liked to get it down fresh and I felt the warm admiration one has for a true professional. But he never told me what he wrote that night.'

Apparently, Hemingway never did write anything about his sole encounter with a V-1 that night or any other night. If he did, it was never published in *Collier's* or in any fictionalised account of the time that he might have written after the war. At all events, that was the end of the writer's association with the RAF, the assignment which had brought him to Europe in the first place. Later Hemingway would maintain that an RAF doctor, who called him 'laddie' (though the 'laddie' looked at least sixty), grounded him for medical reasons due to his head injury. But that unknown RAF medical officer and his laddie, conjuring up that familiar down-to-earth abrasive Scots doctor of the popular 1930s novel and movie, might well have been a convenient fiction. There is no record of Hemingway having been examined by an RAF doctor, Scottish or otherwise. Perhaps he was simply bored by RAF routine on these remote provincial airfields and longed to be back at the comfort of the Dorch and 'Miss Mary', as he was now calling Mary Welsh.

By now, London had been drastically thinned of those chairborne warriors who occupied the Grosvenor Square area for so long. Even the Hollywood Irregulars were on the other side of the Channel, preparing to whore, drink, and film their way across Europe. Miss Mary, like the rest, went to visit an evacuation hospital and watched as a surgeon began to cut open the blood-stained field jacket of a boy who had been wounded by shrapnel in the back. 'Doc, I've got to crap,' the boy said in a hoarse, embarrassed voice. 'I can't help it.'

Mary Welsh stepped back a few feet, but the MO took it in his stride. 'That's okay,' he said. 'Everybody does. Go ahead, in your pants.'

Later, while Mary and Hemingway drank Scotch in the Frisco bottleclub, she told him about the smell of the dead she had come across in Normandy.

Hemingway agreed with her, but apparently was not inclined to go over there himself and sample the sights and sounds of battle, which he had once done avidly. Instead he shaved off his beard, tried hair restorer on his thinning locks, and took up with London society.

One afternoon, accompanied by the fat, ex-Etonian critic Cyril Connolly, he was invited to tea at the immense suite in the Dorchester which Lady Maud (Emerald) Cunard had maintained there since 1943. Hemingway had known Lady Cunard's formidable daughter Nancy back in Paris in the 1920s, where she took drugs, started to indulge herself in the first of a long line of black musicians, boxers, policemen and the like (she even hired rooms above the White Tower to sleep secretly with black men when she came to London), and where she played at being a book printer.

Lady Emerald, who had once left her husband to live with the conductor Sir Thomas Beecham, was now a pillar of conservative respectability. All the same, she still had a sharp tongue and, although she collected celebrities, she was not awed by them. She put Hemingway through his paces sharply and the young novelist Frederic Prokosch, who was present, felt that Hemingway didn't come off too well in the exchanges. He sensed, too, that 'there was a sheen of animal stealth and of carnivorous stupidity, but even the stupidity was part of his charm'. At the same time there was something wrong with the great man, Prokosch decided, although he couldn't quite define what it was. It simply 'hovered in mid-air, like a stench in the jungle'.

Connolly opined, after Hemingway had left, that the first round had gone to Lady Emerald, but after that 'it was all Hemingway'. Old as she was, with her plump body and not too carefully dyed hair, Lady Emerald had good hearing all the same, and a sharp eye. 'I was startled,' she confessed, hearing the remark. 'Not a bit what I expected. You may think it bizarre of me, but he struck me as androgynous!' Connolly thought that 'androgynous' was a peculiar word to apply to a man like Hemingway, but Lady Emerald stuck to her guns. 'I am sure that it is,' she said. 'It is not the *mot juste* perhaps. But that's how he struck me. Distinctly emasculated!'

Naturally, Hemingway did not know about Lady Emerald's comments about the ambiguity of his sexual persona, but he must have sensed something of her attitude to him. Later he railed against and her kind to Mary Welsh, maintaining that type of upper-class woman was out to seduce him. All they wanted to do was to 'bag' him like some sort of sexual trophy, so that they could boast about their conquest afterwards without any sense of shame. He grumbled to Mary that 'he had been invaded by London society. Emerald Cunard was often leading a gaggle of beautiful and famous-named ladies to [his] room at the Dorchester for drinks and flirtations.' They were immoral, he declared.

'I trust you didn't lure any royalty?' Mary teased him, not knowing that her new suitor was not in a position sexually to lure any woman, royal or otherwise.

'No, but those others,' Hemingway retorted hotly, 'they want to stay all night and then have you take them home just in time to meet his Lordship leaving for the office in the morning.'

'You poor innocent country boy,' Mary chided him. 'What about that Bible thing, "He who is without . . . let him cast the first stone?"'.

Some time later, after Noel Monks, Mary's husband, had come and conveniently disappeared again very quickly for his new assignment in Normandy for the *Daily Mail*, Mary Welsh met Hemingway in the Dorchester. Lady Emerald had just departed from his room, but Mary noted she had left 'small mementos of her self around Ernest's room . . . rather like an animal staking out its territory.'

'Too bad you have to go off to France, dusty, dangerous France, and leave your fascinating friends,' Mary Welsh commented.

Hemingway snorted, 'I'm a five-day wonder for them! Next week, somebody else . . .' Then he said, 'Could I ask you something, a favour? Would you write me a letter, any small thing to France? I've got an address here.'

'Sure,' she answered easily. 'Any favour for the troops.'

It was now six weeks since Hemingway had arrived in England and he knew that he, too, must finally go to France, but he would go reluctantly. He liked the Dorch and perhaps he liked the fawning attention of the 'upper-uppest-classes' (as he called them) too, whatever they thought of him behind his back. And he certainly liked 'Miss Mary'. His wish for her to write to him showed that. So, almost as if he were forced to do so, he contacted a cousin of the senior *Time-Life* staffer in London, Charles Wertenbaker. This cousin, 'George', was a full colonel in the US Army Air Corps based in Issigny, France. There he possessed a twin-engined light aircraft, which, according to Wertenbaker, he was allowed to use to transport war correspondents back and forth across the

Channel. The 27-year-old cousin agreed to ferry Hemingway across. He was on his way to France, but he would be back – soon.

At the end of June 1944, General Eddy, the heavy-set, bespectacled commander of the 9th US Infantry Division had a problem. Eddy, who would conceal a bad case of high blood pressure from his superior officers right to the end of the war, now felt his hypertension begin to mount dangerously. Ever since his men had captured the major port of Cherbourg, they had become increasingly difficult to control. The one-time German-occupied harbour area was packed with wine, champagne and spirits. Almost immediately after the port's capture, mass looting had commenced. Even the top brass had taken a hand in it. His corps commander General 'Lightning Joe' Collins had taken enough drinks to last him all the way to the German frontier, which he reached two months later. General Bradley, the army commander, had sent home half a case of looted champagne to be used for toasts for when he finally reached home. From top to bottom, those concerned with this first important port to fall into Allied hands seemed out of hand. In despair, the 9th Infantry Division Commander ordered: 'Okay, everybody take twenty-four hours – and get drunk!'

His men took Eddy at his word, but the drinking continued long after the Ninth had departed from Cherbourg to fight its next battle. Those GIs left behind went on the rampage. Bored, drunk GIs used their firearms indiscriminately on French civilians. There was looting and rape, and in many cases the rapists were black soldiers. But there were enough white soldiers involved too. In the end, according to an official report sent to Eisenhower afterwards, 'the victims could not be brought back to life, but the assailant could be punished. To prove to the civil populace we were doing everything possible to bring about justice, executions were held at or near the scene of the crime. The immediate family of the victim and civic officials of the towns were present to see the execution.' It was against this background of looting, heavy drinking and some serious crime that Hemingway took up his residence in a large stone house in Cherbourg, which was inhabited by Bill Walton, who had been dropped as correspondent with the US 82nd Airborne Division on D-Day, and Charles Collingwood of the Columbia Broadcasting System, aged 26, who had landed on Utah Beach with the US 4th Infantry Division that same day.

The correspondents started off drinking from the moment of the much older man's arrival. 'We had a memorable bash in honour of his arrival,' Collingwood wrote afterwards. 'It was lubricated with compass fluid [pure alcohol] obtained by the Navy, plus some booze we had come across in captured German submarine stores deep in a cliff overlooking the harbour. . . . The festivities were enlightened by a group of Irish deep-sea divers who were engaged in clearing the harbour of the fiendish . . . mines and other obstructive devices the Germans had sown. They stayed up most of the night drinking and singing, slept it off for a couple of hours on the floor and then . . . disappeared beneath the surface of the most dangerous body of water in the world. Very tough characters.'

They were indeed, for these men belonged to the Royal Navy's élite frogmen who, clad in fantastic rubber suits, crawled about the muddy bottoms of harbours looking for mines, bestrode torpedoes to attack enemy ships, or slipped into the attack in midget submarines. This particular group of 'Irish deep-sea divers' were the two 'P-1' and 'P-2' teams of 'human minesweepers', commanded by the English-born Canadian Lieutenant Commander J.L. Harries, and a bearded, irrepressible Irishman, Lieutenant H.J. Horan of the RNVR. On loan to the US Army, it was their job to clear Cherbourg harbour of mines, obstructions and booby-traps as soon as possible so that it could start taking vital supplies. They did so in record time and one of them, Able-Seaman M.H. Woods, would win the George Medal for his outstanding bravery during these highly dangerous underwater actions.

Hemingway had a tremendous story right under his nose, for up to now no one had latched on to the activities of these first frogmen. But it didn't seem to interest him, just as what was happening at the nearby front also didn't.

Perhaps some of his lack of interest was due to the stalemate which existed those first two weeks of July on the US 1st Army Front. In all the months, perhaps years, of planning for the Liberation of France, most attention had been concentrated on the Invasion beaches and D-Day. Far too little thought had been given to what happened next. So it was that the Norman *bocage* country came as a tremendous shock. In those tight Norman fields surrounded by thick, very high hedges, some centuries old, Allied superiority in armour and aircraft meant nothing. The average Allied tank couldn't get through the hedges and close support aircraft could not be used for fear that they might hit their own men.

The battle for the *bocage* boiled down to a slogging match between two sets of infantry with the advantage being on the side of the German defender, fought in what one observer called, 'a sort of gigantic shrubbery'. There were just three ways that the US infantry could get through the *bocage* country. They could march down the roads between the hedgerows – something which was highly dangerous and not to be recommended. They could attempt to get through the gaps in the hedges, which inevitably were covered by German snipers and machine gunners. Or they could rush the field beyond in a skirmish line. This third method, as one battle-worn US officer commented, would have been 'a fair way of doing it, if there had not been a hedgerow!'

Losses were very high. The US 90th Infantry Division, for instance, lost all sense of direction and cohesion inside the *bocage*.

The result was that the unfortunate American division had suffered the loss of 150 per cent of its officers (including replacements) and 100 per cent of its enlisted men by the time Hemingway reached Normandy. Its running mates, the American 2nd and 30th Infantry Division, had similar losses, men being killed and wounded by the hundreds each new day. For an advance of a mere seven miles, the twelve divisions finally involved suffered no fewer than 40,000 casualties, the population of a good-sized town vanishing in just over a month.

Understandably, given his temperament and short attention-span, this kind of slow, bloody, undramatic slogging match did not appeal to Hemingway. Dutifully, of course, he took off for the front every morning in a jeep, as did the other correspondents, to return in the evening to the comfortable house in Cherbourg to write up his notes. But he made no effort to transcribe them into any kind of coherent shape. It was as if the whole dreary, bloody business bored him. Instead, he found solace in the evening in singing, drinking more of the 'compass fluid' and telling tall tales about his exploits in Wykeham Barnes' 'Mossy'.

Unknown to the writer, his new hero Wykeham Barnes was in action every one of those evenings – right above his head in fact. As he told the BBC correspondent that week: 'Our job is to hinder and destroy the enemy wherever movement can be found and we try to ensure that the ground forces get neither sleep nor peace and that the enemy faces his day's battle with tired troops and insufficient equipment.' By blasting and gunning their troops, trains and road convoys, Wykeham Barnes' pilots hoped, as their Group Commander expressed it, that 'when their divisions reach the front line . . . they shall be demoralised, decimated, tired and late. This is our ambition but we shan't know for some months how near we are to achieving it.'

But a bored Hemingway was in no mood to find that out or wait for the more fluid and exciting warfare that would surely follow the breakout from the *bocage* country. After a week in the house in Cherbourg, he decided he had had enough. As quietly as he had arrived, he returned to Issigny and Charles Wertenbaker's obliging cousin, George.

Here too, the war seemed to have gone to sleep ever since the day a month before when the British and American invaders had linked up in the village. Indeed, the only action in the area appeared to be that of a few overworked Norman prostitutes now offering their services to the Americans, instead of their former customers, the Germans, as General Bradley discovered to his surprise that week. Together with General Pete Quesada of the 9th Tactical Air Command, which ran Issigny airfield, he came across an 'Off Limits' sign in a part of the village. Curious, he and Quesada drove on and came across a house marked 'Prophylactic Station', containing three sleeping GIs. None of them recognised their army commander when he awakened them and asked what kind of business they were doing. One of the medics shrugged and said, 'Well yesterday there was just one for the MPs and one for me and that was that'. Characteristically, Bradley and the Air Corps General went on their way without identifying themselves.

From sleepy Issigny Hemingway flew back to England. Hours later he was at the Dorch with Mary Welsh. Two days later on 17 July, he took her for a last lunch at the White Tower where they had first met. Things were beginning to move in Normandy now and he could not justify staying in Britain any longer. What transpired at that last lunch we do not know. Something did, however, for in her diary Miss Mary recorded: 'Wonderful lunch with Hemingway, though terribly sleepy.' Thereafter, as she described it herself, she was 'like a cat in heat' in her attempts to get to France and find Hemingway again.

The days in 'dear old London town' were over. Hemingway was moving to France. At last, Papa was going to war.

Book Two

FRANCE, SUMMER 1944

'Hell, I had to go to war to see my wife!'
Ernest Hemingway to John Carlisle, August 1944

THE IVY LEAGUE DIVISION

In the Second World War they called it 'the Ivy League Division', which gave the American infantry outfit a rather classy image, as if it were made up of young men from the East Coast, who had attended Harvard, Yale, Princeton and the like. In fact, the nickname did not originate from the outfit's divisional patch, which was shaped like an ivy leaf, as many thought, but from the Fourth Division's classification in Roman numerals, 'IV' – ivy, in other words.

The Fourth Division was, and still is, a regular army formation, which had first been raised in 1917. A year later, the Fourth had sailed for France. During the course of its passage from the United States, one of the troopships carrying the division, the British liner *SS Maldovia*, had been torpedoed off the Isle of Wight and fifty-six doughboys had been killed before they had fired a single shot in anger. It was yet another sad event in the tragic history of the fourth which would be strangely paralleled in the Second World War.

In 1940, months before America entered the war, 'the Ivy League' was reactivated under the command of Major General Raymond 'Tubby' Barton, whose ample middle-age spread gave him his nickname. After training for nearly four years, the 4th Division finally sailed for England in January 1944. It consisted of three regiments: the Eighth, formed originally in 1838; the Twelfth, which traced its lineage back to the Civil War; and the 22nd ('Deeds Not Words' as its regimental motto proclaimed it), which had fought in the Indian wars, including the battle of the Little Big Horn in Montana.

In England the Division settled in Devon, with the divisional headquarters being located at Tiverton. Here, one of its members, an intense-looking staff sergeant named J.D. Salinger, made the setting for the first section of his famous post-war story *For Esme – with Love and Squalor!* Salinger was an exception. Most of the Fourth Division were kept too busy preparing for D-Day in early 1944 to have time to take tea with that pert little aristocrat in the local tearoom.

That April, while training for the real thing on Utah beach, the Division suffered a loss that strangely resembled the sinking of the *SS Maldovia* off the Isle of Wight. During the night of 28–29 April in an exercise called 'Operation Tiger', a convoy of Royal Naval craft bearing the Division for a mock invasion at Slapton Sands, was attacked by a flotilla of fast German E-boats. Wild firing broke out everywhere as the motor torpedo boats zipped in and out of the transports firing their torpedoes. By the time it was all over, 749 men of the Division had perished and for weeks after the authorities were kept busy searching for 'bigots' – officers who knew the secret of D-Day, and had gone to the bottom of the sea during that disastrous attack.

Shortly afterwards, General Eisenhower and his personal aide and publicity man Commander Butcher visited the Division in Devon. Butcher, whom Hemingway would later describe maliciously as 'a nylon-smooth captain of the Navy who could not command a cat-boat', was dismayed by the state of the Division, as was his boss Eisenhower. There were too many full colonels, he thought, who were 'fat, grey and oldish. Most of them wear the Rainbow Ribbon of the last war and they are still fighting it.'

Nor was Butcher impressed by the Fourth's younger officers. He wrote in his diary: 'I am concerned by the toughness and alertness of young American officers I saw this trip. They seem to regard the war as one grand maneuver in which they are having a happy time. Many seem as green as growing corn. How will they act in battle and how will they look in three months' time?'

Two months later the Division landed on Utah beach 'under heavy shelling', with a total of 16 casualties. There they 'moved rapidly inland across the inundated area, made a 45-degree right turn and attacked with lightning speed an alert and determined enemy'. Thereafter, the Ivy League Division was involved in the hard slog of the Normandy *bocage* country and by the time it was all over, the elderly colonels had gone and those younger officers who had survived were no longer 'as green as growing corn'. The Fourth was on its way to becoming one of General Bradley's veteran divisions. But the 'butcher's bill had been, and would continued to be right to the end of the war, very high.

Hemingway returned to Normandy for good on 18 July. According to his own statement, he first attached himself to one of General Patton's armoured divisions. Patton himself had landed on Omaha beach, in secret, on 6 July. But while he was waiting for his jeep to be readied, he gave the assembled troops an impromptu speech declaring: 'I'm proud to be here to fight beside you. I am going personally to shoot that paper-hanging goddamned son-of-a-bitch just like I would a snake.' (The reference was to Hitler, who supposedly had been a house-painter at some time in his career.)

But, although Patton was ready to fight, his troops weren't. Indeed, the second of his two armoured divisions, the 6th Armored, was landing at Utah beach on the same day that Hemingway arrived. Both these units, the 4th and 6th Armored Divisions, would not be activated for combat until 25 July, one day after Hemingway severed his attachment to General Patton's 3rd Army.

How then could Hemingway have attached himself to Patton's armour, complaining about the dust his Sherman tanks raised, which irritated his eyes and always sensitive throat? As he noted in his diary: 'This was the summer of the dust and mud. The metal fighter strips would be ankle-deep in dust and huge clouds of dust would billow, blinding and chokeing [sic] you, as the P-47s.'

In his one novel to come out of the Second World War, *Across the River and Into the Trees*, Hemingway makes his hero, the dying Colonel Cantwell, tell his Italian girlfriend: 'I was thinking just now of a man named Georgie Patton who possibly never told the truth in his life.' According to Cantwell, Patton was 'a poor man all his life – although rich in money and with a lot of armour.'

One might apply the same statement to Colonel Cantwell's creator, for here again he appears to be telling an untruth. What was Hemingway really doing during that week of 18–24 July 1944, which he later described as an 'abortion'? He certainly was not with the 3rd Army's only armoured division on the Continent, the 4th Armored. Had he, instead, gone to General Patton's headquarters, located in an apple orchard at Nehou, and been rebuffed by 'Ole Blood and Guts' himself or one of his staff officers?

We don't know. But thereafter Patton, a womaniser and man of action who should surely have appealed to Hemingway, came in for a great deal of slander by the author whenever his name was mentioned. In one case, in a letter written to his publisher Charles Scribner in 1950, Hemingway stated he knew a woman, 'whose daughter was allegedly raped by the Hon. Georgie Patton when she was a child!' Strong stuff, but typical of Hemingway's attitude to the 3rd Army Commander thereafter.

On 24 July, whatever the cause for his leaving Patton's 3rd Army, Hemingway appeared at the divisional press camp of the

Ivy League Division and asked to see its commander. He was taken to Tubby Barton's trailer where he met the thick-set general, with a trim military moustache, for the first time. Later he would write to Mary from France that 'the general is an educated, talented and charming man and a fine soldier'.

What Barton thought of this war correspondent butting in on him at a critical phase of the breakout from the beachheads is not recorded. But he did recall that he remembered Hemingway as a sports reporter who had got into a fistfight with some prominent person or other. (During his lifetime, Hemingway often got into fights with persons, prominent or otherwise.)

The two of them hit it off right from the start and a Captain Stevenson, the general's aide, felt Barton was 'a natural for herd-guarding Ernie'. He, too, shared Hemingway's liking for violent action and the frontline. But at that moment Barton had little time for writers. He assigned Stevenson to look after Hemingway, and the following morning the Captain took Hemingway to meet Colonel Lanham, who had newly taken over the Division's 22nd Infantry Regiment, at his headquarters in a small farmhouse in the crossroads hamlet of Le Mesnil-Herman.

Colonel Charles Trueman Lanham was a short, wiry, ex-West Pointer with a short fuse and a fiery temper, endowed with a gift for profanity. He was also something of an amateur poet and writer, who had written some of the US Army's training manuals back in the States. Hemingway would take to him right from the start and they would remain firm friends right to Hemingway's death, long after Lanham had left the Army to become an executive with the Xerox Corporation. Hemingway always thought very highly of Lanham, but others did not share Hemingway's opinion of the 43-year-old future general who greatly resembled Hemingway's fellow writer Dashiell Hammett (still serving in the Aleutians as a sergeant, although he was

52 years old and a millionaire, thanks to the sale of his *Thin Man* books to the movies). Bill Walton, Hemingway's new paratroop-correspondent friend, later described Lanham as 'small, delicate – and very neurotic'. Gregory Hemingway, the writer's son, thought he was a bore. For, although he was a brave and gallant soldier (he would be wounded in action soon), he was also strait-laced, old-fashioned and very set in his ways. That did not deter Hemingway. For the rest of his war in Europe, Hemingway had found a perfect comrade-in-arms, whom he could idealise into heroic proportions; Lanham, in return, would confirm Hemingway as a man of great daring and high military expertise. For the man who had boasted he was the 'first American officer to be wounded in Italy' had never had a day's military training or fired a shot at a fellow human being. Now through Lanham he was going to make up for those deficiencies, something that was greatly necessary in a writer who glorified action, violence and war.

Somehow, Lanham got hold of the idea this day when Hemingway first entered his life that the author was a 'Colonel Colliers' on a visit from Washington: a kind of non-combatant military tourist, common at that time in France. As he recalled after the war, 'Our respect for visitors diminished in direct proportion to the level of their echelon above our own. A visitor from Washington was therefore at the bottom of the scale. I told Colonel Edwards to show the gentlemen in and went back to my maps.'

Lanham was not prepared for the huge figure who shouldered his way through the narrow door of his farmhouse headquarters, with, peeping in behind him, the smaller shape of Ira Wolfert, novelist and fellow correspondent. Colonel Edwards said, 'This is Colonel Colliers and Mr Wolfram'.

Swiftly, Hemingway corrected the mistake. 'I'm no colonel,' he said, 'I'm a correspondent for *Collier's*. My name is Hemingway.'

'Ernest, no doubt?' Lanham reacted quickly, for he knew his American literature.

'Yes,' Hemingway acknowledged modestly. 'My name *is* Ernest.'

Lanham warmed to the newcomer immediately. He knew all too well how valuable the press could be for one's image – and promotion! Like no other campaign previously, the 1944–45 battle for Western Europe was conducted under the all-seeing, total scrutiny of the media. Daily, hundreds of correspondents, cameramen, radio reporters and photographers swarmed out from their 'press camps' to cover every aspect of the conflict. Suddenly, obscure generals became household names. Their photographs and deeds appeared on the front pages of the papers back home. Those middle-aged gentlemen, who a few years before had been looking forward to a slippered retirement on a modest pension in a warm climate where it was cheap to live, loved it.

Abruptly, their divisions adopted bold exciting names – 'The Hells on Wheels', 'The Screaming Eagles', 'The Rock of the Marne', while they, the divisional commanders, took on all the allure of a Hollywood diva. They had themselves photographed in unorthodox uniforms and were always depicted carrying weapons, a pistol in a shoulder holster, a grenade attached to the webbing of their uniform, perhaps a carbine slung heroically over their shoulders; although usually they never came within ten miles of the fighting front.

These middle-aged gentlemen, who had never heard a shot fired since the First World War (if then) adopted brash, bold nicknames like 'Wild Bill' Weaver, 'Howling Mad' Smith and 'Iron Mike' O'Daniel. And that vain desire for self-publicity seeped down to their junior commanders, who, if they were Regular Army, also had a weather eye cocked for personal publicity which might ensure promotion. As Lanham realised that this was, indeed, the well-known writer Ernest Hemingway, his attitude changed. He briefed Hemingway and

Wolfert on the Twenty-second's current battle, and then invited the two civilians to eat with him and his staff.

Hemingway described the meal three years later: 'There was roast chicken to eat and a great atmosphere of calmness and no one was nervous. Everyone was very cheerful and gay and efficient without haveing [sic] to drink to be gay nor tighten up to be efficient. I was very impressed. Buck [Lanham's nickname] talked on literature.'

Hemingway made it quite clear that he wasn't here for classy chats about the cosmos. For the time being, literature didn't interest him. He was here purely and simply for the war.

Then, 'Wolfram [Ira Wolfert] asked some idiotic questions which embarrassed me, so we left very promptly'.

'France is fun now,' Hemingway wrote to Mary Welsh that month after he had joined the Fourth Infantry Division. 'We have had a tough, fine time. This is the eighth day we have been attacking all the time. Have been with very good guys. . . . Anyway been very happy here and had a good time with infantry again. . . . I make as good a war as I can . . . am very happy at Front.'

Despite the strange new syntax, which Hemingway presumably lifted from Army 'officialese' (which leaves out the personal pronouns in favour of the collective 'we'), it was quite clear that Hemingway was really enjoying the war at last. Tubby Barton was very co-operative and would receive him at night in his headquarters in his underwear to quiz him on the correspondent's activities.

'I was worrying about you,' he told Hemingway one evening in his 'kind warm voice'. 'What made you so late?'

'We ran into some armour,' Hemingway replied, 'and I came back the long way around.'

The general was immediately interested and asked Hemingway for the details before remarking, 'The people are very tired, Ernie. They ought to have a rest. Even one good night's rest would help. If they could have four days . . . just four days. But it's the same old story.'

'You're tired yourself,' Hemingway commiserated. 'Get some sleep. Don't let me keep you awake.'

It was all very chummy (according to Hemingway), and no doubt General Barton was pleased when Hemingway's account of him and his division duly appeared in *Collier's* magazine under the nicely democratic title of 'The GI and the General'.

But if the Ivy Leaguers and their general were tired in those nine days which Hemingway spent with them that summer, Hemingway was not. On 31 July, he acquired a motorcycle with a sidecar and then an abandoned Mercedes which had been shot up and still had a bullet in its steering column. Obligingly, General Barton assigned Hemingway a driver from the Divisional Motor Pool so that he could go where he liked. Now he was able to shoot off all over the place, having, as he wrote to Mary Welsh, 'a very jolly and gay life full of deads, German loot, much shooting, much fighting, hedges, small hills, dusty roads, metalled road, green country, wheat fields, dead cows, horses, new hills, dead horses, tanks, 88's, Kraftwagens, dead US guys'.

Now he was free and at war. No demands were being made on his intellect; he didn't have to write. He missed nothing of his previous life save her, as he carefully pointed out to his new love. Nor did he think of his children because he knew he 'wouldn't see them for a long time'. He certainly didn't miss 'the selfish chickenshit prima donnas', who were presumably his first three wives, and in particular Martha Gellhorn. He was free to go as he pleased, without responsibilities and obligations (he wasn't even accredited to the US 1st Army to which the Fourth belonged), and have adventures with lethal outcomes. It was the middle-aged man of action's dream come true.

His accomplice on these adventures was a 29-year-old private soldier Archie Pelkey, assigned to him as a driver by General Barton. Born in New Jersey, Pelkey, red-haired and minus his front teeth, had served two hitches in the Regular Army before the war. By the time Hemingway had finished with him, Pelkey would be speaking only broken English and be in the process of being referred to a 'shrink'. Twenty-five years later 'Arch', as Hemingway called him, would die drinking beer in front of the television. It would be two days before anyone found the body.

Now, however, the two adventurers set off to enjoy the war, unrestrained by the bonds of military discipline, which irked Pelkey and which Hemingway refused to acknowledge even existed. On the morning of 3 August, the two of them drove up to the little town of Villedieu-les-Peoles. For two days now the Germans had been attacking the flank of General 'Lightning Joe' Collins' VII Corps here in the area. Now the men of the Fourth were going on the offensive though the Germans had brought up fresh troops in the shape of the 9 SS Division. All hell was let loose. There were snipers of both sides in the houses, many of which were on fire, and the combat medics were running back and forth among the flames trying to pick up the wounded lying in the gutters moaning.

Pelkey and Hemingway entered in their motorbike with its sidecar full of hand grenades. According to Hemingway's own account, he quizzed some of the locals in French and found the Americans had by-passed a cellar in which a number of last-ditch SS troops were holed up. Now they offered to show him where the cellar was located. Hemingway took them up on their offer. Arming himself and Pelkey with the grenades, they crept forward to the spot indicated, where Hemingway yelled down into the cellar for the supposed SS men to come out, repeating his order in both German and French.

If there were really SS men in the cellar they did not obey him. Hemingway didn't hesitate. He tugged out the grenades' cotter pins and yelled, 'All right, divide these among yourselves!'

Anyway, that was his story. True or false, it was the first indication that Hemingway was not prepared to abide by the rules of land warfare which prohibited war correspondents from bearing arms in combat. That was the first time. It would not be the last.

Later that same day Hemingway bumped into a weary Buck Lanham who was 'slightly whiskery, dead-eyed tired but very gay and cheerful'. Earlier on, Hemingway had been given some bottles of champagne by a French innkeeper who had thought he was the personal representative of General Patton. 'Ah, General Patton, how we admire and revere him,' the innkeeper had apparently exclaimed to an amused Hemingway. (How a provincial French innkeeper would know anything of General Patton at that stage of the war is a mystery, especially as Patton's 3rd Army was not even fighting in Normandy, but in Brittany.) Now, after killing his SS men in the cellar, Hemingway presented a bottle of the vintage champagne to Buck Lanham from the sidecar of his motor-cycle combination and they drank a toast to victory. For Hemingway it was going to be that kind of war – grenades and champagne!

Two days later, the Fourth was temporarily withdrawn from combat to act as a kind of flank guard in the area around St-Pois. Now Hemingway asked General Barton for permission to bring over one of the Hollywood Irregulars of his Dorchester days. Bob Capa, the *Life* photographer, was currently in Granville some twelve miles away. Could he use the Mercedes to have him over for the weekend? Barton agreed. The weekend jaunt nearly ended in tragedy for Hemingway – as he put it later in a letter to Mary Welsh, 'all our jolly futures were on the bum yesterday for a while'. After Capa arrived, he was transferred to the motorcycle combination with Pelkey driving. Hemingway was going to take the photographer to meet his new friend Colonel Lanham. Unfortunately, Pelkey missed the turn-off to Lanham's Command Post. Instead the three of them went racing down a hill at full speed to take a sharp curve only to find themselves facing a dug-in German 57mm anti-tank gun. Pelkey reacted first. He hit the brakes. The combination skidded to a stop, and they all leapt in panic for the nearest ditch. Hemingway landed hard on his already injured head, while a German machine-gun with the anti-tank crew opened fire.

As Hemingway described it to Mary Welsh, he 'had to pretend to be dead until quite a while later and could hear Germans talking on the other side of the hedge at about ten feet. They spoke very disrespectfully of your big friends, who they considered dead.'

How Hemingway would know the two Germans armed with machine pistols spoke 'disrespectfully of your big friend', he never explained, for his knowledge of the German language was exceedingly basic. That accident ended his first spell with the Ivy League Division. Barton gave him a bottle of Bourbon and wished him well saying, as he departed, 'Ernie, I will miss you very much. . . . Both personally and officially.' For Hemingway now had a new bump on his head, had hurt his back and was urinating blood. Later, he maintained that the second heavy landing on his head had given him double vision. He told Mary Welsh that he was also suffering from 'slowness (of thought and speech), loss of verbal memory, tendency to write backhand and backwards and the headaches, condition Mr S [his abbreviation for 'Mr Scrooby', the suggestive euphemism he had first used with Martha Gellhorn for his penis] was in and the inertia, headaches and ringing in the ears were all symptoms of what had been done to head'. Hemingway definitely needed a rest.

Thus he had ended his fist real taste of combat with an infantry
division. As he wrote to his son Patrick: 'You will be very
proud of what the Division [Fourth] has done and I have never
been happier nor had a more useful life ever.' But, of course, he
had not truly experienced the life of a fighting infantryman. His
days in that first week of August had been spent behind the
fighting front. Despite what he said and wrote himself, he had
been essentially an observer and not a participant. He had not
spent miserable, interminable nights in a fox hole, living off
C and K rations; nor had he slogged along those blinding-white
French roads, lathered in sweat and laden like a pack animal, to
be ordered at the end of the road to form up in a skirmish line
to attack yet another German position.

What did Hemingway know of the reality of that attack on
Percy, for example, where the French innkeeper had given him
the bottles of champagne? He had not been in that attack up
the hill where the slope was soon littered with the dead and
dying of the Fourth Infantry Division. It was 'like some terrible
war film', one observer remembered. 'I saw one tall, very thin
man drop his rifle and start to run away down the hill. Then
I caught sight of holes in his head and he crashed full tilt into an
apple tree. He was running dead! . . . I'll never forget the
dedication of those men of the 4th Infantry walking up that hill
over their dead bodies like British redcoats attacking in
Revolutionary War days. It was magnificent. We got to the top
with about ten tanks and about thirty-five foot soldiers.'

Hemingway knew nothing of this. His nine days with Buck
Lanham's 22nd Regiment passed in exciting, free-wheeling
jaunts along roads and in places already captured, with much
wine, and cosy boastful chats afterwards in the relative comfort
of the regiment command post, where a man could wash and
shave, change his shirt and socks, and enjoy fresh food and not
some nauseating goo out of an olive-drab can. Here no one
asked, as the frontline infantry did, when yet more canned

rations were passed among them for their supper, 'and which one's got the cunt in it, sarge?' For the staff officers at regimental headquarters were gentlemen and this was a gentleman's war.

Nearly forty years after the Second World War had ended, American writer Paul Fussell, who had been wounded leading an infantry section of the US 103rd Division in France, summed up the difference between the men at the front and the 'feather merchants' to the rear like this: 'Those who actually fought in the line during the war, especially if they were wounded, constitute an in-group separate from those who did not. Praise or blame does not attach: rather there is the accidental possession of a special empirical knowledge, a feeling of a mysterious shared ironic awareness manifesting itself in an instinctive scepticism about pretension, publicly enunciated truths, the vanities of learning and the pomp of authority. Those who fought know a secret about themselves.'

Hemingway never had an opportunity to learn that secret. That summer Hemingway wrote: 'I love combat!'

THE HEMINGWAY IRREGULARS

Now peace was returning to the Normandy countryside. The Anglo-Americans had broken out of their beachheads at last and were surging east at a great rate. The beaten Wehrmacht in France were in full retreat.

Now the locals could return to what they had been doing before their rural peace had been so brutally disturbed by the Invasion: getting on with their lives dedicated to the production of fine Camembert and Calvados. Let the 'Boche' and the 'Rosbifs' carry on with the bloody business of breaking each other's heads, as long as they did not do it any more in Normandy. What had the silly war got to do with them anyhow?

Hemingway and Capa, who had had a fairly rough time of it on D-Day (an NCO had literally booted the little Hungarian out of the landing barge when he had thought that Capa was too scared to get out), and six other war correspondents decided they would spend a little time out of war, too. They picked the peninsula of Mont-St-Michel.

The peninsula had been recently liberated by Patton's 3rd Army and was still out of bounds to all save general officers and war correspondents. But as Patton's general officers were presumably all busy fighting in Brittany, the war correspondents, who included one woman, Mrs Helen Kirkpatrick, who worked for the *Saturday Evening Post*, had the place all to themselves. Hemingway and his colleagues moved into the one hotel which had remained open during the war when most of the French coastal areas had been placed out of bounds to non-residents by the Germans. It was the Hotel de la Mère Poulard.

The original Mère Poulard had been famous before the war in the 1920s for the beauty and lightness of her omelettes. Indeed no less a body than the Academy of Gastronomes had written to her in 1922 asking her for the secret of her omelette. Annette Poulard had replied she just threw in eggs and Normandy butter and shook her pan over the wood fire constantly, ending with, 'I am happy Monsieur, if this recipe please you'.

Now the original Madame Poulard had departed, but here successor as *patronne*, Madame Chevallier, was equally obliging. Hemingway flattered her into giving the thirsty correspondents some of her fine wine. According to Madame, the bottles of wine had been hidden from the Germans during the Occupation *dèrriere les fagots*. This raised a laugh from the others when Hemingway told them. In those days, long before gay rights (something which probably made Hemingway rotate in his grave), 'faggot' was the usual derogatory term for homosexual. The wine and the weak joke set the tone for the brief holiday. The correspondents prepared to enjoy themselves in the August sunshine. All were perceptive men with a journalist's trained eye for observation, and they were offered a unique chance to view the real Hemingway when he was not surrounded by his usual cronies, hangers-on, and admirers, who would accept his most outrageous behaviour, as if he could do no wrong.

One of the youngest among them was Charles Collingwood, then aged twenty-six, who had first met Hemingway the previous month back in Cherbourg. He felt Hemingway was 'a marvellous talker and raconteur and a boon companion [who] was often very indulgent to those younger than he'. But

Collingwood noted that Hemingway had a dark side to him, as well. Whenever he could not dominate the conversation or group, he would relapse into a gloomy silence, almost sulking. Collingwood thought: 'In those periods he seemed to belie the complete assurance and self-confidence he usually sought to convey. From time to time one sensed a certain vulnerability about him.'

Bill Walton, whom Hemingway always called 'Willie', also got on very well with the author. Indeed, they remained friends long after the war, although Hemingway did criticise him – behind his back. He described his attitude to Hemingway as 'always kind and loving'.

'Mr Wolfram' (Ira Wolfert) didn't hit it off altogether with the writer. Hemingway described Wolfert as a 'brilliant reporter', but he had no faith in Wolfert's ability to sort the grain out from the chaff. Hemingway pointed out a little maliciously to the others that if he, Hemingway, remarked in a joking manner that he had just seen a wounded cow suckling its calf or a farm dog barking at a bomber, Wolfert would surely have the tall tales in his paper the following day.

So they enjoyed themselves, drinking the fine wines from 'behind the faggots' and eating Madame Poulard's celebrated three-inch thick omelettes, cooked over a fire of wood in copper pans with four-foot handles. Occasionally, Hemingway would slip into one of his dark brooding moods. When that happened, the writer could swiftly turn, even on his friends, as Charles Collingwood was soon to learn that second week of August.

During his stay at Mont-St-Michel, Hemingway finished his flattering portrait of General Barton, which would appear as the 'GI and the General'. For some reason, he showed his draft to Collingwood (the latter had already noted 'there was a didactic streak in him . . . he loved to instruct younger writers'), and asked Collingwood what he thought of the piece.

Collingwood, as he said himself, was then 'a brash youngster'. He did not realise that Hemingway had long given up wanting to know the truth about his work. He boasted that his editor Max Perkins had never changed a word he had written for years. Collingwood blurted out, 'Well, Papa, it sounds like a parody of Ernest Hemingway.' This was very true. Most of the stuff he sent from Europe did. Hemingway's reaction was sour.

'His face froze and I forget whether he actually ushered me out or made it very clear I was to leave, which, of course, I did – feeling like the most insensitive clown after so flattering a gesture on his part. He cut me dead for weeks.'

One unqualified, one-hundred-per-cent admirer of the writer was the enthusiastic, talkative correspondent of the *Detroit Free Press*, John Carlisle. He arrived at the hotel two days later after he had been told by another newspaperman that 'they have a place there . . . where they make omelettes the size of birthday cakes'. At first he thought there would be no room for him, but when Carlisle explained he was an acquaintance of Hemingway, he was told: 'Papa runs the hotel. He'll get you in. He's the boss.' Papa did so and Carlisle, as a one-man admiration society, basked in the sunshine of Hemingway's presence.

For him, Hemingway could do no wrong. He knew all about the war, loved the average GI (when Hemingway certainly did not) and was 'one of the happiest men I ever knew, a guy with a great zest for life and who enjoyed every minute of it'. Although Carlisle himself was bored by the war, he thought Hemingway's whole life centred on the battle. 'I told him one time, "Goddamnit, you must have been born for war. I think you like war." I don't remember his reply. I thought he could have a good time brushing his teeth over a helmetful of water.' Carlisle was typical of many who came into contact with Hemingway during the war. They suspended all judgement, lost all critical faculties, became wide-eyed admiration societies, accepting Hemingway's wildest statements as gospel truth.

When Carlisle once asked the great man why he had left his 'beautiful home in Cuba' to come to France, Hemingway snorted: 'Hell, I had to go to war to see my wife!'

It was a blatant lie. But another little bit of the 'Hemingway myth' had been created, just as was the case with Carlisle's enthusiastic statement that 'In four days Ernie was a legend in the division [the Fourth Division]'. In truth, most of the Fourth's weary young soldiers had never heard of Ernest Hemingway, even by the time the war was over in 1945 and they had endured eleven months of combat – those who survived.

The correspondents had arrived at Mont-St-Michel on a Friday. On Monday, after a weekend of heavy drinking and practical jokes (Wertenbaker of *Time-Life* had driven Hemingway to distraction with a left-handed corkscrew he had found in a joke-shop on the peninsula), Hemingway decided to visit his new friend Buck Lanham at his new command post. It was located in a Norman château some fifty kilometres east of Mont-St-Michel in the little hamlet of Château Lingeard, where Lanham's kitchen staff were busy preparing a special festive meal for the regimental commander. As Lanham explained after the war: 'I had known Hemingway only a short time when I ran into him on 8 August 1944. The following day was my twenty-fifth wedding anniversary. I had mentioned it to my staff, and since we were supposed to be pulled out of the lines the next day, the decided to have a little party at the command post, featuring roast goose which I had never tasted. I asked Hemingway to join us at the party. He said he couldn't and that was that.'

Hemingway who always liked a party and good food (there was going to be a special surprise cake for the Colonel, too), felt a premonition. Later he would tell Lanham, using a phrase from his own book, *For Whom the Bell Tolls*, that 'the reason he had not accepted my invitation was because the place had the stink of death about it'.

Lanham wondered later about Ernie's premonition. 'I said to myself "that's a coincidence maybe".'

Whether or not Hemingway made up the story later to excuse his somewhat brusque refusal of a meal at Château Lingeard is open to question. In the event, however, something did happen at Colonel Lanham's château command post on the very next day. 'Beware of châteaux,' Hemingway would write to one who would suffer there the next day.

Ever since the beginning of August, Hitler personally had been behind the plan to launch a counter-offensive in France to stop the rot. The spot he picked for the breakthrough, which would send the Allies reeling back to the sea, was the little French town of Mortain, defended by the US 30th Infantry Division. Fortunately, General Bradley, the US Army Group Commander, knew the attack was coming. This was thanks to those British 'boffins' grouped in Hut Three, perhaps the most famous little Nissen hut of the Second World War. There, at Bletchley in the Home Counties, these former Oxbridge academics of the 'Ultra Secret' organisation had been deciphering Germany's most secret codes since 1940.

But Bradley could not alert General Hobbs, the commander of the 30th Division. That might have compromised the war-winning secret decoding operation. But he could strengthen his flanks and prepare for an American armoured counter-thrust. Both these measures would not make the German suspicious that their codes had been compromised when they learned of them later. Thus it was that the Fourth Infantry Division was withdrawn to the left flank of the 30th Infantry Division for a brief 'rest' just before the German attack commenced.

On 7 August all hell broke loose on the American front. Hobbs' 30th Division was badly hit. Here and there his men withdrew. Some didn't, but decided to slog it out although the Germans penetrated to their rear and cut them off. The Fourth did not come under direct attack itself, which was just as well because by this time one of its regiments, the Twelfth, had had a complete turnover of personnel (some 4,000 men) due to casualties. But its massed artillery battalions did clobber the advancing Germans of the 116th Panzer Division and help to stop the surprise attack. In their turn, however, the German counter-fire fell on the positions of Colonel Lanham's unsuspecting 22nd Infantry Regiment, which naturally had not been warned by Bradley what was going to happen.

While Hemingway and the other correspondents watched through their binoculars the sudden battle which had flared up so surprisingly on the mainland fifty kilometres away, Lanham's château headquarters was straddled by heavy German artillery fire. Hits were registered on the roof of the château and a little later shells began to fall on the cobbled courtyard. Several regimental staff officers were killed and many wounded straight away. A little later Colonel Lanham was slightly wounded himself and borne away for treatment.

The anniversary dinner was postponed indefinitely, and three days later the 22nd Infantry Regiment was ordered to move to another position some thirty miles to the west.

Hemingway had, therefore, now lost contact with Lanham and his 22nd Regiment for the time being. But already, great new possibilities for adventure and his personal, if selfish, enjoyment of a campaign, in which a quarter of a million men would die before it was all over, were beginning to open up. Suddenly the Ivy League Division was forgotten.

Back in July, General Bradley, the American overall ground commander, had told his staff that Paris was 'nothing more than an inkspot on our maps to be by-passed as we headed toward the Rhine'. The French capital was to be avoided at all costs. Apolitical as he was, Bradley did not want to bog his troops down in any kind of mini-Stalingrad. It was the same kind of purely military argument he would use throughout the campaign, which resulted in Berlin, Vienna and Prague being handed over to the Russians to capture. But Bradley had not reckoned with another general, whose aims were more political than military – the 'new Joan of Arc', as President Roosevelt called him, or that 'damned French prima donna', in Churchill's words, General Charles de Gaulle.

Now on this wet Sunday, 20 August, General de Gaulle confronted the Supreme Commander Eisenhower in his seaside headquarters at Granville. Eisenhower was not in the best of moods. He, too, just like de Gaulle, had been forced to make an emergency landing on the beach in his private plane. While helping to push the plane through the sand he had wrenched his 'football knee' and was now virtually immobilised, when the war in France was reaching a crucial phase.

Just as de Gaulle had learned earlier on that wet Sunday, Eisenhower had now been informed that there had been an uprising against the Germans in Paris. He was not pleased by the news. An uprising by civilians against the German occupiers was 'just the kind of situation I didn't want, a situation that was not under our control, that might force us to change our plans before we were ready for it'.

That was exactly what de Gaulle was here for. He *wanted* Eisenhower to change his plans, for he feared that the Communist-inspired rising in Paris meant that the Communists were out to take control of the government. If they did, that would mean an end to his own aim of forming a provisional government for the country.

Dour and moody, de Gaulle stepped forward to meet Eisenhower. He knew he was a ghost to most French people; they knew his voice from the radio, but they did not know his face. Now his future in France depended upon this American, who he knew didn't like him. Eisenhower didn't waste any time. Using his situation map, he explained to de Gaulle that he had no intention of taking Paris. Instead he would envelop it and leave it to wither on the vine, while his troops pushed on to the German border. De Gaulle, as Eisenhower recalled later, made no bones about it. 'He said there was a serious menace from the Communists in the city.' But Eisenhower refused to change his plans. It was 'too early' to attempt to take Paris, for 'we might get ourselves in a helluva fight there'.

Morosely, de Gaulle left to cross the wet grass to his waiting car, a requisitioned pre-war automobile powered by a gas boiler towed behind the vehicle. It seemed to represent the state France was in during that summer of 1944.

On that same wet Sunday, Hemingway and his driver Red Pelkey, whom Walton called an 'uneducated red neck', had been trying to find a US outfit with whom they might travel to Paris. Why he selected Paris is not recorded. Perhaps it was because he had spent some of his youth there and had a romantic attachment to the place. His generation of Americans, after all, maintained that when a 'good American died, he went to Paris!'

For two days Hemingway had bothered the officers of first the US 7th Armored Division and then those of the 5th Infantry Division for information on the subject. The 5th Infantry Division, commanded by General 'Red' Irwin, a veteran of the fighting in North Africa and Sicily, informed him he should try an outpost at Epernon, a few kilometres closer to Paris. Eagerly, Hemingway and his driver set off in the jeep, borrowed from Tubby Barton, for the outpost and there bumped into two truckloads of Free French fighters under their commander, Tabon Marceau.

That summer 'freedom fighters', who had never lifted a finger against the Germans in four years of Occupation, were springing out of the woodwork everywhere. Many of them were simply young men out for excitement, adventure, loot, and a chance to play soldier. A few were young men with dark pasts, who had worked actively for the Germans, and were now trying to prove that they had been in the Resistance all along.

This band encountered at the outpost seemed to belong to the first group. They were stripped to the waist, with sweat-bands around their heads, and heavily laden with captured German lugers, knives and two sten guns which had been dropped to the Resistance by the RAF. Obligingly enough they took the two Americans to a roadblock, where there had been a skirmish of some sort. A tree had been felled across the road upon which two wrecked jeeps and a damaged US truck lay sprawled at crazy angles. In the field nearby, next to a minefield, the bodies of seven dead Americans had been hastily buried. Hemingway surveyed the scene and noted two German tanks squatting in the ditch, which had been 'fitted with wire controls which ran back to gun pits so as to hit an approaching column in front and back'. What Hemingway had spotted were the German 'Goliath' radio-controlled mini-tanks, which carried an explosive charge of half a ton. One day it would be the forerunner of the vehicles used in Ulster in the 1980s to defuse and explode booby-trapped cars.

The French assured Hemingway that the next town, Rambouillet, had been evacuated by the retreating Germans. The Americans, they maintained, could easily take it without casualties. This seemed a good idea to Hemingway who now realised he was beyond the point of the American troops nearest to Paris, Irwin's 5th Infantry Division. For the first time, not only was he in the frontline, but beyond it, too!

He set off back up the road he had come and bumped into Lieutenant Irving Krieger of the Fifth's 2nd Regiment's anti-tank platoon. Kreiger, who had been digging in his six-pounder anti-tank guns at the side of the road, was approached by Pelkey, who asked the officer if he knew about mines. Krieger, a 'short, stocky exceedingly tough and very cheerful' officer answered that he 'was the regimental mine platoon leader and that it was my job to know about mines'.

Hemingway heard the reply and invited the young officer to come along to see the mines. 'I thought he was going to show me some mines a few hundred yards ahead. . . . Instead we drove ahead about 10 miles to Rambouillet.' Again, like Wykeham Barnes, Pelkey and all the rest of the soldiers and airmen he met during his time in Europe, Krieger soon found himself involved in a wild adventure that went against his better judgement. For, once they reached the former summer residence of French presidents and the royal hunting lodge (where Marie Antoinette, during her 'simple shepherdess' phase, had built herself a model dairy), Hemingway 'wanted to keep on going to Paris!'

Krieger refused. 'I told him what I had done could be explained but to go farther and jeopardise my soldiers more would require further interrogation. . . . The only reason I got out there 10 miles in front of our own troops was due to Ernest Hemingway's aggressiveness in his desire to get a story and get to Paris first. I was too concerned for the safety of my men to wander out 10 miles in front of our troops. But through a series of happenings, there I was, 10 miles out with my platoon and the Battalion Commander and higher authority knew that there were no Germans at least 10 miles out.'

Krieger, who had seen through Hemingway early enough, left. An angry Hemingway, thwarted in his first attempt to get to Paris first, jeeped back to General Irwin's command post to ask for machine guns for his 'irregulars' as he was now calling the handful of French partisans, to 'defend Rambouillet'.

Wisely, Irwin, who had a temper that matched his hair and who had seen much of war over the last two years, declined. What did a civilian war correspondent, even if he were called Ernest Hemingway, need with machine guns? Still angry, Hemingway, who was now advancing from 'Capitaine' to 'Mon Général' in the eyes of his young partisans, returned empty-handed. Fortunately, however, before he was forced to make any further decisions about whether to stay in the place or not, a reconnaissance troop from the 5th Infantry Division arrived at Rambouillet under a Lieutenant Petersen.

Again Hemingway returned to 5th Division Headquarters with a request for supplies for Petersen and this time he struck lucky. 'He got co-operation,' as Petersen recorded, 'and enough arms to take care of his irregulars.' He was in business. The adventure could begin.

When the forerunner of the CIA, the OSS (the 'Oh So Secret' as the cocktail party circuit in Washington had mocked them) had arrived in London, Malcolm Muggeridge had thought them, 'like *jeunes filles en fleur* straight from a finishing school, all fresh and innocent, to start work in our frowsty old intelligence brothel'. Two years later, under the command of Colonel David Bruce, a tall courteous Virginian of impeccable breeding who one day would be the US ambassador in West Germany and Britain, they still seemed very innocent. On D-Day, for instance, Bruce and his boss, General 'Wild Bill' Donovan, who had won America's highest honour of the Congressional Medal of Honor in the First World War, landed on the beaches. 'What a better end for us than to die in Normandy with enemy bullets in our bellies', 'Wild Bill' had declared stoutly.

What other major intelligence service would have tolerated an officer who knew his country's greatest secrets endangering his person thus?

Later Bruce and Wild Bill had come under German machine-gun fire and the latter had declared: 'David, we mustn't be captured, we know too much . . . Have you your pill?'

Bruce confessed he was not carrying the 'L' (for lethal) pill.

'Never mind,' the ever-resourceful Wild Bill answered. 'I have two of them.' He started to empty his pockets. Out came keys, money, snapshots of his grandchildren, newspaper clippings, but no pills. 'Never mind,' Wild Bill said, 'we can do without them.

But if we get out of here you must send a message to Gibbs, the Hall Porter at Claridges [the OSS stayed only at the best hotels], telling him on no account to allow the servants to touch some dangerous medicines in my bathroom.'

Thus, humanitarian disposition having been made, Wild Bill whispered to Bruce, 'I must shoot first.'

'Yessir,' Bruce whispered back, 'but can we do much against machine-guns with out pistols?'

'Oh, you don't understand,' his CO said. 'I mean, if we are about to be captured, I'll shoot you first. After all, I *am* your Commanding Officer!'

Now on this wet Sunday afternoon, the *jeunes filles en fleur*, in the shape of Colonel Bruce and his OSS staff, arrived at Rambouillet to find Ernest Hemingway setting up his 'command post' in the four-square, grey-stucco Hôtel du Grand Veneur, which naturally had a fine cellar.

Bruce knew 'Capitaine Hemingway' from his days with the Hollywood Irregulars, for the London Headquarters of the OSS had been located in Grosvenor Square and Hemingway had attended several boozy sessions, together with Burke and North of the OSS, in pubs frequented by his own office staff. Besides, Hemingway's son Jack was in the OSS too. Bruce was 'enchanted' to see Hemingway. 'Agents and patrols kept rushing in with reports, some of them contradictory, but all indicating that the Germans were laying mines down the road toward us about eight miles away, with a force of approximately 150 men. As there were no American troops in Rambouillet, Hemingway and the French had become more or less convinced the Germans would retake the town [that night]. We grilled the only Boche prisoner we could find. He either knew nothing or was a good actor, so we turned him back to the French, who he was firmly convinced intended to execute him!'

Bruce, the chairborne warrior, now found himself after two years at war in an active post. By now he had some thirty

Americans under his command, including two drunken US paras who were absent without leave, fourteen local *gendarmes* and Hemingway's Irregulars (some ten in number). With this force he proposed to resist any German attack. But what was he to do about Hemingway, who was the only one who spoke passable French and controlled the Irregulars and the *gendarmes*? By the rules of land warfare, war correspondents were not allowed to bear arms. According to one of his biographers, Professor Carlos Baker, Hemingway, realising this dilemma, asked Colonel Bruce for a hand-written statement authorising him to command the Irregulars in whatever battle might ensue.

But this was a justification of Hemingway's role in the 'defence of Rambouillet', given *after* the event, when Hemingway was being investigated by the US Army's Inspector General. At the time, Colonel Bruce, like Wykeham Barnes, Pelkey and Lieutenant Krieger, was swept up by the sheer enthusiasm of Hemingway and his desire for action. Colonel Bruce, chairborne warrior or not, should have known that war correspondents were not allowed to bear arms; not were they allowed to participate in military actions.

However, as depicted by Bruce himself, 'Ernest's bedroom was the nerve centre of these [intelligence] operations. There, in his shirt sleeves, he gave audience to intelligence couriers, to refugees from Paris, to deserters from the German Army, to local officials and to all comers. Within, Ernest, looking like a jolly dark Bacchus, dispensed the high, low and middle justice in English, French and broken German. His language was strong, salty and emphatic.

When German deserters or prisoners were brought in, they were stripped of their pants and made to work in the kitchens of the hotel. Two French women accused of sleeping with the Germans were given the same treatment, though they were allowed to keep their pants and their hair (although

Hemingway's Irregulars had wanted to shave it off as was the custom that summer with such women).

Hemingway himself boasted later that his operations were 'straight out of Mosby' (the celebrated guerrilla warfare leader of the US Civil War). By 23 August, according to his own statement, he had learned the 'entire Kraut MLR' (main line of resistance – by now Hemingway was an instant expert on military terminology), including the location of all roadblocks, radar installations, anti-aircraft, anti-tank defences, and so on, and so on, between Rambouillet and the southern suburbs of Paris.

It was an incredible assertion. How could Hemingway with his ten Irregulars cover such a large area, controlled by an estimated 20,000 German troops? But Colonel Bruce evidently believed him, though he did note that 'Ernest liked to dramatise himself'. All the same, he entertained a 'great admiration' for Hemingway 'as a cool, resourceful imaginative, military tactician and strategist'.

But Colonel Bruce was perhaps in a minority of one in his admiration for Hemingway in his role as *Le Grand Capitaine* during the 'defence of Rambouillet' in those hectic August days.

According to the way that Hemingway portrayed this most controversial and famous period of his time in Europe during the Second World War, it would seem as if he were almost alone, save for Bruce, in Rambouillet. In fact, by Monday 21 August, the place was crammed with war correspondents and others waiting for the fall of Paris. Colonel George Stevens' Hollywood Irregulars were there in full force. Stevens, the professional, was not going to miss the greatest photo-story that would come out of the campaign in France – the Liberation of Paris. Irwin Shaw, Mary Welsh's most recent lover, was with the team and Hemingway, spotting him, said, 'I have a motorcycle. Let's look

for Germans and draw fire.' Wisely Shaw declined. Perhaps he
suspected Papa's motives. At all events, he survived Rambouillet
and was still writing two decades after Hemingway's own death.

Others were not so fortunate in their dealings with
Hemingway. In particular, the war correspondents, now
clamouring for rooms at the Hôtel du Grand Veneur, did not
like Hemingway's high-handedness, the fact that he had
commandeered about fifteen of the place's thirty or forty rooms
for his own purposes, and his swaggering *grand capitaine* manner.

William Randolph Hearst, son of a famous newspaper tycoon
father and representing the Hearst Group, recalled afterwards:
'Hemingway was carrying a gun side-arm and he shouldn't have
been. He was only a reporter the same as us but he thought he
was the Second Coming and acted like it. He took messages
from army messengers, regular official messages from one
headquarters to this headquarters'. And I challenged him. I said,
"You'll get those kids into trouble". Oh, he was very nasty. He
was just as officious as all hell. I don't think anybody liked him
to tell them the truth. . . . He was a pain in the ass all round.'

Matters came to a head in the crowded dining room of the
hotel when the veteran Chicago newspaperman Bruce Grant
started 'complaining loud and clear' that he couldn't get a room
because Hemingway had them all tied up. Hemingway stalked
across to where Grant was standing and knocked him to the
floor. According to Irwin Shaw, not one of Hemingway's
greatest admirers, naturally, Grant provoked the fight because he
mocked. '*General* Hemingway and his *Maquis*'.

Humourist Andy Rooney, who was also there, stated
afterwards: 'It [the fight which now started] was the damndest
thing I ever saw. Bruce Grant was taller than Hemingway, but
thin and in his late fifties or even sixty. And they started this
brawl. Then Harry Harris, a good war photographer with the
Associated Press, who was only about five feet four, got
between these two giants. It was really comical.'

At this point, after they had been separated, Hemingway went outside and yelled to Grant to come out. Grant refused to do so, as Rooney remembered. 'About a minute later Hemingway threw open the door in a very dramatic way and said: "Hey Grant, are you coming out to fight"? Well, I could never take Hemingway seriously after that. I'd always liked him as a writer, but this was such a schoolboy thing.'

But someone would take the events at Rambouillet seriously and Hemingway would live to regret that punch in the dining room of the Hôtel du Grand Veneur.

Standing in that same dining room two days later, Lieutenant Sam Brightman, in charge of the war correspondents, stared out at the packed main street. It was crowded with troops, civilians and vehicles of all kinds. Brightman thought the street would make a tempting target for German long-range artillery. 'The only thing they need is de Gaulle,' he told himself, 'and the Germans will have their best goddamned target since D-Day.' With that, he returned to his table where he could wash down his C-rations with the last wine from the hotel's cellars, an ice-cold bottle of Riesling.

A few moments later a pretty waitress brought the food. Just as she reached his table, she gasped for some reason, dropped a plate, and knocked over his precious bottle of wine. Brightman cursed. But the waitress kept staring out of the window, as if transfixed, tears glistening in her eyes. Her lips moved and she began to say, over and over again, *De Gaulle . . . de Gaulle . . . de Gaulle!*

Brightman's mouth dropped open. What he had just feared had happened. General de Gaulle *had* arrived in Rambouillet!

Hurriedly, de Gaulle, impatient and nervous, chain-smoking as usual, drove through the town, heading for the Château de Rambouillet, the summer home of the French presidents. Here he and his three faithful aides also dined off C-rations, cold in their case, though they did so in the magnificent splendour of the *Salle des Fêtes*. Then de Gaulle, not wanting to appear to have touched anything in the presidential home (though he hoped it would be his soon), 'borrowed' a volume of Molière from the library while he waited.

He would have a long wait, but that didn't matter, as long as the correspondents in Rambouillet did not see his visitor.

But one of them already knew who that mysterious, unauthorised visitor would be. Charles Collingwood of the Columbia Broadcasting Service (CBS), who had run foul of Hemingway earlier that month, was not going to miss the greatest scoop of the campaign so far. Already the day before he had used one of CBS's two experimental tape recorders to tape a 'canned' message. When the actual liberation of the French capital came, he could be far from a communications transmitter. Now, however, his canned account would be soon sitting safely in London, whatever happened in the future. 'The 2nd French Armoured Division,' he dictated, 'entered Paris today after the Parisians rose as one man to beat down the terrified German troops who had garrisoned the city.'

And the 2nd French Armoured Division was commanded by the man de Gaulle was now impatiently awaiting, Vicomte Jacques-Philippe de Hauteclocque, known for these last four years simple as 'Jacques Leclerc'.

THE ROAD TO PARIS

In that dark summer of 1940 when Paris fell to the Germans, Ernest Hemingway, living at Finca Vigia, San Francisco de Paula, Cuba, was occupied with another war – the Spanish Civil War – which had ended the year before. He still did not have a title for the book which would be called *For Whom the Bell Tolls*, but the manuscript was nearing completion. Hemingway was glad about that; his energy was about exhausted.

Still he found time in the afternoons to go to his cock-fighting club, shoot live pigeons at the Club de Cazadores and spend his nights watching jai alai games and drinking. The new conflict in Europe and the terrible things happening on the continent seemed furthest from his mind in that very pleasant pre-Castro Cuba; pleasant for rich Americans, that is. However, he did find a little time to write to his editor in New York, Max Perkins. In it he informed that long-suffering man, who never took off his hat even in the office, that he had thought of a new term to describe the British who always seemed to withdraw at the expense of their allies – *coitus Britannicus*. It translated: 'F-ked from the back with withdrawal. Coitus Britannicus; that's the thing, or appeasement carried even on to the field of battle.' He concluded about the British at that moment that Churchill would call their 'darkest hour' – 'what a degenerate people the English are!' Then, presumably, he went back to his 'heroic' war in Spain and the pleasures of Cuba.

In that same summer on the other side of the world a wounded French captain, Vicomte de Hauteclocque, who had abandoned his wife and six children for the sake of France, wandered southwards with every man's hand against him. Not only were the Germans after the 37-year-old captain, but most of his own people had turned against him, too frightened or too complacent to offer him aid in his attempt to fight again. They cared nothing for the honour of France, which was now uppermost in the mind of the hawk-faced, lean aristocrat. But there was one faint gleam of hope. One 24 June, 1940, de Hauteclocque had heard the first broadcast of an obscure French general who had also fled to England. Of the some 20,000 French soldiers and sailors who had similarly fled to that country, only a mere 7,000 had rallied to his appeal to fight on for the honour and glory of France. But it was a start and the hunted man knew that he too must be one of those who now risked the death sentence being imposed upon them by the French Vichy Government. He *must* join de Gaulle!

One year later, now known as 'Leclerc', he marched, with the aid of the British, right across Africa. At the head of the motley, poorly armed force, he besieged and captured the Italian outpost at the oasis of Kufra in Libya. It was de Gaulle's first victory, after a year of setbacks and defeats. It was not a big victory, but it was a significant one, and for Leclerc it symbolised the start of the long road home to France. From Kufra, Leclerc cabled de Gaulle that the 'tricolour' now waved above the fort at Kufra, and that 'we will not rest until the flag of France also flies over Paris and Strasbourg'. In due course, Leclerc personally would realise both those promises.

But it would be a long haul, involving many a battle and bitter defeat. The years soured Leclerc. He became a sharp-tongued, hard, bitter man who was destined to die young. When the French Army in North Africa finally rallied to the Allied cause, after tamely serving the Vichy Government for two years,

Leclerc swore: 'I will not serve with any commander who previously obeyed Vichy and whom I consider to be turncoat!'

But that was a hard promise to keep, in view of the shortage of French troops. So he compromised when the Americans offered him the equipment for a full armoured division, even accepting a battalion of the *Fusiliers-Marins* from the pro-Vichy French Navy to make up his anti-tank battalion. In late 1943–44, that new division, the *Deuxième Division Blindée*, was brought to East Yorkshire, where Leclerc set up his Headquarters in Dalton Hall, and placed under the command of an American general, Patton.

Leclerc was the man whom Hemingway was about to meet: proud without conceit, brave, selfless and ruthless, a man with little tolerance for fools and *poseurs*; a man concerned solely and totally with the restoration of *la Gloire de la France*.

On the afternoon of Wednesday 23 August, while the rest of his division was 120 miles short of the capital, Leclerc, travelling at the point, reached Rambouillet and went straight to the château to confer with de Gaulle. There he found the future president killing time with English cigarettes and Molière's *Le Bourgeois Gentilhomme*.

Both de Gaulle and General Leclerc knew that time was of the essence. German strength between them and the capital was growing. If Leclerc failed to move swiftly and decisively, the insurrection in Paris might develop into an all-out fight, such as was currently taking place in Warsaw. Just as would be the case in the Polish capital, the only gainers from an all-out battle would be the Communists. 'You are lucky,' de Gaulle said when Leclerc told him he was going to go hell-for-leather for the capital. After a long pause, he continued, 'Go fast! We cannot have another *Commune*.'

These military and political concerns of the French generals were, of course, totally unknown to Hemingway when he met

Leclerc that afternoon. Even if he had known of them, they probably would not have interested him, for his sole concern was to continue playing soldier until they reached Paris. Colonel Bruce, who was present at that meeting, should have known better. But the future ambassador was mesmerised by Hemingway still, and seemed totally unaware of the political considerations involved in an uprising which was Communist-inspired. Indeed, only the day before the French in London had just managed to stop Bruce's OSS office there from arranging a large-scale arms drop by air, which would have fallen straight into Communist hands!

Hemingway and Bruce were presented to Leclerc, whom Bruce described as 'tall, spare, handsome, stern-visaged'. Hemingway immediately began offering his advice on the way to get to Paris, trying to 'fill the General in' with the vast amount of intelligence he had acquired.

Leclerc was not impressed. He had other things on his mind than pandering to a war correspondent turned amateur soldier, even if the war correspondent was a famous writer. He indicated to an angry Hemingway that he should indulge in some sexual intercourse combined with travel. As Hemingway put it more delicately to the readers of *Collier's* in his article 'How We Came to Paris', published in October, 1944: 'Buzz off, you unspeakable, the gallant general said, in effect, in something above a whisper and Colonel B [Bruce], the resistance king, and your armoured correspondent withdrew.'

But although the tone was humorous and light-hearted, Hemingway would never forgive Leclerc till the day he died. From now onwards the Frenchman was always 'that jerk Leclerc'. In his next dispatch he planted a vengeful comment about him – 'a rude general is a nervous general'. Even when Leclerc was dead, killed in a mysterious air crash (which some thought was Communist-inspired), Hemingway could not forgo sniping at him. In a letter to Tubby Barton in 1948, after stating that 'the OSS got a DSC for work I did about Rambouillet', he maintained he had laid out 'everything so Leclerc (am glad that prick is dead) went in on a dime where it would have cost him at least 8.95'.

Leclerc, for his part, had other things on his mind than worrying about injuring the sensitivities of a famous American writer. The time had come for him to honour what was called the *Serment de Koufra* – the oath of Kufra. He had promised to raise the flag of France over Paris once more. Now he was going to do it. Dismissing the Americans, he started to make his plans.

On the morning of Thursday 24 August the great drive commenced. It was raining and progress was slow. For a while Hemingway, still angered by 'that jerk' Leclerc's decision not to take him and his offer of assistance seriously, tried to beat the French to Paris by taking back roads. But it didn't work out. That same afternoon with the rain still falling, soaking the soldiers packing the backs of the open half-tracks, Red Pelkey and Hemingway rejoined the column of the French 2nd Armoured Division. Trouble started shortly thereafter.

The two Americans and the French came under concentrated fire from German guns and tanks. Kenneth Crawford of *Newsweek*, who only five minutes before had been assured by Hemingway that his Irregulars had scouted the whole area – there were no Germans there – now found himself crawling down a wet ditch on his belly for dear life. Later he came across a smirking Hemingway and bellowed, 'You son of a bitch, I thought you'd told me you'd scouted this place out and there weren't any Germans here!'

Hemingway shrugged. 'I had to find someone', he answered, 'to be my guinea pig.'

Shortly thereafter Hemingway and Pelkey came across a ruined café, with the not very original name of 'Clair de Lune'.

Here Hemingway met Colonel Sam Marshall, the controversial army historian and a former newspaperman. Hemingway took an instant dislike to Marshall, who was saturnine and firm-jawed and who would one day report that most American infantrymen in the Second World War never even fired their rifle, even those in élite combat divisions. In a letter he would write to Mary Welsh that month describing his experiences on the road to Paris, he stated: 'Fortunately in phase of advance Rambouillet: Paris had official war historian with us. Otherwise everyone would think was damned lie.'

According to Marshall's account, Hemingway appeared at the door of the café, yelling, 'Marshall for God's sake, have you a drink?' Marshall, who had last met Hemingway at Key West in 1936 said, 'We've ransacked the place. We don't have. We have not.'

But Marshall, who didn't particularly like Hemingway (later he would discover the feeling was mutual), had not reckoned with his skinny assistant, Lieutenant Westover. He objected, 'But, Boss, there's a fifth of Scotch in your back pack in the jeep. You put it there three weeks ago and forgot it.'

'Okay, bigmouth,' Marshall snarled, 'for having such a good memory you can walk back through that fire and get it.'

While Westover brought the bottle, Marshall, who spoke Spanish like Hemingway, introduced the latter to an 18-year-old Spanish girl from Bilbao, named Elena, whom they had discovered in the café. 'She was small and slight and much too ill-clad and dirty to be described as a gracious figure,' Marshall recalled much later. 'Her dark face was marred by conspicuous buck teeth . . . her gown looked like a cut-down Mother Hubbard, once black faded to grey, and frequently slept in.' Maliciously, he noted afterwards that 'the great American novelist' (Hemingway), 'was later to picture her as a gorgeously bewitching siren who held every man in the column in the hollow of her classic hand. Also, he made of her a profound philosopher, spouting great words about noble causes, whereas I have know few women who had such an appalling gift of reticence.'

According to Marshall, they downed the whiskey (in twenty minutes), 'and Hemingway was in search of a friendly wall'. Elena, ugly or not, proved her usefulness. 'She wants to find her husband,' he decided, 'and she has been on the lam since *we* [author's italics] lost the Spanish Republic. I've talked to her and know she is OK. She may be a little bit pregnant.'

Outside, the firing had ceased now and Hemingway asked Marshall, 'Can she go in your jeep?'

Marshall agreed and then Hemingway said, 'If we get in any trouble, I will take care of you'.

This, according to Marshall, 'gave Westover such a giggle that he almost split his Silver Star ribbon'. But then, he concluded, 'such cracks were a habit with Ernest due to his owning the copyright on war'.

So they set off again, with the ugly Spanish girl accompanying them on their way to Paris: a ride which, according to an equally malicious Hemingway, 'provided an occasion for Dr Marshall to hear a shot fired in anger, or at least in irritation'.

Perhaps at this juncture, it might be apposite to quote Marshall, a direct observer, who had the advantage of being a newspaperman and a soldier who had served in both wars. His comments on Hemingway in the summer of 1944, when he was supposed to be serving as a war correspondent, but, in fact, was attempting to play soldier, are relevant.

Marshall noted: 'He [Hemingway] loved soldiering, with reservations. Being in an armed cap exhilarated him and he had a natural way with the military. The excitement and danger of battle were his meat and drink, just as the unremitting obligation to carry on was his poison. To put it more accurately, he loved playing at soldier on the grand scale, with shooting irons; yet in him it was not a juvenile attitude. I truly believe he played at it because he enjoyed the game more than because he was interested in studying men under high pressure. . . . I have always looked at war as a matter-of-fact business, requiring the rejection of every unnecessary risk and the facing of any danger along the path of duty. A man fully aware of his genius can afford more than that.'

But while Marshall and Hemingway, plus the ugly Spanish girl, headed for the French capital, the American top brass was becoming increasingly alarmed at Leclerc's supposed slow progress to Paris. They had heard of the spontaneous parties welcoming the French columns everywhere and believed that the Leclerc Division was 'dancing' its way to its objective. In particular, General Bradley, the US Army ground commander, was annoyed at the way that Leclerc had left the army to which he belonged, Patton's Third, and was now taking part in operations being conducted by General Hodges, the Commander of the 1st US Army. Swiftly, orders were passed down the chain of command and on Thursday 24 August, Tubby Barton's battered 4th Infantry Division was alerted to help the drive on Paris.

The order came like a bolt from the blue. It was so totally unexpected that Barton did not have the requisite maps for an advance on Paris. Others thought they were being sent to the French capital to parade through for the benefit of the French, just as the conquering Germans had done on 14 June 1940, straight from the battlefront. There was an urgent call for neckties, an item of clothing that most of the Fourth had last worn in England before they had departed for Utah Beach. But there were some among the Fourth who were genuinely excited at the prospect of marching on Paris. For these few it would not be merely an adventurous jaunt, but a kind of spiritual pilgrimage.

Sergeant Larry Kelly, for instance, had an almost mystic affection for France and Paris which dated back to the First World War. In 1917 he had enlisted in the US Army, aged 15. In the trenches he had been wounded twice. That hadn't stopped him joining up again in the Second World War. On D-Day he had jumped with the US 82nd Airborne and had been wounded once again in France. Now he was a forward artillery observer with the Fourth and delighted with the news that they were going to attack Paris. That Thursday he promised himself he would be the first American soldier to enter Paris. He would almost make it. But by a tragic error he would be mistaken by a young French patriot for a German. The young man did not recognise the helmet. Kelly would die of the wounds he received then one year later.

Such men, whose life in combat with the infantry was calculated to be less than a month (in the Second World War infantry casualties were fifty per cent higher than in the First World War), had no time for the games played by Hemingway and his various Irregulars. They were young and serious, committed to an image of Paris, which might be touristy, but which was genuine, too.

When he heard the news, Lieutenant Warren Hooker, a platoon leader in the 22nd Infantry, recalled all he had ever read about Paris – Notre-Dame, the Eiffel Tower, Sacré Coeur – and told himself that the Fourth's role would be 'to spill blood in the city and then move on'. He remembered the lines of Robert Frost he had memorised in high school: 'But I have promises to keep. And miles to go before I sleep.'

Hooker, too, would be wounded in Paris and go no further. Lying hit in shoulder and buttocks on the banks of the Seine, he would hear a voice calling softly somewhere behind him, 'medic . . . medic . . .' It was his platoon sergeant, 'Speedy' Stone, dying with the tie he had scrounged for the 'parade through Paris' still knotted around his neck. . . .

Now Hemingway, 'Doctor' Marshall and the rest had joined up
with Colonel Bruce once more. According to Hemingway's
own account in his report to *Collier's*, 'How We Came to Paris',
they soon ran into a 'lightly armoured German jeep mounting a
machine-gun and a 20mm', which came 'tearing up the road
firing at the crossroads'.

The Irregulars started to return the fire and 'Archie Pelkey,
my driver, got in two shots'. Two of the Irregulars 'were hit,
but [they were] very happy now that shooting had started again.
"We have nice work ahead of us. Good work ahead of us," the
guerrilla with the sharp face and light blue eyes. "I'm happy
some of the b.....s are still here."'

Hemingway, with characteristic modesty, informed his readers
at this spot, 'My own war aim at this moment was to get into
Paris without being shot. Our necks had been out for a long
time.' But all the same he made sure his readers knew that 'I took
cover in all the street fighting – the solidest cover available',
indicating that he had been involved in 'all the street fighting'.

According to Hemingway's companion Colonel Bruce, the
main danger at this stage of the drive for Paris came from an
exploding German ammunition dump, 'which was annoying'.
'We finally passed within a few yards of the edge of the dump
and I, for one, found this part of the journey terrifying.' Red
Pelkey thought it all great fun, rather like 4 July. 'Sure is
popping off, Papa!' he shouted above the racket, freckled face
happy.

In the end they made it to the outskirts of the city and as they
waited to move in the last mile or so, Hemingway allowed
Pelkey a few moments of sentiment in his report to *Collier's*.
'They're a good outfit,' Pelkey said of the Irregulars. 'Best outfit
I ever been with. No discipline. Got to admit that. Drinking all
the time. Got to admit that. But plenty fighting outfit. Nobody
gives a damn if they ever get killed or not. *Compris*?' It was a
terribly fine imitation of Hemingway – at his worst.

For his part, the great author admitted: 'I couldn't say anything more then, because I had a funny choke in my throat and I had to clean my glasses because there now, below us, grey and always beautiful, was spread the city I love best in all the world.'

A little later they started to move into the centre of the city. The crowds were everywhere. Yet the angry snap-and-crackle of small arms fire indicated the battle for Paris was altogether over. The party came across a wounded Tonkinese laundryman, probably shot by French partisans, who probably accounted for as many of their own side as they did for Germans on that crazy day. Marshall and Westover patched him up. They prevented the usual crowd of 'instant patriots', who appeared all over the newly liberated countries that summer, from shearing off the hair of an unfortunate, terrified Frenchwoman, whom they accused of having slept with a 'boche'.

A Spahi Lieutenant from the 1st Spahis Marocains, Leclerc's reconnaissance regiment, which had fought for Free France right from 1940, told Marshall to get rid of the Spanish girl Hemingway had landed him with (contrary to military regulations). '*On fait pas la guerre avec les femmes*,' he yelled.

'Since when?' 'Doctor' Marshall roared back. 'Go away young man, and study a little military history.'

But the ugly Spanish girl got the message. By now she must have realised what kind of crazy dangerous company she had found herself in. Without a word she slipped away. 'We never saw her again,' Marshall reported, somewhat sadly.

They came upon the Tomb of the Unknown Soldier guarded by six veterans of the First World War and a *grand mutilé* seated in a wheelchair. The officer in charge asked them if they wanted to ascend to the roof of the Arc. Just like Hitler had done four years before, they did so. There they were greeted by a squad of firemen, and Colonel Bruce recorded that 'for some reason, their commander presented me with a *pompier's* medal'.

But Hemingway was after bigger fish than a fireman's medal. Later he maintained he went from there to 'liberate' the Travellers Club in the Champs Elysées. But it had already been liberated. However they were offered a bottle of champagne there before they braved sniper fire to drive to the Hotel Ritz in the Place Vendôme, which would become another Dorch for Hemingway for the rest of his time in Europe. The Ritz was deserted, which was not surprising. Its guests, German officers on leave, staff officers stationed in Paris, and the usual collection of collaborators who had grown fat at the expense of the Germans in the last four years, had hastily fled at the approach of the 'liberators'. Neither Charles Ritz nor the redoubtable Madame César Ritz, the widow of the founder of the palatial establishment, was in evidence at that moment. Perhaps they deemed it wiser to keep in the background until they knew which way the wind would blow with their new masters, the Americans. Like the Germans who had almost finished their defence of Paris by now, half-hearted as it was, they were 'prepared like nuns in the path of warfare', as Colonel Bruce phrased it afterwards in his delicate manner; 'for the worst?'*

However, their front man, the 'imperturbable Ausiello', must not have been very sanguine about the establishment's future when he first saw the American conquerors enter his grand portals. For they were followed by a noisy drunken rabble, who made up Hemingway's Irregulars. Some were half-naked, others wore bits and pieces of American uniform, but all were heavily armed and threatening. Were these the new *Communards* of 1944, come to punish the rich for their transgressions during the four years of the German Occupation? He need not have

---

* Among others, *Reichsführer SS* Himmler had stayed there, as well as Minister of Propaganda Goebbels. In 1940, Air Marshall Goering had installed himself in the Imperial Suite while he looted French art treasures, among other things. No wonder the Ritzes were worried.

worried unduly. Suddenly, he recognised the two leading
Americans, Hemingway and Colonel Bruce. They had both
been pre-war guests at the Ritz, when even one of Paris's
leading hotels had been relatively cheap for those who were
paid in the almighty dollar. 'Why,' the little man gasped, 'what
are *you* doing here?'

Hemingway, who was always pleased when he was recognised
in what he liked to call 'a smart joint', replied they had come to
the Ritz for a short stay – that short stay would last exactly
seven months off and on.

The manager beamed, oozing professional charm now. As a
welcoming gesture for the first of these new guests from
America, he asked if he could get the American gentlemen
anything. Hemingway looked at his bunch of excited Irregulars
in their shabby bits and pieces of uniform and overalls and said,
'How about seventy-three dry martinis?'

Now the parties commenced. For the men of the 4th Infantry
who had helped to capture Paris, it would last one glorious
night before, heavy-headed and red-eyed, they were routed out
from the beds of the *poules* with whom they had spent that time
and were moved on. Another battle was waiting for them. For
Hemingway and his friend it would last a week. What was
happening outside the Hotel Ritz had no interest for him. He
had completely forgotten he was a war correspondent now.
Indeed, he lent his portable typewriter to another
correspondent. He did not cover the formal surrender of the
capital; nor did he show any interest in de Gaulle's triumphant
entrance complete with German (or French Communist)
snipers. Now life was simply one great alcoholic party.

That night there was a formal dinner, with General Sibert,
Bradley's Chief-of-Intelligence attending. The guests exchanged
signatures on Ritz menu-cards as mementos of the great day.
'None of us,' Hemingway declared with alcoholic certainty,

'will ever write a line about these last twenty-four hours in delirium. Whoever tries it is a chump.' When the waiter handed Hemingway the bill for this 'Liberation dinner', he snorted, in a not very original parody of those pre-Revolutionary patriots who would not pay British taxes: 'Millions to defend France, thousands to honour your nation – but not one *sou* in tribute to Vichy!' At the bottom of the bill the Ritz waiter had automatically included in the price of the meal the Vichy Government's sale tax. It raised a great laugh from those there who were still capable of understanding French.

The parties continued the next day. There was abundant hospitality for all, and all-too-eager girls for those young (and old) men looking for a taste of 'Paree' and 'oh-la-la'. As Hemingway wrote to Lanham, 'I'm on the verge of losing my standing as an amateur pimp'. Irwin Shaw and Helen Kirkpatrick announced they were off to see the victory parade on its march to Notre-Dame. Ernest argued Mrs Kirkpatrick out of it: 'Daughter, sit still and drink this good brandy. You can always watch victory parades but you'll never again celebrate the liberation of Paris at the Ritz.'

The following day Robert Capa made his appearance. Red Pelkey, who was now speaking broken English, told him, 'Papa took good hotel. Plenty stuff in cellar. You go up quick.'

Colonel Charles Codman, Patton's personal aide who had lived in Paris till 1940, turned up after visiting a well-known pre-war brothel, Madame Hélène's, where the partisans had shaved off the hair from all the whores and pencilled a neat black swastika on their bald pates. Hemingway greeted him at the Ritz, with 'compared to Spain, this is nothing. Just a bunch of crap . . . makes me thirsty to tell it.' The bell was rung. More champagne appeared.

So it went on and on. But there was one problem troubling that particular 'amateur pimp'. All around him, it seemed, Paris that glorious weekend was wild with sex. Yet his own 'Mr Scrooby' was obstinately refusing to function. What could be done about it? On that third date of the partying, 27 August 1944, he wrote to his 'small friend', Mary Welsh: 'Why don't you come over here? Should I ask Wertenbaker [her boss] or would that not be discreet? I can't leave now, but can give you good quarters whenever and wherever you come.' The invitation was all too obvious.

And not a mile or more away that day Sergeant Larry Kelly, who had so wanted to be first into Paris, lay paralysed in a Parisian hospital, receiving a bottle of wine from the sorrowing boy who had shot him by mistake. It would be the last he would ever drink.

A COMMAND POST AT THE RITZ

On the day that Hemingway wrote to Mary Welsh asking her to come to Paris, she was already in the French capital. 'Like a cat on heat' she had gone to her boss in London, and told him 'I've got to go to France.' Although he had his reservations, she had convinced him to allow her to go in order to cover the victory march of Leclerc's 2nd Armoured Division down the Champs Elysées.

After a long drive in a jeep with a stuffy major from Ohio from an Army base camp in Normandy, she arrived in Paris as it was getting dark. After a chaotic night, she decided to go for a walk. The walk took her to the Place Vendôme entrance to the Ritz where the concierge recognised her from 1940. She asked if by any change 'Monsieur Hemingway' was in the Ritz.

He was. '*Bien sûr,*' the concierge answered, and directed her to Room 31 and the lift that would take her to Hemingway's room.

What made her take that lift to the first floor and knock on Hemingway's door? Up to now she had met Hemingway a mere half-dozen times. She had not slept with him and she was worldly-wise enough to discount his strange proposal on the bed with Michael Foot at the Dorch. Both Hemingway and she were still married, and what might happen now could surely, at the most, only be an affair; she had had plenty of those in the war years. What could then have motivated her that hot morning of Saturday 26 August 1944? Was it that old desire to be associated with important men? Or was it something more? Was she deliberately setting her cap at Hemingway, intending to ensnare him? She must have known she would never really amount to much in what was basically a man's world – journalism – and besides, her articles show she had little talent. Whatever it was, the moment she knocked on the door of Room 31, the stamp was set irrevocably on the rest of her life. She would become one of Hemingway's women. She would enjoy the fame, the luxury, the travel. But the price she would have to pay would be high – very high indeed.

Red Pelkey opened it, 'Hey Papa,' he called inside, revealing the gaps in his front teeth, 'there's a dame here.'

Hemingway emerged. His face lit up. He gave her a tremendous hug, swinging her off her feet and carried her inside, where two of his Irregulars were drinking champagne on the floor and cleaning their weapons with bits of rag. Why anyone needed to be cleaning firearms in the opulent security of the Ritz, with its Empire-style furniture and pink satin bed coverlets, never seemed to have entered Mary Welsh's head.

As for Hemingway, used to turning order into chaos, and surrounding himself with cronies, however out of place they might have seemed to anyone sensible, he launched into an animated account of his adventures on the road to Paris. She listened for a while and then told him she had work to do. He extracted a promise from her that she would dine with him later that evening. As she went out, Mary Welsh stopped at the concierge's office once again and asked if there were a room free in the Ritz. There was – Room 86. Thus she came to live near, if not with Hemingway for the time being, in Room 86 with its 'dove-grey walls' and view over the gardens behind the Ministry of Justice. This room would be her home from the 'next morning until late the following March', as she wrote in her autobiography, adding significantly, 'but with complications'.

That night she and Hemingway arrived back at the Ritz when only the night-watchman was on duty. 'I felt I no longer had the strength to organise myself in my quatre-vingt-six room.' Instead, she went up to Hemingway's room on the first floor and, clad only in her underwear, crept wearily into bed with him. According to her story, the other bed was 'entirely occupied with Garand M-1 army rifles, hand grenades and other metal objects'.

Nothing happened!

As with his third wife, Martha Gellhorn, his best times with Miss Mary were before their marriage, during their courtship. Then he was on his best behaviour. But even during those seven months, off and on, that he would spend with Mary in that pre-marital period at the Ritz, his mood could change dramatically and there would be ugly scenes. Then Hemingway gave Mary some idea of what to expect when they were finally married. Indeed, friends who knew Hemingway were giving the liaison six months at the most.

As she was to complain herself, all too quickly she was pitchforked into the 'role of a whipping boy'. Impotent as he was, aware that her last lover Irwin Shaw was close by (once when they had a row, she retaliated by shouting at him that Shaw's penis was bigger than his), Hemingway found himself in a quandary. He could not love her physically, but at the same time, he could not give her up. He needed a woman with whom he could be on an intimate level, if not sexually, then at least emotionally. The result was spates and outbursts of drunken temper. Repeatedly he denounced Mary as, 'You goddamn smirking useless female war correspondent!' On another occasion he told a friend in anger that he wanted to give Miss Mary the clap – something he was manifestly incapable of doing at that moment, even if he had been suffering from the disease.

At the same time he was able to make amends by introducing her to old friends, who were now famous personalities as he was. Gertrude Stein and her companion Miss Toklas were in the country, for they were both Jewish and 'decadent', as Goebbels called them, being lesbians as well. (Interestingly enough, most of Hemingway's old women friends in Paris were lesbian.) But Picasso was still there, together with half a thousand 'decadent' canvases. '*Les Boches* left me alone,' he told them. 'They disliked my work but they did not punish me for it.' Dining in a black-market restaurant with Picasso and his mistress, Françoise Gilot, Hemingway even asked the 'master' if he would do a painting of Miss Mary from the waist up, nude. 'Picasso's enormous black radar eyes turned on to me, shrouded in my uniform, for a moment, smiled and said, '*bien sûr*. Have her come to the studio.'

The painting was never carried out. By the time the practicalities were arranged it had become cold in Paris and, as Mary Welsh wrote later, 'if the maestro were to paint me representationally, as he had assured Ernest he would, he would have to paint me with goose pimples as big as grapes'. They never saw Picasso again.

That August, Hemingway topped the readers' poll of best American novelists in the *Saturday Review of Literature* and that attracted other less important visitors to him and Mary at the Ritz, which Tubby Barton was now calling the 'Fourth's advance CP [Command Post] in Paris'. They included a member of that division, Staff Sergeant J.D. Salinger, who heard that Hemingway was holding court at the hotel. 'Let's go see Hemingway,' he told a buddy. Surprisingly enough, he was admitted to the presence and Hemingway had actually read one of Salinger's stories, *The Last Day of the Last Furlough*. Salinger was impressed and his account of the visit in a letter home was almost reverential.

Later, however, like so many ordinary people who came into contact with Hemingway during the war, he became less enchanted with Hemingway's macho posturing. He would meet Hemingway again as a war correspondent with the 'Ivy League' in Germany where some of the soldiers got to 'arguing about the merits of a German Luger, he [Hemingway] was carrying [again contrary to regulations for war correspondents] as opposed to the US 45'. Hemingway reacted instantly and 'blasted the head off a chicken to prove his point'. This apparently shocked Salinger, for his heroes never had much taste for war and violence.

Hemingway had that taste, it seemed. Although he and Mary seemed to be settling down into some sort of routine at the Ritz – 'a drink or two at the Ritz Bar on the rue Cambon side before lunch . . . drinks again after my [Mary's] return in the afternoon' – Hemingway's inability to perform continued to irritate him and make him uneasy. All the visitors and the heavy drinking were not able to conceal his nervous tension.

Mary felt, too, that Hemingway did not understand her world either. 'I had no time for a mid-morning *quart de champagne* with light conversation at the bar. Ernest kept forgetting that I lived by deadlines. Moreover, I was beginning to feel that I was being swallowed by him . . . he seemed to me to melt away my identity.'

She sensed, too, according to her own statement, that although she was happy enough with him for a short period, especially when they were alone and he was not performing for his cronies, 'I felt dubious about the wisdom of any formal commitment between us,' and Hemingway knew it.

'With extra-sensory perception,' she wrote – he called it his 'built-in shit detector' – 'Ernest identified my apprehension and attempted to alleviate it with small gestures'. The 'small gestures' were expensive gifts, for Hemingway knew, using that new 'folksy' language he was beginning to acquire from being around the infantry of the Ivy League Division, 'wimmeys love presents'.

But both of them were really playing games for their own separate reasons and perhaps Hemingway was only too glad to escape the 'Command Post at the Ritz', when out of the blue he received a strange message delivered by hand at the grand hotel. It came from Colonel Buck Lanham, whom he had last seen before he had been wounded at the château ('never trust a château', Hemingway would write years later to someone else who had been wounded there). It was taut and cryptic, and read: 'Go hang yourself, brave Hemingstein. We have fought at Landrecies and you were not there.'

Hemingway, who was not the illiterate oaf he often made himself to be, understood the connotation. It was an updated version of King Henry IV's joyous taunt to the Duke of Crillon after a victory at Arques. He took up the challenge immediately, perhaps to get away from the unresolved problem of his impotency for a while.

Red Pelkey was not available to drive his jeep which he still retained from the Fourth's motor pool. He had been sent back to the Division after the Liberation of Paris, where he had some kind of a crack-up. He would neither obey orders, salute, nor say 'sir'. They took him to the divisional psychiatrist. The latter seemed unable to help Pelkey, who told the 'trick cyclist', as they were called in those days (according to Hemingway after the war) that 'his life had been changed by being with Irregulars and if he could not be with Papa he wanted to die!' Instead, Hemingway set off north with a French driver, Jean Decan, armed to the teeth (again contrary to the regulations for war correspondents), heading for Landrecies, not far from the Franco-Belgian border.

It was a foolhardy mission, for although the Wehrmacht was in full flight north to Belgium and from thence to the Reich, there were little pockets of Germans everywhere, moving to safety in what they called *Wanderkessel* – wandering pockets – who would have found the lone jeep a tempting target.

Steadily, the two adventurers pressed north following the track of the Ivy League Division. All went well the first day, 2 September, and they spent the night in a field. There, according to Hemingway's roughly scribbled notes, they saw 'five V-2s'. These were the supersonic successors to the V-1, which had now commenced their campaign of terror against the long-suffering civilians of the United Kingdom.

As these new 'vengeance weapons' were not normally visible to the human eye after they had been fired, save for a brief terrifying moment when they fell out of the stratosphere, Hemingway must not have been very far from the launching sites at Mimoyecques, Siracourt, Watten and Wizernes, which had been under constant attack from the air for the last six months by the RAF and the US Air Force. Indeed President Kennedy's elder brother, Lieutenant Jack Kennedy, was killed in one attack when his explosive-packed Liberator blew up in mid-air.

Hemingway and Decan reached Tubby Barton's divisional headquarters at six the next morning, the fifth anniversary of the outbreak of the Second World War, and were directed to follow a column heading for Lanham's 22nd Regiment. But they had to fall out due to repeated punctures. They pushed on once more and, according to Hemingway's own account, ran into trouble just outside the village of Wassigny on a side road leading to Le Cateau. Here, though Hemingway did not know it, he was on hallowed ground, at least for the British Army. Back in the last week of August 1914, the retreating British Army had made a stand in the area against the advancing Germans, suffering more casualties than they had done at the Battle of Waterloo. In one day alone they lost 8,482 men. It was a shocking defeat for the British Army, but it was the start of the rise to fame for a slight young lieutenant of the Royal Warwickshire Regiment, who would soon be gravely wounded and left for dead on the field of battle. He was 'that jerk Montgomery', one day to become a British Field Marshal.

Hemingway's role as a field commander in that area, which was dotted everywhere with British cemeteries from the First World War and those which were springing up to take the dead of 1940 and the new ones of 1944, was less auspicious. A reconnaissance group from the Fourth had discovered that the main road from Wassigny to Le Cateau had been cut by retreating German tanks. It was suggested that the 'D-road' leading out of Wassigny should be used instead. There was a problem, however. There appeared to be a dug-in German 57mm anti-tank gun covering it.

One of the locals, a bold young man, came up to Hemingway saying, '*Mon capitaine, on ne se bat pas* [sic]?'

Hemingway thought not. He told the eager young man that there was American infantry in the area. They'd take care of the Germans in due course.

According to Hemingway, the French youth then spat on the ground in front of him.

Hemingway flew into a rage. He told the youth, if he thought he could take the gun out, then he was to do so.

The youth and his *copains* took the 'Captain' at his word. The attack, if it could be called that, lasted exactly four minutes. When it was over, six young Frenchmen were killed and two wounded. All this had occurred, Hemingway said afterwards, because he had lost his temper.

Later that day, Hemingway reached Colonel Lanham at his new Command Post at Pommereuil, where the 22nd Infantry Regiment was poised, ready for its attack into Belgium and from there to the borders of the Reich. Surprisingly enough, in view of the dangers he had run in order to reach Lanham, Hemingway decided to start back for Paris almost immediately. Perhaps he thought now he could solve the problem of 'Mr Scrooby'. At all events, he turned about and drove straight back to the French capital for a reunion with Miss Mary.

According to Mary Welsh's own account, they lived 'on little besides Lanson Brut champagne and the wonder of being together again'. In the morning she would awake, so she wrote, and look for Ernest in the other bed. 'Usually he was there, reading and sipping champagne from a bottle brought up in a bucket of ice the night before.' As Hemingway always boasted he got up 'at first light', and she definitely did not do so, he must have started drinking his 'Lanson Brut' early. But things were moving. What exactly happened those few champagne days in early September is not clear. But in a letter he wrote Mary from Houffalize in Belgium on 11 September, it seems that 'Mr S' (Scrooby) had started to come to life, if only slightly and not in a totally satisfactory manner. In the letter he wrote: 'We loved each other very much with no clothes at all, no lies, no secrets, no pretences (no underwear), and only one shirt apiece and stove, that traitor, sometimes not working.' Later in the same letter, which had to be couched carefully, because even the great author's letters had to go through army censorship (one wonders what Lanham's regimental censor made of it), Hemingway wrote, 'and the never lonely magic touching in bed – and your twice own beloved, lovely to touch, lovely to feel, lovely to be just with and to know that you are there. Dearest lovely, I love you so.'

One can guess roughly what happened between the two of them those couple of nights when they lived off champagne, but, although Hemingway in that same letter explained his current financial position to Mary Welsh, as if to reassure her that she wouldn't starve with him, he was not altogether sure of her affections. He asked, 'What are you doing. Following the Boys?' And one of the 'Boys' in particular seemed to concern him. In a PS he noted that he would dedicate his future book about the war to her, even if 'you've left me and are living with the Shaw of Persia . . . altho might add F-K her the Persian Harlot in parenthesis'. Obviously he was still worried by the presence of Paris of Irwin Shaw, whose penis was longer than Hemingway's.

On the morning of 7 September 1944, still torn between the
excitement of the front and his desire to prove his manliness
and virility with this experienced woman (how frustrating it
must have been for Hemingway to be in the middle of that
sexually-charged war-time Paris and be unable to perform),
he set off to find the 4th Division yet once again. This time he
went north to Belgium in a small convoy, made up of two cars,
a motor cycle and two jeeps. They were manned by the two
drivers, Red Pelkey, reunited with the Boss, Jean Decan, two of
his Irregulars, Marcel and Onesime, the Brazilian correspondent
Nemo Lucas, Captain Marcus Stevenson, his conducting
officer, and a solitary Englishman, Peter Lawless of the *Daily
Mail*, who would be dead before the year was out.

At his letters reveal, his thoughts during this period, moving
through Belgium towards Germany, were always with Mary.
Part of the trouble was probably that Lawless knew Noel
Monks, Mary's husband, and naturally Mary Welsh herself.
'I said [to Lawless] yes I'd met you,' he wrote in one letter, 'and
you were extremely nice and didn't add, "And I love her very
much and would be glad to show you here on the map how
much I love her". But this is only a map 1–25,000 and I need a
Globe and 3 large Atlases to show you how I loved Tom
Welshes' daughter Mary because otherwise you might not
understand.'

But, despite his protestations of love, Hemingway must have
felt inferior (an unusual emotion for him) to both Monks and
the 'Shaw of Persia', for they *had* performed with Mary and he
hadn't. Of course, he had been through it all before and hoped
his impotence would vanish, just as it had with his wife Pauline,
when she had still been his mistress. As he told his post-war
crony A.E. Hotchner six years later in Paris: 'I was in a hell of a
jam – I couldn't make love . . . Pauline was very patient and
understanding and we tried everything, but nothing worked.
I became terribly discouraged. I had been to see several doctors.

I even put myself in the hands of a mystic who fastened electrodes to my head and feet – hardly the seat of my trouble – and had me drink a glass of calves' liver blood every day. It was all hopeless. Then one day, Pauline said, "Listen Ernest, why don't you go pray?" Pauline was a very religious Catholic and I wasn't a religious anything but she had been so damn good that I thought it was the least I could do for her. There was a small church two blocks from us and I went there and said a short prayer. Then I went back to our room. Pauline was in bed, waiting. I undressed and got in bed and we made love like we invented it. We never had any trouble again. That's when I became a Catholic.'

That had been ten years before. Now there was little hope that a sudden religious conversion might do the trick. 'Mr Scrooby' would hardly respond to a whiff of incense and a scrap of Latin prayer any more. But there was still the war as a consolation prize and abruptly Hemingway was feeling happy again. 'Not lonely. Not disappointed – not disillusioned. Nothing phoney. No message,' he wrote to Mary Welsh on 11 September. To his son Patrick, he wrote four days later: 'I have never been happier nor had a more useful life.'

Yes, there was always the war.

THE ROAD TO THE REICH

Victory was in the air now!

First, the retiring Germans had come in small groups, still well organised and still undeniably disciplined soldiers, if dusty and unshaven. But by the first week of September the small groups had turned into a disorganised mass, a frenzied exodus from France, fleeing in trucks, tanks, armoured cars, civilian buses, horse-drawn farm carts, even *gazogènes*, those beat-up French automobiles powered by wood or charcoal.

In these wretched convoys streaming back to the protection of the Siegfried Line, on which five years before confident British Tommys had boasted they would 'hang out their washing, mother dear', every arm of the service was inextricably mixed. There were *Hiwis*, Russian auxiliaries in German uniform; sailors of the *Kriegsmarine*, their ships long lost or abandoned; 'grey mice', the dowdy scared female soldiers of the *Wehrmacht*, cynically nicknamed 'officers' mattresses' by the ordinary German footslogger; still defiant, sullen, young men with the once frightening insignia, those tarnished skull-and-crossbones, of the *Waffen SS*.

With them fled their mistresses, those poor forlorn pregnant girls, who had now found out that it was highly dangerous to have fallen in love with a German *Landser*. There were the collaborators too: French, Belgian, Luxembourgers, Dutch. Once they had thrown in their lot with the Germans because they had believed in the 'New Order', which Hitler had promised would clear away the decadent old Europe, or simply for personal gain. The German New Order had certainly provided rich pickings for those prepared to turn traitor to their native country. Now they fled, too, for as the Flemish peasants watching them go told their fellow Belgians and the Dutch, for them it would soon be *Bijltjesdag* – 'hatchet day'.

Behind them came the British, Canadians and Americans. The latter were divided into two armies – Hodges' First and Patton's Third – their pace slowing a little now as they started to run out of gas, and were advancing on two separate fronts. Hodge's First Army, to which the 4th Infantry belonged, was making its advance in a zone some 65 miles broad, with its armoured divisions out on the flanks, in front of the slower moving infantry formations, like wings.

The strategy this September was the one which had been agreed upon before D-Day. Its objective was to drive as quickly as possible for the Reich, from whence the Allied forces were 'to undertake operations aimed at the heart of Germany and the destruction of her armed forces'. To do this, the industrial heart of the Reich (the Ruhr), would have to be taken, followed by the 'political heart' of that Reich, which Hitler boasted would last 1,000 years – Berlin.

Geography offered four exits from Northern France. For the British and Canadians the route selected was that of Flanders, the flat plain which stretched basically all the way to Germany. For the US 3rd Army, the route was that south of the Ardennes through the industrial area of Mets, Saarbrücken and then to Frankfurt, not the swiftest way to advance on the Ruhr. Finally between those two exits, there were the two routes through the Ardennes: to the north where that area was not so rugged or so well wooded; or directly through the forest on a west–east axis. It was the latter route that Hodges selected for his V Corps, which included the Fourth.

Now, despite the difficulties of the terrain – the narrow winding roads, the steep craggy hillsides, heavy with pine forests – the Fourth was making good progress when Hemingway and his convoy joined them. The Germans were fleeing and victory was in the air. Hemingway was intrigued by the strange mixture of peace and war. Admittedly, here and there he and his party came across traces of the German flight – a burned-out tank with the usual circle of rough wooden grave-markers around it, a few mines, abandoned equipment littering the ditches to both sides of the hill roads. But otherwise it seemed little more than a road march on manoeuvres.

At St Hubert in the heart of the forest, surrounded by clean trickling mountain streams, Hemingway, Red, and Jean Decan had a Sunday breakfast of bacon and eggs while the good local folk went to church in their Sunday best. The hotel where they stayed charged them nothing for the food and wine they drank, or for the services of the *patronne's* tall daughter who had slept with the French Irregular that night. It was all very much of an exciting panic in what might be the final month of the war.

How could those excited confident young men, now working their way down the rugged trails towards the Reich, have realised that September that they were on their way to their deaths? The war wouldn't end this month. It would go on for another eight, long, bloody months. This remote border area between Belgium and Germany would see the decimation of their division, not once but twice over. Before they finally cleared this accursed forest, which stretched right over into the Reich, it would be February 1945 and by then most of them would be dead, wounded or mad.

For Hemingway there was only one discordant note to mar this military jaunt eastwards through the forest. That angry punch at the Hôtel du Grand Veneur at Rambouillet was having its repercussions. Tubby Barton had first informed him of what was brewing by messenger to the Ritz: 'Capt Stevie [Stevenson, his conducting officer from the Fourth] from the outfit with a message from – well I'd better skip it', as Hemingway wrote in a letter to a friend when he was safely back in the States, which resulted in 'Me, with three secretaries trying to turn out some non-incriminateing [sic] account of Rambouillet'.

In that second week of September he learned that his attempts to lie about what he had really done during those six days at Rambouillet, when he had been the *Grand Capitaine* of 'Hemingway's Irregulars', had not worked. The feared Inspector General, in this case the officer in charge of General Patton's 3rd Army judicial department, was investigating his conduct in France. As he wrote to Mary Welsh from his first stop in Belgium, on 5 September, 'I hope I am not in any bad trouble'. He was!

The Inspector General was now taking seriously the allegations of the war correspondents who had been present in Rambouillet and some of the military officers there, too, that Hemingway (while a civilian and under the jurisdiction of the US Army, as his orders to come to France had stated quite clearly) had borne arms against the enemy. For this he could in theory be court-martialled. There was no other court which could try him as he did not come under the jurisdiction of the French authorities, for at the time in question these were the pro-German Vichy régime. Again, in theory, he could be sentenced to a term in a military prison in the United States, or at least sent back to the States in disgrace.

If, on the other hand, he had fallen into German hands bearing arms as a civilian dressed in US Army uniform, he could have prejudiced the enemy against any other correspondent unfortunate enough to be taken prisoner. The Germans had proved themselves very quick to act throughout the war when they had felt that the 'Rules of Land Warfare' had been infringed by the Allies. When, for example, it came out that after the abortive landing at Dieppe in 1942 the Canadians had handcuffed some of their German prisoners, the Germans ordered that all officer prisoners in their hands should be handcuffed similarly for eight hours a day for months on end. Similarly, the secret order two years later to execute all commandos, parachutists and so on found on German-held territory *without trial* followed the alleged 'silencing' of German prisoners who had been taken by Allied commando-para units engaged in covert operations. Hemingway, especially as he was a famous writer whose early books had been translated into German, could therefore not only have endangered his fellow correspondents by his foolhardy actions at Rambouillet, but also have seriously embarrassed the US Army.

Of course, Hemingway had not commenced bearing arms, although a civilian, at Rambouillet. It had started almost as soon as he returned to France the second time.

In that second week of July 1944, young, sharp Iz Goldstein of Brooklyn was 'the regimental GI correspondent', when he was called 'from the safety of his fox hole' to serve 'as a guide for Ernest Hemingway who was visiting our regiment' – Colonel Lanham's 22nd Infantry.

Goldstein, who was soon to be seriously wounded during the shelling of Lanham's château Headquarters 'kept staring at a suspicious bulge in the pocket of his field jacket. Papa noted the question in my eyes. With a grin, almost lost in his bushy whiskers, he pulled out a grenade from his pocket and said, "Just in case".'

Hemingway replaced the incriminating grenade and offered Goldstein a drink from a dented canteen. 'I took a drink. Then it struck! I shook for a moment, my head throbbing, my eyes popping. . . . The gulp I had taken from the canteen was pure unadulterated Calvados . . . regular fare for Papa.'

But Papa was not finished with the young New Yorker yet. He took him into the castle and 'gave me an education on the bidet after discovering many of them in the château'. He told Goldstein about a woman he had once known who 'had filled a bidet with champagne when she could not find water and [who] had performed her ablutions with the wine. Upon completion of her bathing her external genitals and the posterior parts of her body, the woman remarked that, "I feel very bubbly and ready for anything you can offer".' After that, Hemingway said, he had advised all his bidet users to use champagne.

It was such a good story that Iz Goldstein forgot all about that grenade. Others did not. All the while Hemingway was journeying ever closer to the frontier of the Reich, the Inspector General was avidly collecting more and more evidence against him.

On the afternoon of 11 September, Hemingway and his band of companions, Americans, Brazilians, French and the lone Briton, Lawless, came to the last decent-sized Belgian town before they reached the German border. Houffalize was set deep in the valley of the River Ourthe, surrounded by steep high grey cliffs. It was the centre of a small road network and a bottle-neck. In three months' time it was to be the centre of the great link-up between the 1st and 3rd US Armies during the Battle of the Bulge and then it would be wrecked completely. Now, however, although Bomber Harris's aircrews had already worked it over the previous night, the lovely little resort in the heart of this beautiful mountain country was still relatively intact. Yet there was a strange kind of vacuum about the place. The enemy had apparently gone, but where was the liberator?

The liberators, if that is what one could call Hemingway's band, were sitting above the town on the heights, drinking and waiting for Lanham's 22nd Regiment to catch up with them.

Now, however, Belgian partisans clad in the white overalls, dropped to them by the British, of the *Armée Blanche* (the colour of the overalls gave them their name) ventured into the silent town.

But the Germans had not gone after all. A small party of the 2nd SS Division shattered in Normandy, but still retreating and fighting, had stayed behind to fight it out. As always they fought on when the ordinary *Landser* thought there was no more hope and the only solution was *Heim zu Mutter* ('home to Mother').

Thus Hemingway and his companions had a ringside view of the unhappy partisans, ripping off their armbands and fleeing for their lives, while they continued 'drinking happily' in their 'roadhouse, awaiting the arrival of the armed forces of the United States'.

But in the end the SS withdrew too, slinking away through the deep defiles towards the border and the safety of the West Wall (though it would not be the last that the 22nd Regiment and Hemingway would see of the 2nd SS Division), and Hemingway decided to descend into Houffalize. A local volunteered to guide Lanham's vehicles around the town in order to continue the chase, while Hemingway and Lawless went down the winding main road. Lanham joined them and soon they were surrounded by townsfolk talking the harsh, strange French of Wallonia and bearing gifts of wine, cakes and eggs. Lanham asked the locals to repair the bridge over the Ourthe, just blown up by the SS and they set to work willingly, while Hemingway perched himself on a fence to watch.

Some of the locals started to address the imposing figure of the author as 'general'. Modestly, Hemingway said he was only a captain. According to his own statement they asked him why he had not achieved a higher rank at his age. 'Alas,' he answered, 'it is because I never learned to read and write.' While Hemingway played his little games, sitting on the fence with Lanham, some twenty kilometres to their south on the

River Our, which together with the Sauer (or Sûre in French) formed the border between Germany, Belgium and Luxembourg, Staff Sergeant Warner H. Holzinger of the US 5th Armoured Division carried out his CO's orders.

Lieutenant Vipond of the 85th Reconnaissance Squadron's Troop B had earlier told Holzinger that if he wished to claim the credit of being the first enemy soldier to enter Germany during wartime since Napoleon nearly 150 years before, he'd better hurry. On this Monday afternoon, 11 September 1944, other US outfits of the 1st Army were hurrying to the German frontier in half a dozen spots. Now as evening started to fall and shadows raced down the right valley of Our, dominated by the great height on the east bank, Sergeant Holzinger and his little patrol decided to stick their necks out. There would be a medal in it for them anyway, however silent and threatening that cliff-like bank on the other side of the little river looked.

The little stone bridge located between the village of Stolzemburg on the Luxembourg side, and Gmuend, a hamlet in Germany, had been blown by the retreating Germans. But the River Our was shallow, brown and sluggish. It presented little danger. The four American soldiers and one French officer, crouching on the Luxembourg side of the river, could see the bottom quite easily. They decided to risk it. Holzinger went first. Behind him came Corporal Ralph Diven, T/5 Coy Locke, Pfc George McNeal and their French interpreter, Lieutenant Lille. They crossed safely, their gazes fixed apprehensively on the silent cliff on the other side. Nothing happened when they clambered on to the enemy bank. Here the war seemed to have gone to sleep. They crossed over the narrow road that curved along the cliff parallel to the River Our. Almost immediately they stumbled on their first bunker, part of the vaunted Siegfried Line – *der West Wall*, as the Germans called it. It was empty. They staggered up the steep height and came across another three. They were all empty too.

Finally they came to the top, puffing and panting – even for young men it was a tough climb. To their front was the rolling plateau, empty of troops, though dominated by other bunkers. For a while they poked around, completely undisturbed, finding some twenty-odd pillboxes, all empty, their guns long gone, the dust thick on the concrete floors, as if they had not been used since 1940 when Hitler had first marched west. Around one bunker, a local farmer – vanished, seemingly like everyone else – had built a chicken coop. It seemed that the much vaunted Siegfried Line, the Reich's last bastion, was yet another of Doctor Goebbels' propaganda tricks. . . . Now it was really beginning to get dark and Holzinger had no desire to linger any longer in Nazi Germany. Medals or not, the first Allied soldier to penetrate Hitler's Reich thought it was high time he beat it back to the other side of the River Our.

Together, he and his little patrol splashed through the shallow water. The sun was sinking behind the high hills to his front and night poked dark shadows down the tight Our Valley. Hurriedly they doubled back to their white scout car parked under the trees on the narrow little river road. After a few moments they were gone.

Thirty minutes later an excited Sergeant Holzinger was relating his discovery to Lieutenant Vipond. Sixty minutes after that, the information was on its way to no less a person than General Courtney Hodges, the commander of the half a million-strong US 1st Army. That night, Hodges's First Army issued a statement, couched in the dry, unemotional prose of the military. It read: 'At 1805 hrs on 11th September, a patrol led by S. Sgt Warner W. Holzinger crossed into Germany near the village of Stolzemburg, a few miles north-east of Vianden, Luxembourg.'

That night patrols from other American outfits slipped across the Our-Sauer rivers everywhere. A reinforced company of the 28th Infantry Division, for instance, crossed between the

Luxembourg village of Weiswampach and German Sevenig. They brought back with them some worthless German marks – a black farmer's cap and some German earth in bottles to prove that they had actually been on the sacred soil of the 1,000-Year Reich. Perhaps today those bottles hold pride of place in some suburban front parlour – that is, if their possessors lived to bring them back!

That same night a strong reconnaissance patrol from the 22nd Regiment was organised to do the same. First Lieutenant Robert Manning, the Regiment's Scout and Raider Leader, was selected to lead the patrol. It consisted of the scouts and raiders, plus two self-propelled tank-destroyers and five jeeps. Their mission was to obtain information about the enemy and collect a jar full of German earth which would be forwarded to the President of the United States. The 4th Infantry Division always had a keen eye for publicity! After a journey of eight miles, the patrol came across the wrecked railway bridge high above the fast-flowing River Our. Beyond lay the tiny hamlet of Hemmeres: a dozen or so battered old houses straggling on either side up the very steep dirt road leading to the main road to the nearest German town of Prüm.

The self-propelled guns were not prepared to risk driving through the water (though at that spot in summer it can be easily waded) and so the two officers with the patrol, Manning and Lieutenant Shugart, flipped a coin to see who would lead the patrol across on foot. Shugart won and crossed to Hemmeres at half past nine that night.

Although both the 5th Armoured and 28th Infantry Divisions had already beaten the Fourth across, Captain Stevenson, the Division's publicity officer, was quicker off the mark in reporting the news to the Press. Under the headline 'Crackers of Hindenburg Line, First to Break Siegfried Line', the US Army newspaper recorded: 'The US 4th Infantry Division, first American Army outfit to crack the Hindenburg Line at Meuse-

Argonne in the last war and first to enter Paris in this one, also was first to penetrate Germany through the Siegfried Line in force, it was disclosed today.'

Little did the Army newspaperman, who wrote that bold heading for the *Stars and Stripes* on 24 September 1944, know that the poor battered 4th Infantry Division would still be attempting to break its way through the Siegfried Line in that very same area five months later, but by then most of the old Fourth had vanished, destroyed in the battles of the winter to come.

Now things moved fast. Further patrols from the Regiment's 1st and 2nd Battalions were alerted to cross the Our. At twenty-nine minutes after eight on the following morning Tuesday, 12 September, Battery C of the 44th Field Artillery Battalion fired the first light artillery shells into the Reich. Again the Fourth claimed these were the first 'shells to strike Germany proper.' They weren't. The US 1st Infantry Division, 'the Big Red One', lying further north south-west of Aachen had beaten the Fourth to it.

At quarter to nine, the whole regiment was ordered to move to the high ground just west of the German border and Hemingway was present when Colonel Lanham gave his morning briefing at the 'little polyglot town', as he called it, of Beho. (Beho is on the linguistic border, dividing French-speaking Belgium from the mainly German-speaking population of the two border cantons of Eupen and St Vith.) Proudly aware that Colonel Lanham thought highly of him, amateur soldier Hemingway jotted down notes of what the Regimental Commander said, just as if he were a battalion officer. Then they were off.

In a column of tanks and half-tracks, containing Lanham's infantry, they rattled across the hills towards Germany.

'Then the rat race went on again through rolling, forested country.' Hemingway described that trip in his report to *Collier's*

– 'War in the Siegfried Line'. 'Sometimes we would be half an hour behind the retreating enemy's mechanised force. Sometimes we would get up to within five minutes of them. Sometimes we would overrun them and, from the point of the recon, you would hear the fifties hammering behind you and the 105mm Wump guns going on the tank destroyers and the merging roar and rattle of enemy fire and the word would come along, "Enemy tanks and half-tracks in the rear of the column. Pass the word along."'

Now they were almost there. Allied planes came in to strafe their front. Hemingway saw 'two enemy half-tracks tearing up the white road that led into the German hills'. American artillery shells began dropping around them. 'You watched one half track slither slither sideways across the road. The other stopped on the turn of the road after trying twice to move like a wounded animal. Another shell pounded up a fountain of dust and smoke alongside the crippled half-track and when the smoke cleared, you could see the bodies on the road. That was the end of the rat race.'

Some time later they crossed the Our. (Tubby Barton would later boast that he was the first general officer to pass into Germany in the Second World War – the water was 'brown over brown mossy stones' – and had watched the first US tanks to enter Germany.) It was 4.27 p.m. Tuesday, 12 September 1944.

They came to Hemmeres, an untidy hamlet made up of a few dozen cottages and farmhouses, painted a dirty white, in the style of the Eifel region of Germany where the poor peasants lived side by side with their animals in the same dwelling and where they still ploughed their medieval strips of land with lumbering oxen. 'Ugly women and squatty, ill-shaped men' came sidling towards the Americans bearing bottles of schnapps, drinking some themselves to prove the liquid was not poisoned. Others held up their hands in token of surrender. Two days before, the local party bosses had ordered the evacuation of the 'Red Zone'. They had done the same in 1939. This time not all had obeyed the Party's orders. These villagers were the ones who had stayed behind in hiding to tend their animals.

But the rest of the low houses were empty and Hemingway took over one of them, built in 1732, where he found the warm remnants of an officer's meal on the table. While Lanham's men swarmed forward unopposed to the next ridge which, unknown to them, they would still be fighting for again six months hence, Hemingway set about finding a billet for himself and the two drivers, plus anyone else who had attached himself to his new band of Irregulars in the meantime.

He discovered an empty farmhouse at the edge of the hamlet and set up his 'Headquarters' there, taking over the animals he found there. Thereafter he sent Jean Decan to milk some abandoned cows which were complaining piteously because of the milk they carried in their swollen udders. That done, he invited Colonel Lanham and his staff to dinner. C-rations had palled and his generous way with money was no use here. So he shot the heads off a small flock of chickens which he 'liberated', as the cynical phase of the day had it, and ordered a German woman to pluck them and make a fricassee with them. Wherever he was, Hemingway regarded all non-Americans, especially Europeans, basically as servants.

That evening, Lanham arrived with his staff and three battalion commanders and briefed them on the operations of the morrow, while Hemingway, Lawless, and the Brazilian war correspondent, now nicknamed 'the Brazilius', poured the drinks. Indeed, by the time the briefing was over, 'all our booty [was] drunk up', Hemingway wrote. But more wine arrived and the party could settle down to their first dinner on German soil, with plenty to drink to celebrate the great event.

That night, while Allied bombers from the RAF and 8th Air Force in far away England droned over their heads to hit targets further inland, they dined in style. There was 'chicken, peas, fresh onions, carrots, salad and canned fruit'. As Colonel Lanham recalled long afterwards, it was his 'happiest night' of the whole war. They were *all* happy that night. The Brazilius, or the 'Pest of the Pampas', as Hemingway was now calling him, had made them all laugh with his 'rear-ass theory of pursuit', leaping about the room to illustrate his crack-pot theories. Hemingway, who always loved dogs, had found a 'fine, lovely intelligent, so confused dog who is heart-broken that everybody is gone and all routines are broken'. There was wine and good company and they had entered Germany without losses. Naturally it was a happy night.

'The food was excellent, the wine plentiful,' Lanham wrote, 'the comradeship close and warm. All of us were as heady with the taste of victory as we were with the wine. It was a night to put aside the thought of the great West Wall against which we would throw ourselves within the next forty-eight hours. We laughed and drank and told horrendous stories about each other. We all seemed for the moment like minor gods, and Hemingway, presiding at the head of the table, might have been a fatherly Mars delighting in the happiness of his brood.'

It was the last happy day. Now the bad times would commence.

Book Three

GERMANY, AUTUMN 1944

'In the next war, by God, I'm going to have the Geneva Convention tattooed on my ass in reverse so I can read it in a mirror.'

Ernest Hemingway to Colonel Lanham, November 1944

THE BATTLE FOR HITLER'S WALL

On that same Tuesday night when Hemingway presided over the happy dinner party in Hemmeres like a 'fatherly Mars', Colonel Thomas Ford, G-2 of the US V Corps, to which the Fourth belonged, was highly optimistic. Once General Hodges, the 1st Army Commander, gave the green light for the V Corps to attack, he felt they would have little trouble with the Siegfried Line.

The line – *der West Wall*, the Germans called it – which had been built in the late 1930s in response to the French Maginot Line, was outdated, incapable of housing more modern weapons such as as the feared German 88mm cannon or new multiple mortars. Besides, it had not been manned by the Germans since 1940 and he had heard from Intelligence that German officers had been unable to find the keys which opened the doors to the bunkers. They had been missing for four years now!

'There seems no doubt,' he concluded his briefing to his staff, 'that the enemy will defend the Siegfried Line with all the forces that he can gather.' Then Colonel Ford smiled and added that what the enemy could gather was 'very much to be questioned'.

From the German side, it seemed that Ford was right. Confusion, even chaos, reigned on the enemy side of the Siegfried Line. While the frightened Party bosses, the 'Golden Pheasants', as they were mockingly called, because of their love of gold braid, frantically tried to evacuate all civilians from the area, the army equally frantically tried to rally their demoralised troops.

In Trier alone, the greatest city of the area, there were reported to be some 40,000 German soldiers, stragglers and deserters, without any kind of leadership. A hard-pressed General Keppler, commander of the battered, decimated 1st SS Corps, found he was so short of effectives that he could form only two divisions from his original four to oppose any attack launched by the American V Corps. Everywhere in the small towns and villages behind the Siegfried Line, *Alarmeinheiten* (emergency units) were set up from convalescent soldiers, leave men, new recruits, indeed anyone capable of holding a rifle, and dispatched to the *West Wall*.

'Today I was transferred to the 42nd Machine-Gun Fortress Battalion as a messenger,' a young German soldier wrote in his diary that day (it was taken from his dead body some time later), 'destination *West Wall*. This battalion is composed of Home Guard, soldiers and half-cripples. I found many among them who were quite obviously off mentally. Some had their arms amputated, others had one leg short, etc., etc. – a sad sight. "We're the V-2 and the V-3," they called themselves jokingly. A bunch of fools!'

All the same, as Keppler's 1st SS Corps took up its position around Prüm, and the depots at Bitburg, Wittlich, Kyllburg and all the other Eifel townships near the *West Wall* were hurriedly emptied of troops, Field Marshal von Rundstedt, the German Commander in the West, was relatively sanguine.

At his headquarters, some seventy miles away at the confluence of Moselle and Rhine at Koblenz, he learned that his troops were already manning some of the first bunkers and that the Americans had not yet attacked. Old, cynical, incredibly wrinkled, much given to cognac, but very wise in the ways of war, von Rundstedt reasoned that, although he might be deficient in troops and weapons, his men did have the protection afforded them by the thick ferro-concrete of the bunkers. And he was right. As one disgruntled American infantryman, who would soon attack the Siegfried Line, commented bitterly afterwards: 'I don't care if the guy behind the gun is a syphilitic prick who is a hundred years old – he's still sitting behind eight feet of concrete and he's still got enough fingers to press triggers and shoot bullets!'

On the night of Wednesday 13 September, Colonel Lanham, commander of the 22nd Regiment, briefed his officers on the attack to come on the Siegfried Line at the German village of Schweiler. All day his patrols had been probing deeper into the Reich from the biggest village of the area, Bleialf, some four kilometres from Hemmeres, where Hemingway had set up his base.

They had discovered that the enemy held the ridge line some two kilometres to their front and the village of Brandscheid to the centre of that ridgeline was part of the Siegfried Line. Indeed before Brandscheid (a straggle of houses, a pub, and a couple of farmyards with open manure pits in front of the kitchen door) was finally captured for good in February 1945, it would become known as the 'German Verdun'. But by then it would have been virtually wiped off the map.

At the conference, Lanham told his officers that the Regiment would jump off to the attack at 1000 hours on the morning of 14 September.

The Regiment would attack in a column of battalions. The 3rd Battalion would lead and assemble at Buchet to the north of Brandscheid. Here it was to take the road network, poor as it was in that poverty-stricken area, and work its way to the rear of the first line of fortifications. The Third would be followed by the 1st Battalion jumping off from Bleialf. It would move through the gap blown in the Siegfried Line by the Third and continue the good work. The 2nd Battalion would remain in reserve and prepare to move against any German counter-attack, though, as Lanham concluded as the meeting ended at midnight, that was a very remote possibility, indeed. It all seemed very cut-and-dried. Simple. Colonel Lanham would have been even more sanguine if he had known the kind of opposition he would face on the morrow. It was 'Battle Group Kuehne', named after its commander, a Major Kuehne. Two days before it had been hastily thrown together in Wittlich, fifty miles away, from the recruits and invalids of the German 105th Training Battalion. For two nights (Kuehne, an experienced soldier, was afraid of Allied air attacks during the daylight hours) the new unit had marched back and forth through the Eifel until it finally reached Prüm, where the weary, apprehensive soldiers were hurriedly loaded into the waiting half-tracks of the 2nd SS Panzer Division 'Das Reich' and rushed to the *West Wall*.

Now they waited, some eight hundred half-trained men and boys. On the morrow a whole US regiment, some 3,000 strong, plus attached artillery and tank units, would attack them. What chance did they have of stopping the *Amis* with such a handful of soldiers?

At 1130 hours on that Thursday morning, the 22nd's attack took form. At first everything went well and by one o'clock that day, the 3rd Battalion had reached the Siegfried Line bunkers and were within 900 yards of their first objective, Buchet. But now the men of the 'Kuehne Battle Group', plus the handful of SS men who were assisting them, had begun to react. Enemy machine-gun fire and mortar shells intensified. There was that old, familiar, frightening ripping sound that the 100-pound 88mm shell made when it zipped through the air. A Sherman was hit and jolted to a stop. The crew baled out rapidly. They knew the 30-ton tank's bad reputation. It was not for nothing that they called it a 'Ronson'. It could ignite just as easily as the well-known cigarette lighter!

The attack began to bog down. As Hemingway described it (though he wasn't there): 'They [the infantry] started coming back down across the field dragging a few wounded and a few limping. You know how they look coming back. Then the tanks started coming back and the TD's coming back and the men coming back plenty. They couldn't stay in that bare field and the ones who weren't hit started yelling for the medicos for those who were hit and you know that excites everybody.'

Captain Howard Blazzard of the 3rd Battalion, who was with Colonel Lanham observing the battle, said: 'Sir, I can go out there and kick those bastards in the tail and take that place.'

Lanham replied: 'You're an S-2 [operations officer] in a staff function and you stay where you are.'

The two of them remained there for another fifteen minutes with more and more wounded – and others – drifting back. Blazzard thought gloomily, 'We're going to lose this battle'.

Lanham must have thought the same, for (according to Hemingway) he said suddenly: 'Let's get up there. This thing has got to move. Those chickenspits aren't going to break down this attack.'

The two of them, with Lanham carrying a drawn pistol in his right hand, moved up to a kind of terrace on the hillside where his men were lying down, taking cover. 'Let's go get these Krauts,' he cried. 'Let's kill these chickenspitters. Let's get up over this hill now and get this place taken!'

He fired a couple of shots in the general direction of the Germans and encouraged his reluctant heroes with: 'Goddam, let's get these Krauts! Come on! Nobody's going to stop here now!'

He kept shouting and gesticulating until finally his men got up and advanced into the woods at the top of the hill. Then darkness fell and to avoid confusion and his troops firing on their own comrades in the tight fir woods which marched up and down the hillsides to their front like spike-helmeted Prussian grenadiers, Lanham ordered his men to dig in. On the morrow they would change the direction of their attack and assault Brandscheid.

One of the problems facing the men of the 22nd Infantry Regiment was how to tackle the many pillboxes and bunkers which were everywhere. Back in England they had received some training in attacking concrete fortifications in readiness for D-Day. But most of those men who had trained at Slapton Sands and similar spots along the British south-west coast had long vanished. By the end of the Regiment's first month in combat, the Twenty-second had suffered 3,439 casualties, more than the Regiment's total strength on D-Day. Now they had to learn anew.

The technique was to chase the defenders to the floor of their concrete fortification by firing at the bunker's embrasure or door with machine-gun fire, or by using an anti-tank gun. Then a tank destroyer would crawl to within twenty yards of the position and begin pounding holes in the concrete, while the infantry moved in, ready to mop up with demolition charges, flame-throwers and hand grenades. If that approach failed, then the last resort was to use a 'tank-dozer', a Sherman tank fitted with the earth-moving metal scoop of a bulldozer. This would effectively bury the defenders alive, by sealing off the slits and doors with piled-up earth.

But it was the use of the tank-destroyer which most intrigued Hemingway. It seemed to appeal to his juvenile blood-lust and delight in the *grand guignol*. In his account of that September battle – 'War in the Siegfried Line' – Hemingway twice menions gleefully the use of what he called 'the Wump gun' on a pillbox or bunker.

'The Krauts still wouldn't come out when talked to, so we pulled that TD right up to the back of that steel door we had located by now and the old Wump gun fired about six rounds and blasted the door in and then you ought to have heard them wanting to come out. You ought to have heard them yell and moan and moan and scream and yell Kamerad.

'They started to come out and you never saw such a mess. Every one of them was wounded in five or six different places from pieces of concrete and steel. About eighteen good men came out and all the time inside there was the most piteous moaning and screaming and there was one fellow with both his legs cut off by the steel door.

'They were SS boys all of them and they got down in the road, one by one, on their knees. They expected to be shot. But we were obliged to disappoint them. . . . There were legs and arms scattered all over the goddamn place.'

But while Kampfgruppe Kuehne – the name means boldness in German – and the comrades of the 2nd SS Panzer Division were suffering (in the end when Kuehne's men were pulled out of the line there were only 120 left of the original 800), Lanham's 22nd Regiment was taking heavy casualties too.

As soon as their attack commenced on the following day, the Twenty-second was hit by a spirited German counter-attack. Colonel Dowdy, commanding Lanham's 1st Battalion, was killed, and his Company A was beaten back, returning with only two officers and 66 men left. That meant they had suffered fifty per cent casualties.

All that weekend of 15–17 September 1944, the battle raged for the ridgeline around Brandscheid, while Hemingway took himself off for a few days to Miss Mary and the Ritz in Paris, and the steam was beginning to go out of the 22nd Regiment's attack.

Already there were the first cases of combat fatigue, which would soon become endemic during the winter battles of the German frontier, not only among the rank-and-file of the Fourth's 22nd Regiment, but also among the officers. As the official US

War History notes for 17 September when the 1st Battalion renewed its attack under the command of a new CO Major Latimer: 'Enemy shelling so unnerved several officers including the commander of the attached tank platoon that they had to be evacuated for combat exhaustion. About 0830, as Company A moved to the line of departure, another severe shelling so upset the company commander that he, too, had to be evacuated.'

By Sunday night it was pretty obvious that Lanham's attack was stalled. He ordered his battered 1st Battalion to withdraw, while the Fourth's assistant divisional commander Brigadier-General George Taylor drove to Corps Headquarters to report on the situation.

He emphasised the casualties the 22nd Regiment had suffered and pointed out how vulnerable the 4th Division, as a whole, was to counter-attacks on both flanks. He requested that the attack on the Siegfried Line should be halted for the time being.

Taylor did not really have to sell the idea to V Corps Commander, General Gerow. Already one of his divisions, the 28th Infantry, had suffered 1,200 casualties in the attack on the Siegfried Line, nearly a tenth of its strength, and he had ordered it halted. Now he indicated to Taylor that he could inform his boss, Tubby Barton, that he would call off the attack that Sunday evening.

The battle, the first fought on German soil by a US Corps, was over. In four days of combat, the 4th Division had torn a gap of about six miles in the *West Wall*. But it had captured no ground or road systems (save some country tracks) of any strategic importance which could be used for the dash to the Rhine, which Eisenhower had envisaged. At a cost of 800 casualties, the Fourth had merely inflicted a dent on the German defences and the latter were hardening by the hour. That night, with the connivance of his corps commander,

Tubby Barton called off the assault and ordered his division to go over to what he phrased 'aggressive defence'; and that was what they would do for the next two weeks until they were relieved by the 2nd Infantry Division on 4 October 1944.

From now onwards until 16 December, when the great last German surprise attack erupted in the Ardennes with such fury, the tiny American Salient into Germany would be part of the 60-mile-long 'ghost front', where nothing ever really happened save for a little shelling and patrol activity; and to which new, green divisions were sent to be 'blooded' before being dispatched to the real shooting war elsewhere.

Thus it was that when Hemingway returned to the 22nd Infantry Regiment on 18 September, he came back to a front which had become strangely quiet. Even the rumble of the once permanent barrage no longer disturbed the rural tranquility of this now military backwater.

Paris had been a failure yet again. 'Mr Scrooby' had refused to perform, despite all Mary's efforts, and the Ritz had soon palled. Besides, Hemingway was still worried about the impending inquiry into his conduct at Rambouillet the previous month and he felt it prudent to be with friends at the front and as far away as possible from higher headquarters in Paris.

Now Hemingway, Red Pelkey, a Sergeant Kimbrough, and what was left of his Irregulars (two French boys in American uniform, Jean and Marcel), took up their quarters in what the author termed grandly 'Schloss Hemingstein'. The Schloss was the farm owned by a certain Herr Markgraff, a hardworking farmer of 73, set on the outskirts of the small village of Schweiler, which was now located about a mile behind the front. It had no running water, no bathroom, no central heating and no electricity. But if it was a poor sort of place, a typical run-down farm of the Eifel area, which before the war had been regarded by the German Government as a *Notstandsgebier* (an 'emergency area'), it attracted a large number of visitors, daily. After all the *Schlossherr* was the world-famous author Ernest Hemingway!

Soon after Hemingway arrived back there, one such visitor came for a day and stayed for nearly two weeks because he was fascinated by Hemingway and the attention he attracted. He was John Groth, war correspondent and artist, a mild-mannered bespectacled 36-year-old, who before the war had worked for *Esquire* and who now worked for *Parade* and the *Chicago Sun*. As Hemingway wrote of him after the war, 'John [Groth] looked so un-warlike that he inspired instant affection in anyone. . . . Everyone liked him and everybody thought he was crazy because he spent so much time in places where people who did not have to go were considered, fairly accurately, to have an odd mental structure, if they went.'

Groth arrived at Schloss Hemingstein in the evening, with the oil lamps flickering in the low-ceilinged farm kitchen to find Hemingway seated at the table flanked by a barricade of bottles. After the introductions, Hemingway asked the new arrivals whether they had eaten and then said, 'have a drink'.

Mellowed by much cognac, Groth 'began to loosen up' and decided to stay. Thus we have an account over several days of Hemingway by a perceptive artist, who, just as Marshall had done on the road to Paris, concluded that Hemingway felt most at home with soldiers. For Hemingway stubbornly refused to be drawn by Groth on literature; indeed, he seemed to have forgotten the titles of his own books! But at the drop of a hat, he *would* talk about war. As Groth wrote just after the war: 'The talk was always about the war. I don't recall Hemingway ever volunteering a literary reference.'

That night, a slightly tipsy, but happy Groth was introduced to the strange routine at 'Schloss Hemingstein'. After Hemingway had safely locked away *Familie* Markgraff, including two nubile if dirty daughters, for the night in their own cellar, he briefed the new arrival.

'Don't be surprised at what I am going to tell you,' Hemingway commenced. Then he told the new arrival that 'Schloss Hemingstein' was in a very exposed position. The two flanks of the 4th Division were wide open and there were no Americans between the house and the enemy. At night there was always the possibility that a German patrol might sneak into the village and be told by the remaining Germans there that there were *Amis* billeted in the Markgraff house. Hemingway informed the somewhat alarmed artist that there was a plan of defence in force just in case they were attacked. He, Hemingway, would stand watch. Meanwhile, if German soldiers did appear in the courtyard outside, 'we should not disclose ourselves. . . . If there is knocking at the door, we are not to answer. . . . Should they begin to try to enter the locked door, we are to open up on them.'

Groth, from his room on the second floor rear, was to drop hand grenades on the road to the rear of the house. Hemingway handed him two grenades and ordered: 'Put these on your night table where you can reach them. If you need more grenades, here they are.' He pulled a case of grenades from under the table.

Although Groth had never even touched a grenade in his whole life, much less thrown one, he accepted the two and went to bed fully clothed, as Hemingway suggested, just in case they had to make a run for it. 'It was fantastic,' he thought later, 'lying in a German featherbed that wasn't very clean and had been vacated only a few days before by a German, with a crucifix on the wall to my left and hand grenades, ring ends toward me, on my night table and Hemingway downstairs on guard. It all seemed something out of one of Hemingway's stories. It was difficult for me to imagine Germans attacking the house and my dropping grenades on men below outside.

I would be ready though. I wondered about my non-combatant status as a correspondent.'

Hemingway, obviously, had long given up worrying on that particular score.

It was all very juvenile, naturally, but Groth overlooked the bellicose melodramatics in his delight in Hemingway's company and the way he charmed and entertained the stream of guests who presented themselves at 'Schloss Hemingstein'. One day it would be the assistant divisional commander General George Taylor, who told Hemingway that on the Fourth's situation map there was a symbol indicating 'a bona fide company holding part of the line' and designated as 'Task Force Hemingway'. A delighted Hemingway believed it, too. Another evening, Robert Capa was present and he and Hemingway spent the hours talking about the Spanish Civil War. Most evenings, however, Hemingway's guests were Colonel Lanham and perhaps his staff or one of his battalion commanders; the officers of the 22nd Infantry, whom Hemingway had now adopted (after the war he would even become a member of the 4th Division's Veterans Association), were his favourite people. With them, Hemingway could relax and while away the night hours – for there was little to do now that the attack on the Siegfried Line had been broken off – with looted drink and good food.

Once, Lanham and his battalion commanders were having a candle-light dinner at 'Schloss Hemingstein', with the farmhouse windows blacked out with coats, when a shell landed in the courtyard outside. The guests ate the rest of their dinner with their helmets on, all save Hemingway, who remained bareheaded.

Later, Hemingway would expand the incident, of which he was inordinately proud, into quite a story for another young admirer, A.E. Hotchner. As he told it ten years later: 'Boy, you have to learn to drink under the withering fire of a fixed stare or the guided missile. During the war I had set up my headquarters for my Irregulars in a farmhouse that was smack on the frontline. It was designated at command headquarters as "Task Force Hem".'

After two untruths, Hemingway continued: 'Well, you know the artist John Groth? He came one night on his way to some assignment and we put him up. During dinner, the German eighty-eights opened up and hit us pretty good, shattering plaster and window glass. When it cleared, Groth crawled out of the potato cellar where he had dived with the other eaters . . . and he said, "Mr Hemingway, how could you sit there eating cheese and drinking wine when they had us under fire?"'

'"Groth," I said, "if you hit the deck every time you hear a pop, you'll wind up with chronic indigestion."'

Then for his new admirer's benefit, Hemingway asked: 'You know what the French call war? *Le métier triste*. You're looking at a man who's been shot at two years longer than General Grant. The sad goddam science!'

The legend was being added to . . .

Once, Hemingway took Groth to visit the front, and as Hemingway mingled with the GIs, exchanging typical GI repartee with the men, who were mostly half his age or even younger, Groth wondered if the infantrymen really knew who Hemingway was. 'Maybe back home,' he mused, 'on Main Street they had seen technicolour posters of Ingrid Bergman and Gary Cooper. Maybe they had even seen *For Whom the Bell Tolls*. But the very name Hemingway meant nothing to them. But here, in the middle of the German forest, he was a big happy-looking guy who spread a welcome mat before the door. He wasn't only Hemingway now – he was someone they all knew. He wasn't a character out of a book. True, he was something like Robert Jordan, except that this was another war and he carried cognac instead of absinthe. But most of all he was familiar – good guy like themselves – a brave man. So they knew Hemingway all right – even if they had never heard his name.'

Happy Hemingway certainly was at the front. As C.Z. Sulzberger of the *New York Times* noted Colonel Lanham saying of his friend: 'Hemingway has the heart of a lion and is first class in war, but horrible in peace.' That seemed to be true. Long after the war when sometimes he was nothing more than a drunken lout for months on end, he retained the friendship of the men he had met at the front, all the way from General Tubby Barton down to Private First Class Iz Goldstein. That September he wrote home to his son Patrick from the front stating: 'I have never been happier nor had a more useful life ever. . . . We have had some tough times and some wonderful times.'

But as the 4th Division prepared to withdraw across the border into Belgium for a refit, training, and the horrors of the new battle to come in Germany this winter, Hemingway knew he would have to leave the Division. There was no alternative for him but that 'command post at the Ritz', and all the problems that the move back to Paris entailed, both private and public.

Although he wrote Mary on 23 September that he hoped to be in Paris soon, confessing he wished desperately to escape this 'hawk and cough and spit' place (once again he was ill, this time with a severe cold), and find a house for the two of them where he could own a pile of clean shirts, he worried too, about returning.

At 4th Division Headquarters the rumours continued to persist that he was going to be called to account for his conduct at Rambouillet. Then 'liars' and the 'phonies' and the 'ballroom bananas' (those envious other correspondents) were trying to pin something on him. They were making something shameful and underhand out of a brave action, undertaken in the course of an emergency. Instead of being punished for it, why, they should praise him for his work at Rambouillet. Later he would always stoutly – and enviously – maintain that Colonel Bruce had been awarded a medal for *his* reconnaissance work outside Paris.

'Suppose someone introduced a rule forbidding accredited journalists from jumping into the River Seine and a friend fell in, what was the journalist expected to do – let the friend drown?' Thus he reasoned scornfully.

His mood started to slump. On the morning of Sunday 24th, it was raining hard and 'Schloss Hemingstein' was crowded with men seeking shelter and free booze. Somewhere a cannon was booming, echoing and re-echoing in the circle of surrounding hills. Sitting in a corner Hemingway tried to compose a poem:

> 'Loseing [sic] the three last night
> Taking them back today.
> Dripping and dark the woods . . .'

In the end he gave up. There was too much talk in the crowded farm kitchen and he was feeling old and sad. As he scribbled below it in the letter he would send that day to Mary: 'Can't write poetry from too much talking . . . it started to come out like chickenshit Hiawatha.' Then as if to indicate just how low his mood was, he printed on the back of the envelope in which he enclosed his unfinished poem and letter, his APO (Army Post Office) address and the words 'Please deliver in case of casualty'.

Perhaps on that gloomy, rain-swept Sunday that was exactly what Hemingway hoped would happen to him. A 'KIA' (Killed in Action) would solve all his problems for good.

THE INQUIRY

October 1944 was a bad month for Ernest Hemingway. Many great writers – and some not so great – seem to live in a world of their own. Graham Greene, it is said, believed he had a *doppelganger*, who travelled the world ceaselessly, impersonating him. John le Carré, who sounds much more ordinary under his real name David Cornwell, apparently thinks he was once an operative in the clock-and-dagger world of British Intelligence. Imagination, it appears, feeds upon imagination!

In that October in France, Ernest Hemingway had two blows levelled at his person, which, for a while at least, wrenched him from the fantasy world which he usually inhabited. So far the war in Europe, which had caused untold suffering and misery to millions of humbler people, had been a kind of game for him. It had provided an exciting means of escape from his personal problems: a fresh chance to run away from that absurd, unreal life in Cuba where he had failed to exercise his craft; and with luck the war might provide him with the material for a new book.

During the last few months he had made periodic and very brief visits to the front, but when the action had died down and life had become the boring dreary routine of the average infantryman's war, he had scuttled back to the champagne rounds of his luxury hotels. In short, the Second World War seemed, in Hemingway's eyes at least, to have been created for Papa to take pleasure in and weave his own highly individualistic and often cruel, even sadistic, fantasies. Now, for a while at least, hard reality struck.

It came just after he returned to the Ritz from the Eifel, in the form of a communication, couched in that unemotional, long-winded officialese of the US Army. 'You will proceed,' it read, 'by military aircraft and/or Government motor transportation on or about 4 October from present station to Headquarters, Inspector General Third Army (Rear) to carry out the instructions of the A.C. of S.H-2, Supreme Hq. AEF.'

Hemingway had been around the military long enough to decipher the gobbledegook and understand the purport of the message. The Acting Chief-of-Staff of the Allied Expeditionary Force had ordered Patton's Inspector General to interrogate him on his conduct back in July–August in Rambouillet and Paris. The inquiry he had feared and dreaded ever since Tubby Barton had told him what was in the wind was now actually going to take place. It was scheduled for Friday, 6 October 1944.

Hemingway set out for Patton's Headquarters in the capital of Lorraine on the Thursday morning, travelling eastwards across the war-torn ravaged countryside from Paris in a jeep. The roads were battered and littered with the already rusting tanks of both the German and American Armies. After Verdun his driver had to make a large detour round Metz, which was still under siege by an exasperated Patton, who was already threatening to sack his corps commanders if they did not take the last remaining major German bastion in France soon. Then fighting the traffic (in particular the black drivers of the Red Ball) bringing up supplies to the 3rd Army front, he and his driver headed south to Nancy.

Nancy had fallen to Patton's 3rd Army nineteen days before, an event which caused the 3rd Army Commander some emotion – 'this is where we came in', he commented when he heard the news – for the capital of Lorraine was one of his old stamping grounds from the First World War. Since then, he had moved his headquarters to the French barracks in the rue du Sergent Blandau, while Patton himself had taken up residence in a villa in rue Auxonne. Now all the city's hotels were packed with American officers and ancillary headquarters.

It was with some difficulty therefore, that Hemingway followed the welter of 3rd Army signs, all phrased in the complicated, confusing shorthand of the military, until he found the old hotel which housed the Inspector General's Department. Stiffly he left the jeep and walked across to the hotel in the cold moonlight to hear the charges against him.

The officer in charge of the inquiry was a Colonel Park and, like all the other senior officers in the Inspector General's Department of Patton's 3rd Army, he was no stranger to scandal and inquiries. General Patton himself had been involved in more than one investigation over the years since he had landed in North Africa back in November 1942. First there had been 'slapping incidents' in Sicily 1943 when he slapped two soldiers suffering from combat fatigue. Patton felt the men in question were simply 'yellow-bellied cowards'. Then there had been the '45th Division Massacre', in which the officer and sergeant accused of cold-bloodedly massacring German prisoners had maintained they had done so because Patton had encouraged them in a rabble-rousing fighting speech he had given to the 45th Division just before it had gone into action for the first time. When Patton himself was not being investigated, then his sorely tried Inspector General's Department were investigating other officers, from generals down to enlisted men, whom the Commanding General wanted court-martialled for crimes ranging from cowardice in battle to the failure to wear a necktie in combat. Yes, Park was well used to investigations, but this was the first he was being ordered to conduct against a civilian.

Solemnly he read out the allegations to a grave Hemingway. They stated that, 'Mr Hemingway stripped off correspondent's insignia and acted as a colonel, French Resistance Troops; that he had a room with mines, grenades and war maps; that he directed Resistance patrols, which action is believed to violate credential rights of the correspondents'. Based on the statements taken from the other correspondents, who had been angered by his conduct at the Hôtel du Grand Veneur in Rambouillet, it was also alleged that Hemingway had employed a full colonel of the US Army as his Chief-of-Staff and that he had declared to a fellow correspondent that he was no longer writing dispatches, which implied that he no longer regarded himself as a war correspondent. Already at the time when he had first taken up with the French partisans, SHAEF had sent an officer to see Hemingway, and warn him that he was on his own if he continued to work with the Irregulars; Supreme Allied Headquarters took no further responsibility for him.

His reaction had been violent. As the officer, a Lieutenant Leary, recalled in February 1945 for the South African correspondent Barbara Loxton: 'This made Hemingway mad, very mad. Little Brazilian correspondent [the same one who had entertained at that first dinner party on German soil] kept saying, "Well Mr Hemingway, what are you going to do now?"' Hemingway's reaction had been violent and constituted another breach of his status as a war correspondent. 'Hemingway whisked out a gun and shot at him, missing his head by a couple of inches!'

Finished with the statement, Park looked at a suitably sombre Hemingway and said: 'In the morning, I will question you and take your statement under oath.' With that the writer was dismissed and walked back to his room, mulling over the allegations, his mood black, very black indeed.

Of course, he knew they were true. He had carried a weapon right from the start of his jaunt to Europe and he would continue to do so, long after the investigation was wound up and he left Europe in 1945. Iz Goldstein had spotted the grenade back in Normandy hidden about Hemingway's person 'just in case'. Later, when Mary had visited him at the Ritz, she had found one of the two beds piled high with weapons and grenades. As we have seen, John Groth was given grenades by Hemingway at 'Schloss Hemingstein'. In the coming December, Hemingway would be spotted carrrying weapons again, after (as his brother Leicester put it) he 'had learned that depressing lesson back in Paris' and realised that 'other correspondents, unless they were genuinely friends, were out to get him'. Now he handed his pistol to his driver or Baron. 'Hold it until we leave,' he would say, 'That way I know I'll get it back.'

But even in Luxembourg that December, three months after the investigation, 'a sottish wreck at the Hotel Cravatte', as British war correspondent and former admirer of his novels, Cyril Ray, characterised him, he took little care to conceal the fact that he was armed and prepared to use those weapons, if necessary. As late as January 1945, when he had finally finished with the front and was planning to return to Cuba, he went 'a little wild' and started firing German machine pistols, which Lanham had given him, at a photograph of Noel Monks (Mary's husband) mounted in a toilet bowl!

Now his love affair with weapons and violence, which had been part and parcel of his whole life, had rebounded. If he were found guilty on the morrow of the charge levelled against him, he would lose his accreditation as a war correspondent. That would mean he would be sent back to the United States as soon as transport was available. In itself, that would be no great hardship. He was already missing the sunshine and the easy life in Cuba. Besides, he felt he had enough material about the war already to start the trilogy of war novels which he had planned. But he still had not made love to Mary and he knew all about her past affairs – and they were many. Would she wait for him, if they were separated by the Atlantic Ocean, especially as he had not yet proved his male potency to her?

There was also the scandal to be considered. At the front and in the Ritz he could get away with his drunken high jinks, but to be sent home in a kind of disgrace would definitely be recorded by the many correspondents who disliked him. The stateside papers would all pick up the news item about America's most popular novelist. What might the impact be on the American reading public?

Finally, there was his third wife Martha Gellhorn. By now he knew their marriage was finished. All the same, he still held her in high esteem, not only as a woman but also a fellow writer, who could stand up to him and had attempted to make him mend his drunken ways in the past. She had forced his hand back in Cuba and made him volunteer for an overseas assignment in the first place. Now if he were sent home, she'd be able to crow over him; point out that he was good for nothing any more if he couldn't even hold the job as war correspondent.

That night in Nancy, as Hemingway finally turned in at midnight, his mind must have been in a turmoil.

While he had been waiting for the blow to fall, Hemingway had worked hard to secure testimonials to his conduct at Rambouillet. The most important, from Colonel David Bruce of the OSS, read: 'I met Ernest Hemingway for the first time on 26 July 1944 at my Command Post in the vicinity of le Mesnil, France. . . . He is without question one of the most courageous men I have ever known. Fear is a stranger to him. His calmness and casual air under fire has always had a beneficial effect upon both officers and men.' Bruce went on to state that he had given Hemingway written permission to bear arms and command partisans under the extraordinary conditions which pertained at that time at Rambouillet. Another who testified to Hemingway's courage, though naturally his testimony had no relevance as far as the business at Rambouillet was concerned, was Lanham. Naturally, Colonel Lanham made no reference to the fact that he knew Hemingway had been armed and prepared to use his weapons during his recent stay at 'Schloss Hemingstein'.

Another testimonial came from Major James Thornton, who had been there with Hemingway at the French township. He wrote: 'It was apparent that we should require the assistance and co-operation of all allied personnel on the spot and the services of War Correspondent Ernest Hemingway were welcomed.'

It was Colonel Bruce, the future diplomat, who stretched the truth, however, and pointed the direction in which he thought the inquiry should go. He stated at the end of his testimony: 'I witnessed no instance of Mr Hemingway having conducted himself in any manner other than appropriate for a loyal American acting efficiently during a period of emergency. I never saw him armed nor did I hear of any instance of his having personally engaged in combat with the enemy.' The 'loyal American', acting 'during a period of emergency' was the clue to the manner of his thinking. How could any American military tribunal penalise a loyal American, even if he were a civilian, for bearing arms when the chips were down?

Neither Hemingway nor Bruce should have worried. For as Hemingway's biographer Jeffrey Meyers has pointed out: 'To justify these depositions and ensure exoneration, Hemingway was ordered by two officers of General Patton's staff to commit perjury to swear that he was not armed in Rambouillet (he did not state that he had been armed *outside* the town) and to deny under oath actions he was proud of.' The Army, especially 'Ole Blood and Guts's' 3rd Army, was going to look after its own, particularly when the accused was a red-blooded American like Hemingway, who, civilian or not, was prepared to take up arms for his country.

On the morning of Friday 6 October, Hemingway faced up to Colonel Park. The writer was asked whether he had taken off his war correspondent's insignia during the events at

Rambouillet. By this he meant the basic American Army blouse, adorned with the title of 'war correspondent' on the shoulder. Hemingway replied that, due to the warmth of the weather then and for the purposes of 'sanitation' (whatever that meant), he had done so, but only momentarily.

Park pointed out to Hemingway that other correspondents at Rambouillet had heard him being addressed as 'captain' and 'even colonel' by the partisans. How did he explain this rank being applied to him by armed Irregulars? Perhaps emboldened by the knowledge that there were those at Patton's headquarters – maybe even 'Ole Blood and Guts' himself – who did not want him convicted, Hemingway replied cheekily that a civilian owning a dory on the New England coast back home was automatically called 'cap'n'; just as in Kentucky everyone of any status was naturally referred to as 'colonel'. Why, even in China, any little yellow man who wore a uniform was addressed respectfully as 'general'.

Colonel Park pressed a little harder. What about the weapons and ammunition which other people had seen littering Hemingway's room at the Hôtel du Grand Veneur?'

Hemingway had his answer ready. After all, for the quick-witted intelligent, inventive man that he was, it wasn't difficult. Why, he replied, his room had simply provided a convenient storage place for the Irregulars' weapons – that's all. . . .

Up front at that precise moment, Patton's men were battering, unsuccessfully, at one of Metz's toughest forts, Fort Driant, named after a French hero of the First World War. They had been attacking the Fort for three weeks, losing on average 100 men a day in a kind of mini-Verdun, with German artillery from covering positions routinely swatting the attacking Americans off the Fort's roof, once they had managed to break through the perimeter defences.

The day before, one of the attackers, a Captain Ferris Church, had sent back a graphic message from the Fort, stating:

'The situation is critical. A couple more barrages and another counter-attack and we are sunk. We have no men, our equipment is shot and we just can't go. . . . We may be able to hold till dark, but if anything happens this afternoon, I can make no prediction. The enemy is butchering these trps [troops] until we have nothing left to hold with. We cannot get out our wounded and there is a hell of a lot of dead and missing.'

While Hemingway played his silly little cat-and-mouse game with Colonel Park, Patton, at his command post in Etain west of Metz, decided he could not take any more casualties at Fort Driant. Depressed and reluctant, he admitted he had been beaten at the Fort – for the time being at least. He ordered a withdrawal. Fort Driant wouldn't be taken till December.

Now, as the inquiry continued, the stream of boxlike Army ambulances, carrying the grim legend in their windscreens, 'Priority. Carrying Casualties', bore their freight of misery back from the front to Nancy and its chain of surrounding military hospitals.

What about the charge that he had employed a full colonel as his second-in-command (Colonel Bruce) and that he had been observed with maps and field glasses? Park asked.

Hemingway admitted he had possessed both glasses and maps. He needed them for his job as a correspondent. Bruce, on the other hand, had not served him. Their roles had been reversed. He had worked for Colonel Bruce merely as a translator, passing on his orders in French to the partisans.

There was some talk now of his actual role with the 4th Infantry Division during its race across northern France, Belgium, and into Germany. Hemingway already knew he was well covered by Tubby Barton, the main figure in that *Collier's* article 'The GI and the General' soon to appear in the magazine, and he replied confidently that while he was with Barton's Fourth, he had been accompanied by the Division's

Public Relations Officer, a Captain Stevenson, who incidentally was the son of the then governor of Texas.

Colonel Park here nodded approvingly, but persisted that other war correspondents had testified that he, Hemingway, had acted like a character out of one of his own novels and not as a war correspondent should have, abiding by the rules of his profession. Hemingway brought his big guns to bear. He said he could produce both character and conduct testimonials from not only Colonel Lanham but also General Barton, if required. That did it.

Colonel Park was outranked. He must have done some quick thinking, reasoning that a divisional commander was not going to risk his career in the Regular Army by lying to save a civilian, however famous that civilian was. Hemingway had to be telling the truth! Probably he had been the victim of a bunch of envious, back-biting civilians who had been drunk at the time of the events in question. Everyone knew that newspapermen were lushes. Soon thereafter, Park terminated the inquiry, advising Hemingway to set his mind at ease. In due course he would be exonerated; there would be no repercussions. He could stay in Europe.

Shortly afterwards Colonel Park kept his word. In his findings he wrote in awkward officialese '[there was] no violation by him of the existing regulations for war correspondents'. As Jeffrey Meyers, Hemingway's biographer, wrote forty years later: 'Hemingway was licensed to do as he pleased and famous enough to get away with anything.'

Hemingway's relief at being cleared was obvious. In a letter he wrote to Colonel Lanham two days later, he stated: 'I.G. [Inspector General] very sound and understanding. Beat rap by explaining when troops . . . placed themselves under command, refused command explaining impossible war correspondent command troops due to Geneva Convention . . . all other raps [beaten] on same basis. Send you a couple of funny papers on same but do not show to anyone and keep for me.'

But he felt bitter, too, at having been accused by his fellow war correspondents of being 'a show-off and horse's ass'. If he had told the truth and had been sent home, he would have been fêted as a war hero. He could have relaxed in comfort, waiting for a suitable medal to be struck in his honour by 'the Key West Chamber of Commerce' or the 'Havana Pigeon Shooters'. Despite his relief and bitter humour, however, the inquiry at Nancy had been traumatic. Four years later when the inquiry had been long forgotten by everyone else, he was writing to the now General Banham from Cuba on 15 April 1948, stating, 'I know how goddamned busy you are and hate to bother you with it. But I think it is possibly fairly simple employing these steps:

A. Ascertain who was I.G. 3rd Army (Bear) on 5th October 1944.
B. Ascertain from I.G. if this record is available.
C. If I.G. has no information ascertain who was the stenographer who took down the testimony.'

In other words, long after the event, Hemingway was asking a busy general to try to find out the full details of the charges against him, although he had been exonerated in 1944! Why?

His own explanation was: 'Am sorry as hell to bother you about this. But sooner or later, especially if I am dead, there will be a lot of rhubarb about this and I think the record is much the best thing to have.' The truth, it seems, was that the inquiry still rankled so much that he was going to include it in a book – 'now that it [the IG's report] is no longer restricted, I would like to have the damned thing to refresh my memory when I write it' – perhaps even in that one bitter novel he produced about the war, *Across the River and Into the Trees*.

Fortunately, perhaps, Buck Lanham could not turn up the required documents. Probably he never even bothered to look for them. By this time he had got the measure of Hemingway, who in his drunken moods was inclined to write to everybody and anybody, including the President of the United States. So Hemingway was never able to use them in his subsequent writings in whatever form.

Now, however, in 1944 when he returned to Paris, Hemingway was less and less inclined to trust other people, save for the friends he had made in the 4th Division. In particular, he was very wary of his fellow war correspondents. Indeed he did not write another article for *Collier's* after the one on the Siegfried Line was published on 18 November 1944. The correspondents were 'out to get him', he told his brother Leicester a few weeks after the Nancy Inquiry when they met again in Luxembourg City.

So he managed to get himself off the hook that first week of October. But that cold grey month in 1944, when the war in Europe turned against the Allies, was not finished with him yet. In the letter he wrote to Lanham from Paris on 8 October, he mentioned that the only bright spot in the whole miserable business of the inquiry was that the 'kid (Bumby) [John Hemingway, his eldest son] jumping with fish rod is jumped in Jura mts [mountains] where he knows good streams. After job done could fish. Anyway could fish supposed to be German (very blond kid speaks perfect French ok German). Now in Voges [sic] his Col likes him very much. In funny racket had good fight kraut patrol last week. If could do what want to do would see him. His Col offered send him Paris see me but we both knew no and I said no. Col complains he so goddamned military. Can't have any contact with him. Unlike his old man, I was more like that too but that was in another country and besides the wench is dead.'

Of course, Hemingway was drunk when he wrote that letter. Even his new-found basic syntax, which he thought a combination of 'militarese' and the uneducated speech of the average GI with whom he had been associating in the Fourth, could not be *that* muddled. But his pride in his officer son, who had transferred from leading a platoon of 'coloured' military policemen to become an OSS paratrooper, shines through his confused, turgid prose. Suddenly, 'Bumby', whom he had neglected so often in the past, was dear to him, a young man of whom he could be proud: a son doing the kind of things he dearly wished he could do himself and *would* do, if envy and regulations did not stop him.

But Bumby would never use those 'fish rods' in the Jura, the Vosges, or anywhere else for that matter. That cruel October, which had already levelled one blow at his father was reaching out for him again. For the very last time before he placed that sporting gun against his temple on that quiet June Sunday morning and blew away his entire cranial vault, Hemingway would have to face up to reality again. . . .

A COMMAND POST AT THE RITZ

For a man of his fame, gained at an early age, good looks and wealth, Ernest Hemingway had enjoyed comparatively few women. Four of the five women who had been his mistresses became his wives. Although he had had opportunity enough in Paris in the 1920s and later in Cuba in the 1930s, Hemingway seems to have had little to do with whores, save talking to them. Throughout the 1930s when he was in his late thirties and early forties and should have been in his sexual prime, Hemingway had only one affair besides that with Martha Gellhorn, whom he later married. Despite his boastfulness on the subject of sex, Hemingway had, indeed, led a surprisingly unpromiscuous life, having married early and remaining married for the rest of his life. Moreover, by the time he had reached the age of 44, he had suffered two lengthy periods of impotency. For a man of Hemingway's type, much given to the outward show of male virility – boxing, big-game hunting, the company of men in bars, and so on – this recurring difficulty with 'Mr Scrooby' must have been very galling.

Did Hemingway have a hang-up? Was there, beneath that simple, tough macho image – the boxer, the warrior, the bull-fight *aficionado* – a much more complex and complicated individual, especially in matters of sex?

One recent biographer, Kenneth S. Lynn (*Hemingway*, 1987) certainly thinks so. In his account, Professor Lynn blames Hemingway's mother Grace for distorting her son's sexuality at an early age. According to Lynn, Grace Hemingway, a big domineering woman who apparently lived with another woman after her husband's suicide and displayed lesbian tendencies, dressed her son in girl's clothes at an early age and made him grow his hair long to look like a girl. This treatment up to the age of about five gave him, again according to Lynn, doubts about his masculinity all his life.

Allied to this, his father's suicide (for which he blamed his mother), must have created a man of undecided sexuality, who was also assailed by a fear of failing and being a weakling just as his doctor father had been.

His first wife, Hadley, had been eight years older than Hemingway and something of a mother figure. Thereafter, he had picked women whose figures had been as slim as boys (totally unlike that of his mother) and whose hair was cut short, even cropped, when it was no longer fashionable for women to wear their hair like that. In addition, significantly enough, many of his other female friendships were with women who were lesbians or bisexual. According to Professor Lynn, Hemingway could never sort out his sexual identity due to his upbringing, and in his last novel, *Garden of Eden*, he indulged his imagination in the real transsexual fantasies of his own life.

Whatever the truth of the matter, Hemingway had begun to suffer his second long spell of impotency in 1943 and it is apparent that his third wife, Martha Gellhorn, who was independent with a career of her own, and was not prepared to cater to his every whim as his other two wives had done, would not help him. Perhaps that accounted for their many bitter quarrels and his final rejection of Martha?

Mary, his latest conquest, scenting a 'catch', was definitely ready to help. She was eager to go to bed with him and definitely more submissive and loving than Martha. But possibly he was unable to reveal to her the kind of sex which turned him on. As a result, Hemingway was still unable to perform!

So it was that while hundreds, and soon thousands, of young men were being butchered weekly at the front, the major concern of America's most famous writer that winter was the problem of his own potency, or lack of it. Naturally, one could say that a 45-year-old civilian writer had every right to be preoccupied with his own personal problems. However, this particular writer was living in a war zone, despite the fact that he had set up a 'command post' in the Ritz. Around him there were men and women in uniform whose daily concern was the events at the front, even if they were mostly chairborne warriors. Sometimes in the stillness of the dead of night, the thunder of the guns in Lorraine could be heard at the Ritz. Daily, the ambulances poured into and through Paris carrying the torn, battered bodies of the wounded to the rear.

Each new day brought fleets of trucks and lorries bearing swarms of eager, callow, desperate young men form the front, who would spend a seventy-two hours' leave in 'Gay Paree'. Pockets full of back pay, haversacks bulging with goods for the black market, already half drunk, Hemingway could see them any time he chose, heading for 'Pig Ally' (Pigalle) and the hordes of 'good-time girls' in their wooden-heeled platform shoes, flowered dresses and rabbit-skin fur coats waiting for them there. If he had wished to do so, Hemingway could also have seen them at the end of that leave, being herded back into their 'deuce-and-a-half' (two and half ton trucks) like cattle, sometimes by helmeted military policemen, wielding white-painted clubs. Hungover, hollow-eyed, perhaps by now diseased, but all definitely broke, they were being shipped back to the front up to that new section, which the GIs called the 'death factory'. With a life expectancy of a month, if they were infantrymen, they knew they would never see 'Gay Paree', or their homes ever again.

But Hemingway never saw those sights or, if he did, he never recorded them. During his October stay in the Ritz he was concerned solely with his own problems – and pleasures. As always, even in the midst of a cruel, savage global war, Hemingway, a writer, supposedly sensitive to the emotions of his fellow men, remained totally unaffected by the sufferings of the 'little man'. His colossal egotism and vanity left no place for such things. Reality in the shape of the Nancy inquiry had infringed upon his life for a day or two in the first week of that grey October. Now all he wanted to do was to play and drink, and if at all possible, induce 'Mr S' to start functioning once again.

Now from his room 31 at the Ritz, with Mary living officially at room 86 a couple of floors above him, Hemingway entertained all-and-sundry at this palatial 'command post', which now, as the notice at the desk proclaimed 'Provides accommodation for VIP [Very Important Persons] personnel only!' And for the most part, Hemingway's guests were VIPs as the new word labelled the élite. In particular there was one who not only visited, but immediately took up residence when she knew her old acquaintance Hemingway was staying at the grand hotel.

She was Marlene Dietrich ('diet-rich' as she parodied her name for Hemingway's entertainment), who had been entertaining US troops overseas off and on for two years now; not that her absence from Hollywood meant much, for her career had been in the doldrums for the last few years since movies featuring European vamps had gone out of fashion in a now deadly serious wartime Tinsel Town.

Marlene Dietrich had always been contemptuous of Hollywood and its emphasis on maintaining an outward show of morality. She was and would always remain her own woman, oblivious to her reputation in the movie capital as a woman who repeatedly fell love with her leading men. Once, for instance, she told a journalist that her leading man and lover Jean Gabin 'had the most beautiful loins I've ever seen in a man'.

When she saw John Wayne in the studio canteen for the first time, she exclaimed, 'Daddy, buy me *that*!' According to some sources, the glamorous 42-year-old star was also one of that group of females to whom Hemingway was always attracted, like Gertrude Stein, Janet Flannery, Nancy Cunard, all of whom were lesbian or bisexual. Dietrich certainly had a bisexual aura about her which helped to make her a star. In his own autobiography she maintains that her reason for cross-dressing (in the late 1930s she was photographed wearing male suits, something very shocking in those days) was because she wanted to sing 'men's songs' – 'the best songs are written for men'. This explanation ignores the fact that she had been dressing as a man for two decades, long before she thought of a singing career. In fact, as one critic, Christopher Tookey, has noted, 'her escapades with various woman friends were . . . notorious. The screenwriter Budd Schulberg has recounted, for instance, how Dietrich once tried to seduce his mother with the aid of a bottle of champagne and a book on lesbian lovemaking.' There was also 'Jo Carstairs, a crew-cut millionairess racing driver famous for her tattoos, or Mercedes D'Acoasta, an openly lesbian socialite and authoress who persuaded Marlene to start wearing the slacks which then became the Dietrich trademark'.

Now the famous actress came back into Hemingway's life (she had met him aboard a ship back in the late 1930s) at the Ritz. 'It was a Platonic love,' she maintained in her autobiography, though she did not like Mary at first and seemed envious of her.

'It is impossible to say why a man desires a particular woman. Mary Welsh was stiff, formal and not very desirable. Like most women of her sort she probably would have gone on living sadly and joylessly if she hadn't found a Hemingway along the way, who, for a long time, had had no romantic affairs or sexual adventures. . . . Mary Welsh didn't love Hemingway, of this

I am sure. Yet this modest, inconspicuous woman war correspondent had nothing to lose.'

Mary, for her part, did not seem jealous. For her, Marlene Dietrich was 'a business woman concerned with every detail of her program from transport to accommodation, to sizes of stages and halls, to lighting and microphones. Business seemed to be her religion.'

'The Kraut' or 'Daughter', as Hemingway variously called Marlene Dietrich, treated the writer as if they had once been lovers at some time or other (which they hadn't). As Mary recalled long afterwards: '[She] used to wander down to Ernest's room to sit on his bathtub and sing to him while he shaved and they both forgave me when I mimicked her.' Dietrich also explained to both Mary and Hemingway as one of her 'choice topics of exposition', her plans for her 'funeral which [she had] worked out in elaborate detail'.

There were other visitors, however, who were not so welcome to Mary at that swank command post at the Ritz. Some time that October, three of four battalion commanders from Lanham's 22nd Infantry Regiment came on leave to the French capital from the Belgium–Germany border where the Regiment was preparing for the blood-letting soon to come in the 'Death Factory'.

At first they were all clean, tidy and respectful, as befitted young colonels of infantry who held the fates of some 800 equally young infantrymen in their hands. But Hemingway was always liberal with the champagne (over the six months he was at the Ritz he drank the grand hotel dry of his favourite champagne marque), and they started to get drunk.

Marlene was introduced to them and one of them announced, 'his dearest dream would be to write home that he had lain on a bed with her'. Marlene, always one to support the troops, obliged. 'She promptly stretched out on top of one of my [Mary's] rose satin coverlets and the blushing officer warily arranged himself, as stiff as at attention beside her. Ernest's joy surged over.' Now the infantry officers were getting more and more drunk. They headed downstairs to eat, where they were introduced to Mary's employer, Clare Booth Luce, the wife of the owner of the *Time-Life* set-up.

Clare Booth Luce had just arrived in Paris from Italy where she had been very impressed by the work of the US Army Air Corps. This she pointed out to one of the young infantry colonels.

'You're darned right, babe,' he slurred, 'and don't you put your mouth on it.'

Mrs Luce did not see the way the situation was developing. For she said: 'The infantry – they pinpoint the advance, don't they?'

That did it. By now the 22nd Infantry Regiment had had nearly twice its establishment turned over due to casualties. The colonel was in no mood to play games with this stupid civilian lady, however important she might be. As far as he knew, he might be dead before the month was out in what was soon to come. (He was too.) 'Pinpoint!' he exclaimed. 'Sweet Jesus! You ought to read a book, you dumb broad. What are you doing here anyway?'

Mary wished the earth would open up and swallow her. Already she could see the terse note from her employer the next morning: 'Your service with Time Inc is terminated!' Hurriedly she left without saying goodbye.

Hemingway was in an ugly mood when he came to her room later. He was pretty drunk, too. For a while he prowled around her room angrily until she said, 'Well, I have to go to bed now. I'm tired, if you'll excuse me.'

Hemingway's rage bubbled forth: 'You insulted my friends,' he cried, 'all evening and without cess, you insulted my friends! You could not have behaved more horribly!'

Mary had had enough. 'Your friends,' she cried, 'are drunks and slobs! They threw up all over my bathroom! They probably lost me my job! They drove Marlene away. They may be heroes in Germany, but they stink, stink, stink. But I did not insult them, your boorish friends!'

Hemingway did not hesitate. He was not taking that kind of 'crap' from a woman. He hauled back and slapped Mary.

It was not a really hard slap, but the first one she had experienced 'since my mother used to spank me with the back of a hairbrush'. She fell back on her bed, crying, 'You poor coward. You poor, fat, feather-headed coward. You woman-hitter!'

She rose to her feet and pranced around, half-crazy with rage and bitterness. 'Knock my head, you coward,' she taunted him. 'Why don't you knock my head off? Show what a big strong coward you are. Take it to the Twenty-second. On a platter. Show 'em, you won't let me insult 'em, you bully!'

Hemingway simmered down, though he had rarely been able to contain his anger. 'Hold it,' he snorted, putting his hands behind his back deliberately. 'Hold it now!'

Mary could not contain herself, she was so angry. 'You think you can frighten me, you big bully?' she shrieked. 'Why don't you break my jaw in self-defence? Knock my head off!'

Hemingway slumped down on her bed and she pushed him back, straddled his hips and began pummeling his chest. 'You big bully . . . You flyblown ego!' she cried.

'You're pretty when you're mad,' Hemingway said calmly, allowing himself to be struck by his pint-sized girlfriend.

The remark infuriated her even more. 'This is the end of this,' she yelled. She found the bits and pieces of his clothing he had left in her room, thrust them into his hands and declared 'good night and goodbye!' With that she pushed him out of the door.

Next morning there was a polite knock. It was one of the young battalion commanders, now sober. 'Papa really feels bad,' he said. 'He's sorry.'

'Papa be damned!' she replied.

'He wishes you could see his side of it.'

'Tell me about your outfit,' she countered. 'Have you got some smart asses in it? Is your ammo freezing up on you, nights? Tell Papa from me, he's a coward.'

In the end, when Mary remained stubborn and unyielding, Hemingway sent Marlene Dietrich to plead his case. Mary told her she didn't think much of a man who sent others to make his apologies for him. 'Any man worth his salt would come up here himself instead of sending apologies. He's a coward and a bully, as I told him last night and I've had enough of him.'

Stubbornly Marlene Dietrich pressed Hemingway's suit, but Mary turned a deaf ear. 'Finally,' as Dietrich recalled many years later, 'I listed all the advantages of a relationship with him and advised her to compare her present life with what she could expect at his side.' According to Dietrich, 'my efforts bore fruit. At lunchtime her resistance began to slacken.'

Later, while Mary scrubbed Hemingway's back in the bathtub, she told him, 'You drink so much, you lose your mental balance,' and suggested he should return to his second wife, Pauline, to whom he still wrote. She'd be a 'practical nurse for you in your old age and your kids – why can't you be big enough to make a *rapprochement*?'

Perhaps Mary was simply flying a kite, trying to ascertain whether Hemingway was really serious about marrying her. At all events, Hemingway would not return to Pauline. Still in the bath, with Mary drying his back, he told her: 'You are a beautiful and wonderful Pickle. And all I can say now is that I love you truly and that I need you and will love you always and need you always.'

'Always?' she sneered. '*Shit!*'

Now she knew that she had Hemingway and as Dietrich reported afterwards, 'I have never seen anybody as happy as Hemingway'. For better or worse, Mary would have him for the rest of her life.

Still 'Mr Scrooby' stubbornly refused to perform. Try as she might, Mary could not rouse his sagging organ. For his part, Hemingway blamed his inability to perform on the second concussion he had suffered back in July in Normandy. Impotent or not, Hemingway was now determined to marry Mary Welsh, but there was still the problem of his third wife, Martha Gellhorn. The time had come to discuss divorce.

In the last week of October, Hemingway learned that she had finished her 'Cook's tour' in Italy and had arrived in Paris, where she was staying at the Hotel Lincoln for a while before setting off once more for the front in Holland.

He telephoned her and insisted she should have dinner with him. On the theory that it was time that they parted for good, she agreed to do so. It was not going to be a happy occasion.

John Groth, Hemingway's new artist friend, happened to be present and was astonished by Hemingway's behaviour and the way it alternated between submissiveness and open hostility. Martha Gellhorn irritated Groth by the bossy way she corrected his imperfect French and ordered Hemingway about: 'Ernest, get a waiter . . . Ernest, get the wine list . . . Ernest, give me the wine list – you don't know anything about wine . . . Ernest give someone else a chance to speak.'

For her part, Martha Gellhorn thought that Hemingway was deliberately setting out to humiliate her in public. He brought along 'a band of his young soldier pals from "his" regiment', she recalled long afterwards, 'and in front of them insulted and mocked me throughout the dinner. They were miserable and slowly left.'

Mrs Lael Wertenbaker, the wife of Mary Welsh's boss Charles Wertenbaker, who was also present, heard Hemingway read aloud his tender if mawkish 'Poem to Mary' which he had written that winter. This was followed by a crude pornographic verse he had also penned called 'To Martha Gellhorn's Vagina', which he compared to the 'wrinkled neck of an old hot water bag'. That did it. A bitter public quarrel broke out in the dining room and in the end, as Martha Gellhorn remembered afterwards, 'I got up from the banquette where I'd been hemmed in and fled'.

The next morning, filled with remorse, he wrote her a note of apology, in which he likened his treatment of her to having spat on the Holy Grail. The note would cut no ice with her. From Holland she would soon write to him: 'We are honest people, Bug, and this is a no-good silly arrangement. It is not our style. . . . I think it would be best for you to get this finished with me.' Then she asked for a divorce. As usual, Hemingway would twist the matter and claim that *he* had rejected Martha. He reviewed the reasons for the breakdown of their marriage: the claims of her career, her frequent absences during the war and the fact that he couldn't write when he was lonely. He did not mention the fact that when he had once slapped Martha, she had driven his prized Lincoln into a ditch by way of revenge. Martha was not so forgiving as Mary had been recently in a similar situation.

Hemingway also noted that his love and loss of Martha were closely connected to the wars they had seen. 'Once I was gone she wanted me back very much. But we want some straight work, not to be alone and not have to go to war to see one's wife and then have wife want to be in different war theater in order that stories not complete. Going to get me somebody who wants to stick around with me and let me be the writer of the family. Since children have to be in school am not going to be lonely to die and not able [to] work.'

'I got sort of cured of Marty [Martha] [by flying] with the RAF. Everything sort of took on its proper proportion. Then, after we were on the ground, I never thought of her at all. Funny how it should take one war [the Spanish Civil War] to start a woman in your damn heart and another to finish her. Bad luck.'

But the real bad luck for Ernest Hemingway was still to come this October.

It was Sunday, 29 October 1944. At the front a lull had settled in. Both Patton and Hodges, the commanders of Eisenhower's 3rd and 1st Armies respectively, were preparing for new attacks in the first week of November. The Germans had experienced their own 'miracle of the Marne' all along the border with France and Belgium and the Americans were 'regrouping', licking their wounds, and telling themselves they'd succeed next time. All they needed was more men and more machines. Surely the Germans couldn't stand any further losses on the scale they had been suffering up to now. The US commanders were committing themselves to the same kind of war that would fail two decades later in Vietnam: the battle of attrition when enemy 'body counts' were the only successes; for they indicated that final victory was just round the corner.

As a result, Paris and the Ritz were full of chairborne warriors, visiting 'firemen' and high-ranking officers taking a few days' leave in the luxury hotel before they returned to the bloody business (for others) of conducting the new battle in the 'Death Factory'.

Despite the fact that the hotel was crowded and food was getting tighter, Hemingway was always an honoured guest there and received preferential treatment, especially, importantly for him, in matters of liquid refreshment. Every time he entered the lobby or dining room he would be honoured with a slight smile and bow from Madame César Ritz, the widow of Ritz's founder. Mary, however, was ignored. Madame Ritz frowned upon liaisons of this kind, although her husband's hotel had been host to many a rich man's mistress before the war. As Mary wrote long afterwards: 'It was only when I returned to the Ritz after the war, having been properly married according to the Napoleonic Code in Cuba, that Mme Ritz acknowledged my existence and then she was entirely gracious.'

Madame Ritz need not have worried really for 'Mr S' was still not performing. The Hemingway–Welsh liaison was still utterly chaste. But on this pleasant October Sunday afternoon, the two of them were temporarily not concerned with the problems of the bedchamber. Instead, Hemingway and Mary were enjoying a leisurely lunch, concentrating, in particular, on the good wines that Ritz was still able to furnish, conversation becoming more and more animated the more they drank. They were thus pleasantly engaged when the second blow of that October struck home. A young man in army officer's uniform, wearing the silver wings of a parachutist, threaded his way through the dining room and stopped surprisingly at their table. Hemingway looked up. He could see the young man was a mere first lieutenant from the silver bar on his shoulder, and mere lieutenants were a rarity in the now VIP Hotel Ritz.

But this particular young officer was something special. He introduced himself as 'Lieutenant-Prince-Poniatowski', a scion of that famous Polish family, currently serving in the OSS, and the bearer of bad news.

He had been sent personally by the scar-faced commander of the US 3rd Infantry Division, General John 'Iron Mike' O'Daniel, currently fighting in the Vosges Mountains of Eastern France, to inform Hemingway of a family tragedy. His 21-year-old eldest son Jack (nicknamed 'Bumby' since his childhood in Paris) had been wounded and captured while out on patrol. The real war had come home to roost at last.

BUMBY GOES INTO THE BAG

Hemingway had not been very pleased when his first wife Hadley had announced she was pregnant with the future Jack Hemingway in Paris in February 1923. He went over the house of his new friend Gertrude Stein, who, although she was a lesbian, he still wanted 'to fuck'. She recalled that he stayed all day in gloomy reverie until 'all of a sudden he announced that his wife was *enceinte* and then, with great bitterness, "I am too young to be a father". We consoled him as best we could and sent him on his way.'

Later, when his parents were divorced, Jack usually saw his father only during his vacations from school, when the latter made up for lost time by introducing his son to all manly sports, in particular hunting and fishing. Indeed, Hemingway took his interest in his first son's welfare to extremes some times. In the spring of 1943 when Jack came on vacation to Cuba from Dartmouth College, Hemingway felt it was time for his 20-year-old first-born to lose his virginity. He asked him: 'Bum, have you ever been laid?'

His son lied he had not and a concerned Father Hemingway laid on a Cuban prostitute to take care of the oversight. She was named Olga and when she met Jack she burst out laughing. The very night before they had been in bed together! Later she telephoned Hemingway's home and when Hemingway asked how she had fared with his son, she replied confidently that he was *como un toro*!

Later Hemingway grew exceedingly proud of his eldest son when he volunteered to leave a safe job as a military police officer to become an OSS paratrooper. In the summer of 1944, he jumped into France with an OSS team and thereafter carried out reconnaissance and intelligence work with General Patch's US 7th Army as it worked its way up from the invasion beaches on the Riviera to Eastern France. There it was on Saturday 28th that he and some comrades were surprised in the Lower Vosges mountains, not far from Belfort, while on a patrol for the veteran 3rd Infantry Division. According to the report Hemingway received later, Jack, a Captain Green, and the handful of French partisans they commanded, heard the sound of some digging in the woods in which they found themselves. Green crawled forward to check it out.

That was a bad mistake. The Germans of General Wiese's retreating 19th Army, who were now at last trying to make a stand on the Führer's order in the Lower Vosges Mountains, spotted him. They opened fire. Green was hit in the foot. The next moment, Jack Hemingway was wounded in the shoulder and right arm. He dropped to the ground struck by five rifle bullets and a number of grenade fragments.

Minutes later, as they lay wounded on the ground, they were taken prisoner by men of the German 2nd Gebirgsjagerdivision, an alpine formation which contained many Austrians. As Jack Hemingway told it afterwards, 'An Austrian lieutenant who spoke French looked at my dogtags and said: "*Sprechen ze [sic] Deutsch?*". And I said "*Non, je parle français*" [so much for Hemingway's boast about his son's knowledge of German]. The Austrian lieutenant then spoke French and asked: "Were you ever in Schrooms [Schrums, Austria]?"'

Jack Hemingway replied, 'Yes, when I was a little boy.'

The Austrian then asked, 'Do you remember anyone named Kitty?'

Hemingway answered, 'Yes, she was my nurse.'

The Austrian then informed the surprised youngster that Kitty had been his girlfriend and that he had known Father Hemingway and his wife when Jack Hemingway had been two years old. He said, 'Lieutenant Hemingway, do not be nervous. I know who you are and I am a great admirer of your father's work.'

Thereafter, Jack Hemingway's captors arranged for him to be shipped to a hospital in Alsace where he would be patched up and sent to a POW camp in the Reich. Now Jack Hemingway would never have a chance to use that fish rod, which he had brought with him to a kind of total war he and his father could never have envisaged. Instead, he worried what might happen to him on an account of his father's anti-fascist reputation. 'I had read, particularly in his forward to an anthology of war stories *Men at War*, his recommendations about what should be done to SS men if we were ever in a position to do so, including, I think, castration or sterilisation.'

But on that Sunday afternoon, Hemingway knew nothing about the kind Austrian officer or his son's fears. All that was known was that Jack's wound was probably not fatal and that he had been taken to a German forward dressing station.

Hemingway was shocked. He fired a score of anxious questions at the young courier. More wine was hurriedly brought. Next to him, Mary could feel 'Ernest's temperature, blood pressure, anxiety, anger, and frustration rising to some point of explosion with no safety valve apparent'. The wine started to talk. Hemingway began to fabricate all sorts of crazy plans to rescue his son. 'Haven't we got a plan of their hospital system there?' he demanded. His idea was to land a small plane, perhaps an artillery spotter, near the German hospital where Jack was being held and rescue him. 'If we made a quick surprise drop we could get him out,' he urged passionately. 'We ought to be able to make a heist.'

The plan was as novelish as the old gangster word 'heist'. The Prince-Lieutenant replied coolly that some action had been considered at 3rd Division's Headquarters but speedily rejected. As Mary put it: 'We began to understand that to the US Army, Lieutenant Jack Hemingway was merely one of tens of thousands of Allied wounded captives.' But Hemingway, who didn't live in the real world of men, even at times like this, wouldn't give up. He awoke next morning with hundreds of plans instantly hatched in his fertile brain. 'I can't go over there [where his son had been captured]. If the Krauts learned of it, they might put the bite on Bumby. But you could go. You're an innocent *Time* reporter. You could go and re-check and see if there is anything we don't know now and reconnoitre some and find out the true gen.'

Mary replied, adopting the tough talk that Hemingway favoured. 'I can't speak any Kraut. Send Marlene.'

The mind boggles at the thought of that screen vamp 'reconnoitring' in the front line, but Hemingway did not seem to think the suggestion absurd. But he still preferred Mary to go, although, naturally, she wouldn't 'be any good behind the lines'. But 'you could talk to Bumby's outfit people. Poniatowski [he had now slipped away] is only one of them. And to his general. You've got so many friends who are generals.' A sexually envious Hemingway knew only too well that this was true.

In the end, Hemingway convinced Mary. They dreamed up a pretext to visit the area, with Mary purportedly researching a story of the famed Japanese-American combat team, which had won more medals than any other outfit in the US Army in Italy, and which was now serving in France. Her boss, Charles Wertenbaker, agreed to let her go for *Time* magazine and the Army approved.

Of course, she could only go over the same ground as had Jack Hemingway's comrades, and she found nothing. In due course, she would write Hemingway a long report on his son's capture, concluding that '[I] feel encouraged about the whole business and more optimistic than we did here [at the Ritz]. . . . One thing you know I'm not soft-soaping you to save you anguish. I know we understand each other about that. . . . Any kind of anguish is preferable to evasion or deception.'

But by then Hemingway had gone from Paris to the 'Death Factory' and it would be left to someone else (who was losing all contact with reality and was just as larger-than-life as Hemingway was) to institute a crackpot rescue attempt to 'heist' Jack Hemingway, and many others like him, that was doomed to failure right from the start.

One of the few correspondents who ever went up (for this was a loser's battle and they knew it and besides, it was damned dangerous, even for civilian correspondents) called it 'the Green Hell of the Huertgen'. But that name never really caught on. The GIs of the 'poor bloody infantry', who would fight and die there, had another name for it, which never passed the American Army censors; for it was all too true and realistic. They called it the 'Death Factory'.

The place they were talking about was 'der Huertgenwald' (in reality, three forests, although the name of one of them – the 'Huertgen Wood' – was applied to all three of them by the Americans). It lies just south of the great imperial German city of Aachen on the Dutch–German border, some 20 miles long and 10 miles wide. It is a sparsely populated area, with the few villages perched on the top of the ridges, riven by steep gorges, their slopes thick with tall, dark green trees, heavy with resin. It is the kind of forest one reads about as a kid in one of those brooding Grimm's fairy tales, in which it is easy to lose one's way. Indeed, an imaginative person entering these dark brooding woods might well be inclined to drop things behind him to mark his path, as did Hansel and Gretal trying to find their way home and finding instead the dreaded *Pfefferkuchenhaus* with its cannibalistic, warty witch.

The horror of the 'Death Factory' had really commenced in September 1944 when General 'Lightning Joe' Collins of the US VIII Corps had made his first 'reconnaissance in force' over the border into Hitler's vaunted '1,000 Reich'. The real aim had been to head for the Rhine, but for some reason that no one could ever explain afterwards, Collins, a dynamic little American-Irishman who had made his reputation in the Pacific, was worried about a German counter-attack to his right flank from the direction of the Huertgenwald. For that reason he ordered one regiment of the US 9th Infantry Division into the forest.

For five solid days the Ninth, which had fought in Africa, Italy and France, tried to break through, taking appalling casualties (indeed they had a virtual one hundred per cent turnover) in the tight confines of the fir forest. Unable to manoeuvre, the trails and firebreaks were covered by German fixed-line machine guns and thick with a new type of anti-personnel mine. Mounted in a glass or wooden container the deadly package of steel balls could not be located by engineers using the conventional mine-detector, which picked up only metal objects. To find the unseen killers, the hard-pressed infantry and engineers had to crawl on their hands and knees along the forest trails, often under fire, prodding the frozen earth with their bayonets or looted German pitchforks. American soldiers had not fought in conditions like this since the Argonne offensive back in 1918, or perhaps even the 'Wilderness' of the American Civil War.

This was a battle totally unlike the high-speed, mechanised combat they had been used to ever since they had overcome the *bocage* in Normandy. Regiments became battalions, battalions became companies, companies squads, as large-scale formations were broken into little isolated, frightened units in the close-packed fir trees. 'The enemy seemed to be everywhere,' one of the infantrymen who fought in the Huertgen recalled bitterly afterwards. 'And in the darkness of the thick trees, the confusion seemed everywhere.'

'If anybody says he knew where he was in the forest,' one battalion commander spat angrily at the time, 'then he's a liar!'

'The Huertgen was agony,' one sergeant correspondent wrote at the time, 'and there was no glory in it, except the glory of courageous men – the MP whose testicles were hit by shrapnel and who said, "OK, doc, I can take it"; the man who walked forward firing Tommy-guns with both hands until an arm was blown off and then kept on firing the other tommy gun until he disappeared in a mortar burst.'

Overnight, the GIs of the 9th Infantry Division – and all the other divisions which followed them into the 'Death Factory' had to learn new skills in order to survive in the forest fighting.

The kind of fox hole they had patiently dug before was no use when a man's outfit was being shelled in the trees. Here, shells didn't explode on the ground, with the shrapnel erupting upwards harmlessly. They exploded overhead – 'tree-bursts', they came to be called – and the red-gleaming, razor-sharp shards showered downwards with deadly effect, unless the GI had learned from the Germans to cover his fox hole with logs and sods of grass. Nor was it any use throwing yourself flat on the ground when tree-bursts were exploding all around. To do so only exposed more of the body's surface to that killing, flying metal. The thing to do was to press your body against the nearest tree trunk – and pray!

Night movement was taboo. To get out of one's hole at night was a sure invitation to death – not only at the hands of the enemy, but at those of your friends, too. At night, soldiers, German and American, shot first and asked questions afterwards. During the long hours of winter darkness, for sometimes as long as twelve interminable hours, infantrymen cowered in their coffin-like holes, praying desperately for the dawn to come once again. Here, every sound or movement of a tree branch signified imminent danger, and there was little sleep, even if a man was exhausted. They lived off their nerves and if they had to carry out the body's functions, well, they did so where they squatted. Better to be defiled than to be dead!

All American's technical advantages in warfare were useless in the forest. Artillery was of little use. There were thick rows of trees marching up and down the steep slopes everywhere. The forward artillery observers were blinded. They couldn't adjust their fire. Besides, they had to think of the danger to their own men. It was the same with bombers and fighter-bombers. Friend and foe were so close to one another that the pilots daren't risk it. Tanks were of little use either. They were too vulnerable because they were limited to the forest trails and they were always mined and covered by enemy pillboxes.

The hard-pressed infantry and their commanders prayed to be released from the frightening vice-like grip of the forest, where both the most senior officer and the humblest doughboy felt like blind men. They longed for the open ground beyond. But each time they managed to fight their way clear of the trees up to the bald ridgeline beyond, where the few villages of the area perched, the German Panthers, Tigers and self-propelled guns would be waiting for them and they would be forced to flee miserably and in terror back to the cover of the trees.

The days the infantry spent in the forest blurred into one long, never-ending, nerve-racking misery. No one recalled the separate days any more. Each new dripping grey dawn brought up new cannon fodder; bug-eyed replacements in fresh uniforms, complete with necktie – and now death. Many a young man entered combat in the forest for the first (and last) time without even knowing the name of the unit to which he had been sent. Within hours they were being carried back by the cursing, sweating litter men a bloody wreck, yet another casualty of the Huertgen Forest.

Even the Germans, who were more familiar with this kind of warfare from their long experience of fighting in the endless woods of the tundra in Northern Russia and Finland, felt the horror of the forest. It frightened and brutalised them, too, just like the Americans. A young replacement recalled with horror long afterwards, watching as his new comrades cooked their rations over an open fire, seated on the frozen solid bodies of their own dead. When he protested, one bearded weary 'stubble-hopper', as the German infantrymen called themselves contemptuously, said mildly: 'Well, it keeps my arse from getting cold, don't it?'

Colonel Wegelein, the commander of a battle group made up of mainly officer cadets, was spotted wandering alone, save for his dog, in the forest after the battle group's first day of combat. An American sniper promptly shot him dead and took his maps from the dead body. Some time later one of Wegelein's officers tied a noose round his legs under fire and drew the dead colonel back into cover.

But what had an experienced senior officer, who had been in the Germany Army since 1921 and who had had five years of combat behind him, been doing wandering about the forest unarmed like that? Was he, too, sick of the never-ending slaughter and courting a quick death to get it all over with once and for all? Or had he simply lost his way?

Before the whole messy business was over, the 'Death Factory' would claim 29,000 Americans who had also lost their way.

On 16 October, eleven days after the 9th Division had entered the forest, General Hodges, the commander of the US 1st Army to which the Division belonged, withdrew it. The Ninth had penetrated exactly 3,000 yards into the forest at a cost of one and a half casualties per yard – a total of 4,500 men killed, wounded or missing in action. One of its regiments, the sixtieth, had suffered an almost one hundred per cent turnover in personnel.

The Ninth was relieved by the 28th Division, which had fought alongside Tubby Barton's Fourth in that first venture on to German soil back in September, in what now seemed another age. The changeover was not encouraging. The 'Death Factory' lived up to its name. Everywhere the 'new boys' could see the grim waste of battle – empty shell cases, wrecked jeeps, cleared mines, belts of unused ammunition, and the sombre-faced blacks of the Graves Registration Units still removing the rain-soaked stinking, bloating corpses of the Ninth's dead.

The survivors of the Ninth hiking six miles to reach the trucks which would take them away from the 'Death Factory' did nothing to cheer the new boys up. There were none of the usual 'Bronx cheers' (raspberries), the mocking banter, the cries of 'you'll be sorr-ee'. The mud-splattered survivors, unshaven and morose, stumbled out of their positions like sleepwalkers, staring straight ahead and silent. They looked, the new boys thought, like men who had 'been through hell – and worse'.

At dawn on 2 November 1944, while Hemingway in faraway Paris made frantic efforts to find out more about the fate of his missing son and Mary prepared for her mission to Alsace, the morning stillness of the forest was broken by the start of the 28th Division's barrage. Now 12,000 shells would be fired at the enemy positions. It was the Western Front circa 1917 all over again. The Germans were being 'softened up' for the coming infantry attack. The only trouble was, they were not softened up!

At noon precisely, the 28th Infantry went into the forest and they were fated to suffer a worse beating than their predecessors. Almost immediately things started to go wrong for the unlucky Twenty-eighth. The end would be defeat and disgrace.

At the ridgeline village of Schmidt, the Germans counter-attacked with tanks. Panic set in. The men began to pull back, slowly at first, then ever more swiftly. Non-coms lashed out with their fists and boots. More than one officer threatened the waverers with his pistol. To no avail! They wouldn't turn and fight.

The 28th's commanding general ordered the lost village retaken. While the assault force was being mustered, the Germans attacked another village, held by the Division. The defence collapsed. Soldiers started to cry like broken-hearted little children, while their battalion commander slumped in his cellar, apathetic and motionless, seemingly totally unaware of the chaos all around, his face buried in his hands. The Germans pressed home their advantage and the battalion broke altogether. 'It was the saddest sight I have ever seen,' one of the 28th's officers, Lieutenant Condon, reported afterwards. 'Down the road from the east came men from F, G, and E Companies pushing, shoving, throwing away equipment, trying to outrace the artillery and each other, all in a frantic effort to escape. They were all scared and excited. Some were terror-stricken. Some were helping the slightly wounded to run and many of the badly wounded, probably hit by the artillery, were lying in the road where they fell, screaming for help. It was heartbreaking . . . demoralising.'

Another officer, Captain Nesbitt, said that it was no use pointing out to the fugitives they hadn't seen a single German yet; it was just enemy artillery which was inflicting casualties on them. 'They ran as fast as they could. Those we saw were completely shattered . . . there was no sense fooling ourselves about it. It was a disorderly retreat. The men were going back pell-mell!'

Things went from bad to worse. Combat fatigue became endemic. Men, company commanders, even battalion commanders, refused to fight and broke down. In the end, General Cota, the Twenty-eighth's Commanding General, was forced to order a soldier sentenced to death for running away in the face of the enemy. Eisenhower would confirm the sentence. He would be the first American soldier shot by his own comrades since the Civil War. The casualties mounted and mounted. A whole regiment disappeared and its commander, already wounded twice, crawled down the mountainside to report to Cota. When he saw the blood-stained, mud-covered officer, big, tough 'Dutch' Cota, who had been decorated for his bravery on Omaha beach by both Eisenhower and Montgomery, fainted clean away.

In the end the top brass realised it was no use continuing with the decimated 28th Division. They ordered the fighting to continue for a few more futile days, but in its brief seven days in the forest, the 28th Division had lived up to its nickname of the 'Bloody Bucket' Division (so named because of its red, bucket-shaped divisional patch). In that one week in November it had suffered a staggering 6,184 casualties, nearly half its strength. The Twenty-eighth was a spent force. Now it was the turn of Tubby Barton's men of 'my favourite division', as Hemingway called the Fourth, to enter the 'Death Factory'.

Why the top brass continued the attack into the forest no one was ever able to explain afterwards. After what had happened to the 9th and 28th Infantry Divisions, they should have circumvented the Huertgen Forest, sealed the Germans off, bottled them up in their wooded fortress, just as they had done with the German-occupied French ports, or as the British had done with the German garrison on the Channel Islands. But they didn't.

Perhaps it was a matter of military and personal prestige. They had set out to conquer the forest in September. Now, two months later, after so many casualties, they were still determined to take it. Perhaps it was that professional arrogance, lack of imagination and intellectual insensitivity, which was now beginning to characterise the American top brass, swollen-headed with their victories in France and Belgium. They were the symptoms of that institutional illness which might be called 'the disease of victory'; it was the same disease which would make these captains and majors (notably Colonel Westmoreland, or 'Waste-More-Land' of the 9th Infantry), one day to be colonels and generals in Vietnam, continue *that* monstrous struggle when the battle had long been lost by the USA.

In the end, after eight infantry and two armoured divisions had gone into the 'Death Factory' and had finally broken the German resistance in the forest, it was recorded that only one of the many generals involved ever protested this grossly unnecessary battle. He was the youngest of them all, 38-year-old General 'Slim Jim' Gavin of the 82nd Airborne Division, which had dropped on D-Day. Army commanders, corps commanders, divisional commanders, generals all, had accepted the attack orders from above, knowing the kind of slaughter the men would soon face in the forest. Not one of them protested, save the youngest, Gavin. Sickened as he was by the slaughter, for him it was 'a totally unnecessary battle'.

On 5 November 1944, there were the first indications that the Fourth was going to be sent up from its training and garrison area on the Belgian–German border to the Huertgenwald. Totally unprepared for what was to come the Fourth's 12th Infantry Regiment, under the command of James Luckett, was rushed to the front to assist the ill-fated 28th Division. Within hours the new arrivals were fighting for their very lives.

Two companies of Luckett's infantry were surrounded. Desperately, Luckett formed a stop line to the rear. Casualties mounted. By the end of the fourth day in the 'Death Factory', Luckett's 12th Infantry had lost half its effectives in battle due to 'trenchfoot', or that persistent malady which would plague the American Command throughout the winter battles, combat fatigue. The Germans were playing tough, too. One of Luckett's men was found wounded and abandoned by the enemy in the forest. First his discoverers robbed him, then they rigged an explosive charge underneath the wounded man's body. For the next seventy hours (nearly three days) the wounded doughboy lay alone in the cold and rain, racked by pain, the only available water that which he could lick from his cracked lips, fighting desperately to stave off unconsciousness. He was afraid that when the American aidmen came to rescue him, as they eventually would, they would blow not only him but themselves to smithereens when they attempted to lift him. He succeeded. He was found, warned his would-be rescuers and lived to tell his tale – truly a testimony to the courage and endurance of the human spirit!

By the fifth day, the 12th Regiment was burned out. It had already lost 1,600 men, half its strength, and wasn't even within sight of its objective. The top brass, which believed (with Napoleon) that there were 'no bad soldiers, just bad officers', relieved the unfortunate Colonel Luckett and whistled up Tubby Barton's two remaining regiments.

During 7 and 8 November, these regiments started to assemble in the little Eifel village of Zweifall, where Tubby Barton set up his headquarters in the big school building opposite the church. Now it was going to be the fourth's turn to enter the 'Death Factory' and, as one of the handful from Colonel Lanham's 22nd Regiment who would survive the débâcle, T/5 George Morgan, would recall long afterwards, it was to be a traumatic experience.

'Show me the man who went through the Battle of Huertgen Forest,' he recorded, 'and who says he never had a feeling of fear, and I'll show you a liar or damn fool. You can't get all of the dead because you can't find them and they stay there to remind the guys advancing as to what might hit them. You can't get protection. You can't see. You can't get fields of fire. Artillery slashes the trees like a scythe. Everything is tangled. You can scarcely walk. Everybody is cold and wet and the mixture of cold rain and sleet kept falling. Then we attack again and soon there is only a handful of old men left.'

THE 'DEATH FACTORY'

In essence, the task of Colonel Lanham's 22nd Infantry Regiment was to attack up the heights from Zweifall, work its way down the extremely steep slope on the other side to a little brook hidden in the forest called '*Weisse Wehe*'. From there, it was planned the infantry would ascend the equally steep, forested slope on the other side, using two trails through the forest. Once on the summit, the Twenty-second would assault the hamlet of Grosshau, a single street of cottages grouped around a small church, just off the main ridgeline road which led down to the major Rhenish city of Dueren on the Rhine plain below. This time, the Americans in a two-divisional attack (the 8th US Infantry Division would be assaulting the main road to the Fourth's right simultaneously) would be assaulting the German positions from a different direction. That was the only thing which distinguished the new plan from the previous ones, which had failed so lamentably. As the German Chief-of-Staff of the enemy's 7th Army which defended the forest, General Freiherr von Gersdorff, wrote after the war: 'The German command could not understand the heavy American attacks on the Huertgen forest. . . . We presented no danger to them [the Americans] because we did not have the strength. An armoured attack [on our part] was also not possible and was never even planned.'

Again the 'poor bloody infantry' were going to be thrown into an attack which would serve no strategic and little tactical purpose, even if it succeeded, which was hardly likely when the

Germans on the ridges dominated the whole area, even as far back as Tubby Barton's Headquarters at Zweifall. They would have every advantage on their side, including the weather, which had now turned grey, overcast and rainy, precluding any support from Allied air forces, which now completely dominated the sky over Germany (although the meteorologists did hold out a ray of hope for the day the attack would commence – Thursday, 16 November. On that day, after nearly a month of rain, they predicted no precipitation, and possibly even some sun).

For the 22nd Regiment, 'H-Hour' would be at quarter to one on that Thursday afternoon. Again, as in the Eifel, the assault would be in a column of battalions, with Lanham's Second Battalion kicking off the assault. Before that, the attached 44th Field Artillery Battalion, reinforced by the 20th Field Artillery, would fire heavy concentrations to each flank of the proposed breakthrough area, in order to seal it from German reinforcements and as a means of deceiving the Germans exactly where the *Amis* would attack. It was to be a pious hope. The Germans weren't deceived. They would be waiting for the Americans all right.

Late on the afternoon of the Wednesday before the great attack, Lieutenant-Colonel Tom Kenan of the 22nd's Second Battalion looked up from the hole in the ground which served as his command post to see a tall burly man, wearing a helmet and olive drab trousers, but without a weapon and no badges of rank, staring down at him short-sightedly through steel-rimmed glasses. Later it was claimed that the stranger was carrying a Tommy-gun, but after the inquiry at Nancy, it would be hardly likely he would do so so very publicly. Kenan had never seen Hemingway before, but he was impressed by his bulk, accentuated by a sheepskin-lined white jacket the stranger was wearing. In contrast, however, he thought the glasses perched on the writer's nose seemed 'pitifully small and inadequate'.

Hemingway introduced himself, explained he had come up from Tubby Barton's Headquarters at Zweifall, and asked to be taken to Colonel Lanham. If Kenan wondered how a civilian war correspondent had got hold of the top-secret information that a major offensive (there were going to be divisional-sized assaults along the whole length of the 1st Army's front) was to commence on the morrow, he did not put his thoughts into words. After all, this was the famous Ernest Hemingway, the movie of whose book *To Have and Have Not*, starring Humphrey Bogart and Lauren Bacall, had just been premiered in Hollywood.

Obediently, the Colonel led Hemingway to Lanham's caravan, a plywood trailer on wheels, which was towed by a truck or weapons carrier all over Western Europe. Montgomery had pioneered the device back in the Desert, when he had looted such a vehicle from a captured Italian general, nicknamed 'Old Electric Whiskers', by the Tommies. By now any officer in the field, right down to the lowly colonels, possessed one. It was the ultimate military status symbol of late 1944.

Together with Bill Walton, the would-be paratrooper Hemingway had met first at that ill-fated Capa party in London, Hemingway settled down in the caravan, which featured a German steel helmet painted with flowers to be used as Lanham's chamberpot, to 'shoot the breeze' with a worried Lanham. The colonel briefed the two correspondents on the action of the morrow and then after Walton had departed and, in view of the fact that Lanham could not sleep, Hemingway and he talked and drank right into the small hours of the Thursday morning.

Hemingway told Lanham about Bumby. In his turn, Lanham, who was depressed, told Hemingway that he had had a premonition that he might not survive the coming battle. Hemingway exploded. He snarled that he was sick and tired of 'all this shit' about premonitions. His pet hate, fellow war correspondent the American Ernie Pyle (Hemingway often called himself 'Ernie Haemorrhoid, the poor man's Ernie Pyle') was always having the damned things. Then he launched into an attack on Pyle, of whom he was envious because he had served so long overseas and on all fronts (in the end, Pyle would be killed in the Pacific in 1945), but even as he did so, he knocked on the wood of the caravan's table. In fact, Hemingway was as superstitious as the next man.

Finally, the drinking session broke up. But both men were up bright and early next morning as the guns of the 'softening-up' barrage started to rumble and a weak sun, as the meteorologists had predicted, lightened the grey sky to the east. Together with Lanham, Hemingway visited the three battalions preparing for the attack, issuing new orders and encouraging the rank-and-file, many of them replacements who gripped their rifles in damp sweaty hands, although the morning was still cold. They were going into action for the first time, but all of them had heard of the horrors of the 'Death Factory'. They needed all the encouragement they could get.

The attack 'jumped off', in the parlance of the war correspondents, promptly, but there was little dash about the assault. The terrain was too rugged and the trees were too dense. As one of Lanham's staff officers told Sergeant Mack Morriss, the correspondent of *Yank* magazine at the time: '[the advance] is like wading through the ocean. You walk in it all right, but water is all around you.' Almost immediately the advancing battalions started to break up into smaller groupings in the forest. By that evening, the men of the Fourth had already learned that, due to the trees everywhere, 'a man would throw away his rifle before he would give up his axe', as Captain Henley of the 1st Battalion stated grimly, 'because with an axe he could chop wood – and also kill Heinies'.

Darkness came early and, not wanting to make the confusion any worse in the dark green of the forest, where, at the best, anyone off the trail could see a matter of only yards, Colonel Lanham ordered his men to pause and dig in for the night. He would switch his 1st Battalion into the lead. The Second would then follow. In line abreast, the two battalions would attack and seize the high ground which dominated the main trail through the forest. Lanham would issue further orders in the morning.

On the morning of the 17th, Hemingway again accompanied Lanham in his jeep as he went up to brief his officers. They stopped at the dugout of the acting commander of the 1st Battalion, scheduled to start the day's attack. He was Major Hubert Drake, 'a little grey sort of man', in whom Lanham did not have much faith. On the way back to his trailer, Lanham confided his doubts about the officer to Hemingway, mentioning the fact that he might have to relieve him in a few days if he did not shape up any better. Quietly Hemingway said after a moment, as the jeep churned its way down the mud of the trail: 'Buck, you won't ever have to relieve him.'

Lanham, or 'Silent Buck', as he was known behind his back in the Regiment, bristled. 'Why?' he snapped.

'He won't make it,' Hemingway replied. 'He stinks of death.'

The jeep had just reached the regimental command post when the Twenty-second's executive officer, Colonel Ruggles came up, saluted and reported: 'Major Drake has just been killed, sir. Who takes the 1st Battalion?'

Drake had been killed in a sudden artillery-mortar barrage, which had descended upon Lanham's two battalions and which had also wounded the commander of his 3rd Battalion, Colonel Teague.

Hemingway made no comment and walked on alone to Lanham's trailer. Lanham instantly summoned another officer, Major Goforth, to take over the First, giving the latter only one order: 'On arrival I should not get into the same hole with

Captain Henley. We had lost too many officers already.' Before this attack was over, Lanham would lose many more; very many more.

A little while later, Lanham went over to his trailer to find Hemingway seated there with a stiff drink in his hand, although it was just after nine in the morning. After what Hemingway had said to him recently about premonitions, he was justifiably puzzled by the former's warning: 'How the hell did you know?' he barked.

Hemingway didn't have a real answer, although he was pleased that his prediction had come true. He mumbled that here in the 'Death Factory' he had experienced that same curious stench which had stopped him from staying at the Château Lingeard when Buck had been wounded and several of his staff killed in the cobbled courtyard. That had told him all he had wanted to know.

Now for the first time in his career as a war correspondent in Europe in 1944–45, Hemingway spent a considerable length of time at the front, and at an unglamorous one at that. For eighteen long days, while the 22nd Infantry Regiment was shot to pieces, he stuck it out under miserable and dangerous conditions. Hemingway never did report on what he experienced and saw in the 'Death Factory' for his employers *Collier's* magazine. All he ever wrote on those terrible two weeks and a half in November–December were recorded in a few fictional snippets *à la grand guignol*, in his 1950 novel *Across the River and Into the Trees*. Perhaps in that selfish novelist's manner of his he didn't want to waste the 'good stuff' on a magazine public, but wanted to save it for the grand trilogy he planned to write after the war.

But he was there all right and mentally noting what it was like as Lanham's regiment vanished day by day until, in the end, when they were finally taken out of the forest, Lanham could moan, 'my mental anguish was beyond description. My magnificent command had virtually ceased to exist!'

In the sleet, rain and snow that followed that first and only good day of the offensive, the suffering and casualties in the 22nd Regiment were appalling. On the second day of the attack, the commander of the 2nd Battalion was killed, together with two of his staff officers. The now Major 'Wild Man' Blazzard, who as a lieutenant had taken that first patrol across the Our into Hemmeres and beyond, moved up to take command of the Battalion. By the time he reached the Battalion Command Post, not a single member of staff remained. 'Wild Man' Blazzard had to fight his battle aided by a single runner.

The casualties mounted daily. One hundred . . . two hundred . . . three hundred . . . one day, one terrible day, there were nearly five hundred – half a battalion. They were hauled down from the slope where they had been hit by cursing sweating litter parties, carried through the Weisse Wehe stream which had flooded its banks and was neck-deep, to the regimental aid post which was located in a farmhouse on the far bank. Here, blood-stained, harassed, chain-smoking doctors worked them over, dividing the casualties into those who would die, those to be saved after much treatment, and the lightly wounded, who after treatment could be returned to their units. The ones who could fight again received priority.

Behind the front on the other side of the border in Belgium, in the frontier towns of Eupen, Malmédy and Verviers, the military hospitals were filled to overflowing, not only with real casualties, men who had had their bodies torn and ripped by shot and shell, but with men who could stand no more and were suffering from combat fatigue.

'Exhaustion' was written on the evacuation tags tied to their filthy, mud-smeared uniforms. They were sent to the 622nd Exhaustion Centre just outside Eupen. (There were so many of them that a special unit had been set up for them, where they were kept segregated from the genuinely wounded men of the Fourth.) Here they were injected with enough sodium amytal to keep them sleeping for three days, being woken up only for food and in order to carry out their bodily functions. At intervals they were given saline intravenous injections until, hollow-cheeked, bog-eyed and trembling, they were woken to be placed under scalding hot showers and shaved. Then came the questions and perhaps a little elementary psychoanalysis. Thereafter, if a man was simply generally exhausted and had collapsed or broken down because of it, he was sent back to the front.

Dr Boice, the Regiment's chaplain, thought there were too many combat fatigue cases who were 'gold-brickers'. 'Having once found that he could be evacuated with combat fatigue,' he wrote afterwards, 'the soldier instinctively knew that the medical tag reading "Combat Fatigue" represented safety for him and surcease from the danger. Frequently some soldiers made the circuit from the rest centre to the front lines three or even four times. It was another one of the hells of war. The psychiatrists had no choice, for there was no other place to send the man unless he was physically disqualified or mentally unstable.'

Hemingway must have seen all this, although, as one of Lanham's officers noted, 'He kept out of our hair', drifting into Lanham's CP at night 'after things were buttoned up'.

Bill Walton, the other correspondent, who spent more time with him than most of Lanham's staff officers or Lanham himself did during his stay in the forest, remembered that most of Hemingway's talk was about his mother, Grace. He told Walton the reason for his contempt of her was that she continued to accept money from him, money he had earned from his books, which she regarded as immoral. This was unforgivable, he added angrily. There was no mention of the battle raging all around and the sufferings of the young men dying daily in their scores. It was the same in Hemingway's talks with the senior officers of Lanham's Regiment at night in the Colonel's Command Post. The conversation centred on his past experiences, ranging from the mating habits of the African lion to his contempt of 'trick cyclists', or psychiatrists. Hemingway was of the same school of thought as most of the generals who sent young men to their death in the forest and who would, undoubtedly, one day die themselves comfortably in bed of old age.

He didn't believe in 'combat fatigue', or any such nonsense as that. A man either had guts or he didn't, and combat was the test of that. If he broke down and refused to fight any more, then he was yellow – a coward. It was an attitude of which the generals would have approved. Not that Hemingway was not brave himself. All the officers admired him because he had come to the 'Death Factory' and stayed there of his own volition; no one had forced him to come here. Lieutenant-Colonel Swede Henley, one of the 22nd's Battalion commanders, was one of those who admired the man who was nearly twice his age on account of his fearlessness: 'He stayed with me in my command post in the front lines in the rain, sleet and snow. He was always right in the thick of the heaviest part of the fighting, looking for something to write about. He carried two canteens – one of schnapps, the German equivalent of southern corn whisky, and the other of Cognac. He always offered you a drink and he never turned one down. One of the things that amused me was how he always put the canteen to the corner of his mouth and gulped it down.'

Unfortunately, despite his bravery and attempts to find 'something to write about' in the 'heaviest part of the fighting', Hemingway did not write anything about the 'Death Factory' at the time. It would be long afterwards when he did, in a fictionalised form. His bunkmate, Walton, did, and although he was a patriotic American, who like most correspondents thought it his duty to be positive and support the Allied effort, he did reveal some of the terror of the 'Death Factory' from the point of view of the combat soldier. In a long-forgotten article published in *Life* magazine on 1 January 1945, he pictured the scene in Lanham's command post with a rebellious captain, nicknamed 'Swede', a 'stocky wide-faced' young man, facing up to this CO. 'Colonel sir,' Walton records 'Swede' saying, 'I don't care if you break me for it. I meant what I said last night, even though I didn't know it was you on the line. That little patch of woods we're fighting for ain't any good to anybody. No good to the Germans. No good to us. It's the bloodiest damn ground in all Europe and you make us keep fighting for it. That ain't right!'

'The colonel [presumably Lanham], slight of build, keen-faced, intense, and the blond captain, bulky, mud-splattered, a two-day growth of beard on his wide face, a face designed for grinning but dead serious now and pale with fatigue, faced up to each over across the CP's wooden table. Then Lanham spoke deliberately. "There's nothing in the world that I'd like to do better than tell all you boys to call it off and go home. You know that, Swede. But it can't be done. The only way we can get this thing over is by killing Krauts. To kill them, you've got to get them."'

Swede agreed and went back to the 'Death Factory'. Walton ends the vignette on an optimistic note, but the despondency of the man at the 'sharp end' is all too clear.

In another sketch, Walton portrays Major Goforth of Lanham's 1st Battalion dealing with one of his company commanders who had just come in to report.

'"We're hunting for officers," said the new arrival, slumping on to a battered tin water can. "G Company's got only two officers left. Lost three this afternoon. We can't go on like this, Major."

"'I know, boy," Goforth agreed, "but where am I going to get them? Division says we can commission any good man right here in the field. But who?" He looked around a circle of dirty, unshaven faces watching him in the spluttering light, faces drained of colour like those of drowned men.

"'There's McDermott," someone suggested.

"'Can't spare him. Practically runs G-2."

"'He's last available sergeant. We've already commissioned six."

"'Guess we'll have to depend on replacements," said Goforth.

"'The trouble with replacements is that they don't last long enough," observed the company commander. "Trucks brought up 30 for me this morning. Eighteen were hit even before they could get into the line. No percentage in that."

'As he spoke the blanket covering the dugout doorway was pushed aside and three young lieutenants entered, saluted and said they were reporting for duty. "There you are, Jack," said Goforth. "Replacements for you. Take 'em with you when you go back."'

Even the dullest, most insensitive reader of that article in *Life* on that New Year's day so long ago could not fail to comprehend the underlying pessimism of Walton's report from the front. The article clearly made plain the suffering, the high losses and the weary cynicism of senior officers channelling ever more cannonfodder into the forest. Walton's sympathies were obviously on the side of the combat soldier, the one who really paid the 'butcher's bill' and was too tired and too frightened to indulge in macho theatre.

Hemingway, on the other hand, would see the 'Death Factory' (as we shall see in more detail later) from the viewpoint of the staff, from the same way Tubby Barton and Buck Lanham saw it. His protagonist would be a 50-year-old colonel who had been through two wars, not a scared 18-year-old replacement, hurriedly trained and thrust into a battle even before he knew where he was.

Just as any senior ex-West Pointer would, Hemingway maintained that a man who wouldn't fight was a coward. There was nothing to be scared of in combat. Either you were killed or you weren't. If you were killed in battle, that was it; you knew no more. If you weren't killed, you had won. That was his simplistic philosophy. What Hemingway forgot was the constant misery of the poor infantryman, slogging through mud, spending his nights in waterlogged fox holes, living out of cans, mostly cold. They had no canteens filled with spirits. They didn't go back to steak dinners and classy chats about the cosmos. It was the unrelenting misery and ever-present danger which broke men in the 'Death Factory', not the prospect of being killed.

In short, in what little he wrote about battle in the Second World War, Hemingway, the darling of the Left in the 1930s, was as hard-nosed and insensitive to the suffering of others as any hardline colonel on the staff.

During the night of 26 November a patrol from the Twenty-second reached Grosshau, on the ridgeline road to Dueren which was their objective, and reported they had heard digging there and the sound of tracked vehicles. At nine the following morning, 105 men of Company B attacked the high ground outside the hamlet at Lanham's orders. The leading platoon was decimated, every man being either wounded or killed. The following platoon was reduced to ten men and pinned down. A German machine-gun made it seemingly impossible to move. A PFC volunteered to try to knock out the machine-gun. The volunteer was ripped apart before he had gone five yards. A sergeant volunteered to worm his way through the woods around the flank. He, too, was hit. Now it was the turn of PFC Macario Garcia, who had just become an American citizen the previous year. He disappeared into the woods. Grenades were heard to explode. A little later Garcia reappeared, wounded and bringing with him four prisoners. 'God damn,' he exclaimed in his fractured English, 'I kill three Germans and knock out the machine-gun.'

Soon thereafter, Garcia was evacuated to the rear before anyone could find out even his first name. 'That man is going to get the best medal I can give him!' Lanham exclaimed when he heard of the brave exploit, as what was left of Company E started advancing once again. Lanham succeeded and Garcia later received his country's highest award for bravery, the Congressional Medal of Honor.

But by now there weren't too many Garcias left in the Twenty-second, and Tubby Barton was annoyed by the Regiment's slow progress. On the 29th, he ordered Lanham to take Grosshau that day, 'regardless of cost'. Lanham tried a ruse. Under the flag of truce he asked the defenders to surrender. It didn't work. His 2nd Battalion would have to attack the smoking ruins, which was all that was left of Grosshau. Just before one o'clock that day, they attacked from the woods. They were received with a hail of fire from the ruins. By half past four, the attackers had advanced a mere seventy-five yards as far as the first ruin. The Germans threw in a counter-attack. It was repulsed. Lanham sent in some tanks. They ran into a minefield and bogged down. By nightfall the assault battalion had suffered 162 casualties.

Just before midnight, however, German resistance broke at last and Grosshau was American. It had taken over 250 American casualties in thirty-six hours to cover a distance from the edge of the woods from which the Americans attacked to the start of the village, a distance which today can be walked in less than five minutes.

Naturally Hemingway burned to visit the Twenty-second's newly taken main objective although it was still under German artillery, including huge shells being fired from a railway gun down at Dueren five miles away. Lanham agreed to let him go, if he went with Bill Walton. A picture taken of the hamlet – 'a potato village', Hemingway called it – that day in the sloping, thin November sunshine, shows it to be a mass of shattered ruins, the one street a sea of cold mud. Even the place's little church, St Apollonia, had been hit by shells repeatedly and most of its belfry destroyed, though one solitary bell remained hanging there. (It is still there to this day.)

Together with a morose Walton, an excited Hemingway dodged the military traffic and the odd enemy shell. Both men would report on what they saw there that day, but Walton's copy as a war correspondent would be subdued, as if he were sickened by the whole bloody business. Hemingway's account, fictionalised in *Across the River and Into the Trees*, however, was cruel and full of those touches which he felt showed his toughness, but in fact revealed his total insensitivity.

His fictional Colonel Cantwell, Hemingway's protagonist and mouthpiece, is met by a grey-faced GI in the hamlet. '"Sir, there is a dead GI in the middle of the road up ahead and every time any vehicle goes through they have to run over him and I'm afraid it is making a bad impression on the troops."' One wonders how many of Tubby Barton's GIs would use such expressions as, 'I'm afraid it is making a bad impression'.

Cantwell goes to see the unfortunate dead man and decides he should be removed from the road, 'and I can remember just how he felt, lifting him and how he had been flattened and the strangeness of his flatness'. A little later Cantwell recalls how 'we had put an awful lot of white phosphorus on the town [Grosshau] before we got in for good, or whatever you call it. That was the first time I ever saw a German dog eating a roasted German Kraut. Later on I saw a cat working on him, too. It was a hungry cat, quite nice-looking, basically. You wouldn't think a good German cat would eat a good German soldier, would you, Daughter? Or a good German dog eat a good German soldier's ass which has been roasted by white phosphorus.'

Even within the context of the novel, the description of what he might have seen that November day in Grosshau six years before, is out of place. What sane, decent, realistic man, which Cantwell purports to be, would tell his 19-year-old Italian mistress – the 'Daughter' of the conversation – such terrible things, even if she were willing to listen to them?

If, on the other hand, Hemingway really *had* seen that soldier squashed to pulp in the mud by the passing vehicles, and the dead, burned German being fed on by the half-starved dog and later recorded it thus in his novel to give his reader a quick, cheap *frisson* of horror, what respect did he show for all those young men who had suffered and died to take Grosshau?

Between 16 November and 3 December, when the fighting ceased in the 'Death Factory', at least for the 4th Infantry Division, Lanham's 22nd Regiment alone had suffered 2,678 casualties. They included 12 officers and 126 men killed in action, 184 missing, 1,859 wounded and nearly 500 non-battle casualties. This was out of the original 3,000-odd men who had begun the horrific struggle. Lanham, who would soon quarrel bitterly with Tubby Barton over the 'Death Factory' battle, and whose days were numbered, could exclaim with truth: 'My magnificent command had virtually ceased to exist. . . . These men had accomplished miracles. . . . My admiration and respect for them . . . was transcendental!'

If Hemingway, who had lived with them and eaten their food for the last eighteen long terrible days, ever felt any admiration for the men of the 22nd Infantry Regiment, it was never revealed in his work. For him the 'Death Factory' was simply 'material'.

Book Four

LUXEMBOURG, WINTER 1944

'There's been a complete breakthrough, kid. . . . This thing could cost us the works. Their armour is pouring in. They're taking no prisoners.'
  Ernest Hemingway to his brother Leicester, 16 December 1944

1

THE LAST HURRAH

On Monday 4 December 1944, Hemingway said goodbye to the survivors of the 22nd Regiment, now preparing to move to the 'ghost front' in Luxembourg, then, together with Bill Walton, he set off in his jeep for Paris. He was sick and not in a particularly good mood. He arrived at the Ritz 'with a fever and a rasp in his throat like that of a cracked accordion and went to bed in his own room' as Mary Welsh described him, 'his cheeks too pink, his temper variable'. Mary decided to keep out of his way and an angry Hemingway, for whom 'Mr Scrooby' had still not performed, started planning his return to Cuba from his sick bed.

Obligingly the US Army let him have his brother Leicester as nurse, secretary and general dogsbody. (As Cyril Ray, the British war correspondent, who knew Hemingway at this time, has remarked, 'Hemingway had great prestige with the American military; they always gave him whatever he wanted.') Baron was only too happy to perform these duties for his famous brother, especially as he could see he was really ill. 'He was coughing up blood freely. After getting rid of half a cup of the stuff, he'd rasp, "just a little discharge, Baron!" with a tired, almost rueful grin.' Leicester Hemingway thought his brother 'had something worse than pneumonia. His face was pale beneath the beard. He had a high fever; breathing was difficult. For once even he had a conviction that bed rest would be good.'

For a few days Hemingway obeyed the orders of the French doctor who had been summoned by Charles Ritz to attend to their famous guest. But after he had ceased spitting blood, he began to miss the alcohol. As he told Leicester: 'I miss the gastric remorse, Baron. The doctor can't be serious about taking a healthy kid like me off the water of life. Call room service and get us some *fine*.'

The alcohol led to the return of visitors. As Leicester put it: 'He [Ernest] held court afternoons and evenings' propped up in 'a big white bed in the ornate room.'

Once Jean-Paul Sartre came, accompanied by his mistress and companion Simone de Beauvoir. After the third bottle of champagne, the French writer's girlfriend asked how seriously ill Hemingway really was. Thereupon Hemingway kicked off the bedclothes and waved one hairy, healthy leg in her direction. 'Healthy as hell!' he chortled.

After they had departed, Mary dropped in, dressed in civilian clothes and bearing the gift of a miniature bottle of Cognac, which she hoped would cheer Hemingway up. She wore the civilian clothes because she was on her way to a fancy party. Hemingway didn't like that one bit. When she asked, 'Did they [she meant Sartre and de Beauvoir] have anything interesting to say?' he snapped, 'No. . . . Did you know that you look like a spider poised there?' Mary left hastily; later she complained to her diary: 'His [Hemingway's] manners to the public are better than his manners at home. When he is good he is more endearing, more stimulating . . . with gaiety and wisdom than anyone . . . but when he is bad he is wildly, childishly, unpredictably bad. . . . Is it the ego or eagerness which prevents him from allowing me to pass first through a door?'

André Malraux, the French novelist now serving with de Gaulle's First French Army in Alsace, came to visit him again (they had already had a tipsy slanging match back in August). Now, on the surface at least, they were friends once more, as they had been back in Spain during the Civil War. Leicester remembered them 'both talking at the same time', as he 'opened new chilled bottles, filled and rinsed glasses, opened more bottles and listened as rhetoric flowed'.

According to Leicester: 'A great many bottles were uncorked that night. The two men sluiced down amazing quantities of the fermented grape. I went out twice to get some air while they discussed the war. André was commanding troops near Strasbourg. Ernest went into the problems of the line to the north.'

But although they didn't quarrel in public this time, Hemingway could not altogether conceal his envy and contempt of the Frenchman, whose novel *La Condition Humaine* he had described in 1935 as 'the best book I have read in ten years'. The envy was occasioned by the fact that Malraux was a real soldier with an active unit, commanding 2,000 soldiers, while he, Hemingway, was simply an observer, a war correspondent, who had merely played soldier for a few days. After this meeting, Hemingway always wrote of Malraux as a 'phoney' and a braggart. Typical is the letter he wrote to Bernard Berenson in January 1953: 'How you can tell a man who has killed men (armed) is that usually his eyes do not blink at all. A liar's eyes blink all the time. Meet Malraux sometime.' As always, Hemingway detested, even hated, other writers, who had the temerity to take over *his* war.

It must have been about this time, the second week of December, that 'Mr Scrooby' finally functioned. As Hemingway's brother Leicester put it delicately: 'Mary got back and Ernest's morale picked up. She soon had to leave but he *kept on gaining* [author's italics].'

Abruptly Hemingway's plans for returning as soon as possible to Cuba were dropped for the time being. For her part, Mary, flushed with success, ignored the warnings of her head and heart and the fact that she already knew Hemingway could be 'wildly, childishly, unpredictably bad'. The relationship on her side became warm and loving once more. She forgot the tiffs of the last weeks. She also tolerated Marlene Dietrich, to whom Ernest had paid so much attention ever since the star had arrived at the Ritz. It has been a 'friendship [which] naturally gave rise to much gossip and gabble', as Dietrich put it later. Many years after, in her old age, Miss Dietrich believed the 'love that Ernest Hemingway and I felt for each other – pure, absolute – was a most extraordinary love in the world. . . . [He] loved me with all his strength, and I was never able to do the same for him.'

For his part, Hemingway rejoiced that he could make love once again. That December he was delighted he could perform and was exceedingly grateful to Mary who had managed, after so many failures, to make him feel like a real, hairy-chested man once more. 'He talked about it a lot,' Bill Walton, his companion that December, recalled long afterwards, 'and he was proud of this cute little girl on his arm as he swept into the Ritz dining room. . . . She did not play up to him as a man of letters. Instead she treated him as the hotshot warrior, macho man, great in bed.' From now onwards, a grateful Hemingway would begin noting the frequency and dates of all his lovemaking with Mary.

According to Hemingway's most recent biographer, Kenneth S. Lynn, the same diary, with its references to the joys of sex with Mary, also reveals the author's fascination with 'androgyny and sexual transpositions', and Lynn makes a telling quote from it: 'Mary has never had one lesbian impulse, but has always wanted to be a boy. . . . I loved feeling the embrace of Mary which came to me as something quite new and outside all tribal law. On the night of December 19th we worked out these things and I have never been happier.'

Well, whatever the nature of that 'embrace', it worked and continued to work, until the drink and his constant abuse of Mary after the war put paid to 'Mr Scrooby' for good.

While Hemingway recovered and rejoiced, the battered remnants of his 'favourite division', the Fourth, now moved to Luxembourg. As Dr Boice of the 22nd Regiment chronicled the occasion: 'They were really fed up with the set-up. The sick, sweet odour of death was never far away from any man. . . . It was a haggard, whipped, abysmally unhappy, utterly disillusioned remnant of a great combat team that made its heartbreaking move from Huertgen, Germany, to Luxembourg.'

The little Grand Duchy, set on the borders of Belgium, Germany and France, was basically German-speaking with two official languages of High German and French, while among themselves the natives spoke a German dialect, *Letzeburger*. It had been part of the German Reich for four years after the Nazi invasion of 1940. But, although young Luxembourgers had been conscripted into the German Army as *Reichsdeutsche*, and there had been some collaboration with the occupiers, the locals were friendly and had welcomed the Americans as liberators when they had arrived in early September.

Even the friendliness of the natives' welcome and the modern American appearance of the undamaged capital, Luxembourg City, could not shake the men of the Fourth out of this despondent mood. Nor was their mood improved by the fact that, instead of being sent to a rest area, the Division was placed into the line again along twenty miles of the Moselle, which runs between Luxembourg and Germany in the south of the country. Admittedly this was a quiet front – the 'Ghost Front' – where nothing had happened since September, save for patrol activity and some shelling. All the same, it was a front and as Dr Boice noted, 'the Division was in no condition to fight. Nobody expected it to have to fight.' The American High Command might not have, but the German one had different ideas!

Battalion after battalion moved into position along the river line, as the units of the 83rd Division, holding the positions there, moved out. They found all the locals had been evacuated, 'just as though the Pied Piper has passed this way once again. The houses had REAL beds, the bins were full of apples and potatoes, the deserted cafés were full of wine, a few billygoats and chickens disconsolately poked their way around town'. But Dr Boice also noted that 'the Germans were just across the river!' They were, too. In that part of Luxembourg, to the north and south of the largest German city of the area, Trier (one of the four former capitals of the Roman Empire), the River Moselle is less than a hundred yards across in some places. On both sides, in Luxembourg (held by the Fourth) and in Germany, the vineyards which produced the Moselle wine ran steeply up to the heights which dominated the river below. It was here that both sides had dug in back in September when the front had settled down into a kind of armed neutrality.

The officers who guided the men of the Fourth into their new positions told them reassuringly that nothing ever happened here. Occasionally a deserter from the Wehrmacht might swim the river and ask to be taken prisoner. Now and then, some fanatic on the other side would open with a burst of machine-gun fire at some lone American truck driving along the road that ran parallel to the river bank. There were rumours, too, of German soldiers crossing the Moselle, but not on patrol; it was far more serious than that, the guides had joked. They were on their way to assignations with willing local girls, whom they had met in Luxembourg before they had had to flee in such disarray the previous summer. No, the weary survivors were told, they had nothing really to worry about. This, after all, was the 'Ghost Front', where the shooting war had gone to sleep.

And in that second week in December 1944, it seemed to the men of the Fourth that their guides from the departing 83rd Division might well be right. Here the front appeared to have settled into some kind of limbo, a haven of peace in the midst of total war.

Within rifle range of each other on the heights on both sides of the river line, German observers could watch the *Amis* line up for chow; and the Americans watched at twilight as German women sneaked into the bunkers and pillboxes of the Siegfried Line for a night of love. Here, it seemed, it was live and let live, with both sides resting and watching and avoiding irritating each other with anything that might be considered a warlike activity.

Yet all the same there were those among the Fourth, either sensitive or apprehensive, who didn't altogether trust the calm. They were oppressed by a sense of unease and foreboding. What were the Krauts doing over there? What were they planning? After the early snowfalls of that December, soon to be one of the coldest on record, when an army of skeletal, brooding black firs stood out against the glittering white mantle of snow, such men might fight off an unreasoning desire to escape to the rear while there was still time. At night, when on guard, they would hear noises: the muffled clatter of horses' hooves on straw-covered roads; the muted sound of a train whistle in the far distance; the rattle of what might have been tank-tracks.

When morning came, the front across the river was as empty as ever. Here and there beyond the ridgeline, beyond the vineyards and the fringing heights, there might be a stiff plume of new smoke rising into the grey still air, but that was about all. Nothing else moved. Even the birds seemed to have vanished. And the sensitive ones, and the apprehensive ones, told themselves they had been imagining things again, were letting their nerves run away with them. The Krauts were finished. They'd had it! Why, hadn't Monty himself wagered five pounds with Ike, the Supreme Commander, that the war would be over by Christmas . . . and there was only a matter of days to go.

There was no apprehension, no foreboding to the rear. On that grey, gloomy Saturday, 16 December 1944, when their world fell apart, the top brass played. Whatever was happening at the front, whether hundreds of the British, Canadian, American, French soldiers under their command this day died or not, was of little concern to them. After all, it was Saturday, wasn't it and everyone relaxed on Saturday!

Far to the rear at Supreme Allied Headquarters at Versailles, just outside Paris, Eisenhower and most of his staff were going to attend a wedding. For the first time since the days of Marie Antoinette, the chapel at the Petit Trianon was to be used for nuptials – Eisenhower's diminutive valet and ex-bellhop Mickey McKeogh was marrying a bespectacled WAC Sergeant, Pearlie Hargrave. Eisenhower would attend because it was the democratic thing to do, and he liked Mickey as well.

Later Eisenhower would give a reception for the happy couple and the champagne would flow liberally. Indeed, one day later when her boss and lover's divisions were reeling back from the front in disorder, Kay Summersby would record: 'Half the headquarters was soggy with the silence of plain unadulterated ordinary hangovers!'

Eisenhower had another and more personal reason for celebrating this last happy Saturday. He had just heard that he had been nominated by Congress for the newly created rank of General of the Army, which carried five stars. Now in a matter of four years he had achieved the status of old 'Black Jack' Pershing, who had commanded US troops in Europe in the Old War when Eisenhower had been a lowly captain in charge of guarding strategic installations and training troops in the United States. Now, although he had never fired a shot in anger or even commanded a company in action, he was America's most powerful combat soldier in Europe. It was a heady feeling.

That evening he had invited a few old drinking and card-playing cronies to the Petit Trianon. Someone had sent him a bushel of oysters from the States and his 'darkies', as he called them, were already preparing them on the half shell as an entrée, to be followed by oyster stew, with fried oysters concluding the festive meal. Thereafter he and his old friends, all West Pointers like himself, would drink and play cards into the early hours of Sunday. It would be an ideal weekend.

One of his guests that day was General Bradley, the commander of the US 12th Army Group. The official reason for his visit was that he was coming to Paris to discuss the problem of the shortage of riflemen at the front (but that was dreamed up only after the shock of what was going to happen this day had sunk in). The real reason for 'Brad's' visit was that he was driving from Luxembourg, his Headquarters, to party with Ike. (In the event, it was discovered that Bradley hated oysters and Eisenhower's darkies had hastily to scramble some eggs for the 12th Army Group Commander.)

Bradley, together with General 'Red' O'Hare, one of his senior staff officers, and his personal aide, Major Chester Hansen, arrived in Paris about noon. It had been a pleasant drive, despite the weather. The whole of his central front in Luxembourg had seemed quiet and the only real traffic they had encountered in the Grand Duchy had been from the 'Red Ball Express', which brought up supplies for the line. As usual the black drivers of the supply convoys that rolled ceaselessly day and night seemed to think they owned the road and naturally they all drove at top speed, not caring for their engines. But then everyone knew blacks were too simple to understand such things.

Just before he had left his Headquarters in Luxembourg City, there had been some information coming in about enemy activity to the north on the 1st Army front in Belgium. The news had not worried Bradley. He felt the 'other fellow', as he always called the enemy, was simply indulging himself in a 'spoiling attack' to put Hodges, the First Army Commander, off his stroke. For yet once again, Hodges was preparing a new attack in the area of the Death Factory.

The 12th Army Group Commander stopped his olive-drab Packard, adorned with four stars, outside the Ritz. (As 'VIPs',

O'Hare and Hansen were naturally staying at Paris's leading hotel.) Bradley joined them over lunch. The conference with Eisenhower was not due to start till 2 o'clock that afternoon, and Bradley, now completely out of touch with Headquarters and unaware of what was really happening at the front, took his time.

Finally he left, leaving O'Hare and Hansen to their own devices. Not that it would be difficult to find something to do in Paris. The French capital was 'wide open' and after staid old Luxembourg where there was no night life and, as the locals said themselves, everyone went 'to bed with the chickens', a night out on the tiles in 'Gay Paree' was something to look forward to.

It was beginning to grow dark this Saturday afternoon in the conference room at Versailles, where it was pleasantly warm in contrast to the freezing cold outside, when Brigadier Kenneth Strong, Eisenhower's Chief-of-Intelligence and the most junior officer present, noticed his deputy standing in the doorway. The Scot crossed over to him. His deputy passed him a note with a worried look on his face. The Scottish Chief-of-Intelligence read the note hastily and interrupted the conference. 'Gentlemen,' he announced with his pleasant burr, 'this morning the enemy counter-attacked at five separate points across the First Army sector.'

Later, when the top brass became aware that the last German counter-attack of the Second World War in the West had taken them completely by surprise, they fudged the record. They maintained that Eisenhower had been instantly aware of the Germans' real intent and had reacted instantly. 'This is no local attack, Brad,' he was reported to have snapped, and had immediately alerted two divisions to stand by and help Hodges if the need arose.

But that was *afterwards*, when Eisenhower, Bradley and Hodges realised that if the general public became aware that twelve vital hours had elapsed before they had become aware that the 'Battle of the Bulge' had commenced, with 600,000 Germans sweeping all before them, there would be a major scandal: one that might cost some of them their positions.

At the time, with a 60-mile-broad gap being broken into the American line all along the 'Ghost Front', the top brass continued as if nothing very startling had happened. In due course they would eat their oyster stew, drink Bourbon and whisky over cards to celebrate Ike's fifth star, while a frantic Hodges at Spa, Belgium, was still trying (and failing) to reach his Army Group Commander. It was understandable that his two escorts played, too. Hansen spent a boozy afternoon in the company of Hemingway and others. Despite the fact that Hemingway had not really recovered from his illness and was sweating heavily, Hansen, O'Hare and Hemingway went off to the Lido, where the floor show started at eight-thirty.

The drinks at the Lido were more expensive than at most of the other Parisian night clubs, which now catered almost exclusively for American officers, but the music was soft and pleasant and the surroundings elegant. The tall, beautiful chorus girls were as naked and raunchy as at the cheaper places and a delighted Major Hansen noted in his diary for the fatal Saturday, when the top brass's world fell apart, that he and Hemingway 'saw bare-breasted girls do the hootchy-kootchie until it was late and we hurried home'.

Mary Welsh, Hemingway's mistress, had seen it all before when she had worked in Paris before Mary 1940 at the time of the German invasion. For her, the Lido was just another 'girlie show'. She declined to go with the men. Instead she set about netting another celebrity for her collection, in the form of Air Corps General 'Tooey' Spaatz, who, with 'Bomber' Harris, was ruthless advocate of bombing Germany into submission. Tooey was giving a dinner party that night and Mary had wangled herself an invitation. Social climber that she was, Mary Welsh was also a reporter and curious. Now she was puzzled by the constant stream of aides with anxious looks on their faces who kept coming and whispering urgently in the bomber general's ear.

Something – something very serious – had happened, she realised. By mid-meal, she knew that 'I must get out of the way as smoothly and quickly as possible'. As soon as the dinner was over, she excused herself and Spaatz did not attempt to hold her back. Instead, he offered her his car to take her back to the Ritz and then did something strange. He insisted that she should have an escort of an armed airman, together with the chauffeur. Now Mary knew that the balloon had gone up. The Ritz confirmed her forebodings. It was in turmoil. Now the confused reports coming from the front were indicating that there had been a major breakdown on the First Army sector and not a 'spoiling attack', as Bradley claimed. 'Red' O'Hare had been on the line to 12th Army Group Headquarters (the line would soon be cut by the advancing Germans) and the news was bad. That bad news was passed on to a slightly drunk Major Hansen, who, in his turn, might have revealed it to Hemingway, for his brother Leicester recalls him during that night of turmoil and little sleep snorting: 'There's been a complete breakthrough kid. . . . This thing could cost us the works. Their armour is pouring in. They're taking no prisoners!'

After that melodramatic statement, Hemingway now attempted to telephone Tubby Barton in Luxembourg. According to General Barton's statement later, when Hemingway finally got through some time about dawn on Sunday, the author explained he was sick and was in process of trying to go home. 'But he wanted to know if there was a show going on which would be worth his while to come up for. . . . For security reasons, I could not give him the facts over the telephone . . . so I told him in substance that it was a pretty hot show and to come on up.'

It certainly was. Although the 4th Division was not bearing the brunt of the surprise attack on the Ghost Front, the 'Ivy

League' was under serious attack at the frontier township of Echternach on the River Sauer. A little while after the Hemingway call, Tubby, very worried now, was on the phone to Luxembourg. He told Bradley's Chief-of-Staff (Bradley was still sound asleep in far-off Paris) that he had committed all his men at Echternach, but the Germans of the 212 Volksgrenadier Division were already across the Sauer, and he couldn't stop them without armor. Already they were pushing along the dead-straight road which led to Luxembourg City, where Bradley had his Headquarters opposite the main railway station, only 20-odd miles away. 'If you don't get the armor up here quickly,' Tubby warned, 'you had better get set to move!'

By now Hemingway was completely caught up in the great flap. He had contacted Red O'Hare, and although the latter had other things to do, Hemingway's fame worked the trick, as always, and O'Hare obtained a jeep for him. Already having changed his shirt twice due to excess sweating (Hemingway would do so four times before he finally left for the new front) he supervised the preparation for his departure and what lay before him.

This time he was going to carry a pistol openly, telling his brother Leicester, 'General Red O'Hare is sending a jeep over for me. Load these clips. Wipe every cartridge clean. We may have a bad time getting up there. The Germans have infiltrated with guys in GI uniforms.'

While Mary helped him into the two fleece-lined jackets he would wear for the trip, she and he 'speculated to the limit of our imaginations' on what might be coming their way. 'The Krauts might cut off all the Allied armies in the north,' they mused. 'They might launch parachute troops. They might reach Paris.' Mary remembered back to 10 May 1940 when she had seen French government officials outside the Quai d'Orsay burning official papers before fleeing. Was this going to be another complete breakthrough ending in another Dunkirk?

Hemingway seemed to have been taken by the same worrying idea. Just before he left, he handed Mary a 'canvas sack full of papers with instructions to burn them, if she were forced to flee Paris.' Why Hemingway thought his personal papers would be of any interest to a German intelligence officer, he never explained. Perhaps he had even larger delusions of grandeur than normal? Then he turned to Leicester and told him that the jeep was coming in fifteen minutes. 'Try to get up there yourself,' he urged his brother, 'and look me up at the Fourth. Now look after yourself, will you, Baron?' Leicester said he would.

'Good luck, kid,' Hemingway finished with and turned to Mary. He kissed her heartily and then, clad in his two white fleece jackets, he strode through the lobby of the Ritz like an overfed polar bear.

Outside in the grey dawn, the driver gunned the engine of the jeep, the exhaust steaming in the icy air. There were *flics* everywhere. They were waiting for the Germans to drop their parachutists, dressed as American soldiers. Back in 1940 it had been Germans disguised as nuns. Panic was in the air.

Hemingway did not mind. He was cheerful. After Italy in the Old War, Turkey and Greece afterwards, then Spain, the Eifel and the Huertgen, he was going back to the wars again – and he had always dearly loved war. He did not know, of course, but this was to be the last time that he would ever hear a shot fired in anger.

The driver selected first gear. The little jeep lurched forward. The steel-helmeted policeman with the old-fashioned pre-war rifle slung over his shoulder saluted and they were off to the front. Hemingway was off to his last battle. This was the last hurrah.

BLACK CHRISTMAS

Generalmajor Franz Sensfuss, commanding the German 212th Volksgrenadier Division knew exactly what the dispositions of Tubby Barton's 4th Division were when he attacked across the River Sauer at six o'clock on the morning of Saturday 16 December.

German agents had been able to cross the river easily enough during the long hours of the December darkness in the previous week, and in the summer before when the Wehrmacht had fled Luxembourg City, they had left behind a network of male and female informers and agents. These traitors (they were all native Luxembourgers) frequented the bars and few brothels of the old city where GIs from the front on leave were to be found and pumped them for information. As a result, Sensfuss knew that the terribly depleted 4th Division (it had suffered 5,000 battle casualties and 2,500 non-battle ones in the 'Death Factory') was spread out very thinly. All the Fourth's rifle companies, which were down to half strength, were on outpost duty along the length of the River Sauer (which would be the 212th's zone of attack) with their command posts, manned by only a handful of men, at the villages of Berdorf, Lauterborn, Osweiler, Dickdorf, and the only town of the area, Echternach.

In addition to their lack of strength, the American defenders of the River Sauer line were also hampered and further dispersed by the nature of the terrain in what is called locally 'the Switzerland of Luxembourg'. It is an area of deep, thick-wooded gorges, full of huge boulders and caves in which primitive cave-dwellers lived in prehistoric times. Here the roads were few and bad, and radio communications were poor because the Fourth's radios did not work well in that kind of terrain. As a result, Sensfuss felt that, although he would have to attempt a river crossing over the Sauer in darkness under the very noses of the Fourth's outposts on the other bank, he could succeed in overwhelming the *Amis* before they could summon help. Then his men could break through the villages of Dickweiler and Osweiler, take Echternach and cut the main road from there to Luxembourg City.

By the time Hemingway had managed to get through to Tubby Barton in the early hours of Sunday, 17 December, Sensfuss's 212nd Division had succeeded in doing this. Everywhere, Barton's 12th Infantry Regiment which had defended the area under assault, had been forced back with heavy casualties. Barton had thrown in his reserve battalion. He had asked for reinforcements, but had received none save a battalion of engineers. Echternach had been lost, except for a hat factory still stubbornly being defended by the Fourth. Everywhere it seemed that Sensfuss's 'People's Grenadiers' were moving from one success to another.

Now, very worried that the Germans were heading up the Echternach road for Bradley's Headquarters in Luxembourg (they weren't – Sensfuss had a more limited objective), Barton alerted Lanham's battered 22nd Regiment for immediate action. Buck Lanham was to detach his 2nd Battalion at once. It would go to the assistance of the hard-pressed 12th Infantry in the Osweiler-Dickweiler section. The rest of the Twenty-second would stand by for further orders.

That morning, as General Bradley finally woke up and Hemingway, in his jeep, was speeding through northern France towards the tiny Grand Duchy to the north, General Barton was suffering from the same shocked outrage that was the lot of many American commanders. As General Bradley expressed it to Eisenhower's Chief-of-Staff, General Bedell Smith, 'Pardon my French, but where in hell has this son-of-a-bitch gotten all his strength?'

Major Hansen, his young aide, would put it more succinctly when he logged later that Sunday: 'The G-2 section . . . found itself confronted by a situation it did not believe possible.' By then some of Bradley's staff and Eisenhower would be advising Bradley to leave Luxembourg and go to his other headquarters at Verdun, across the border in France. Bradley would refuse, stating: 'I will never move backwards with a headquarters. There is too much prestige at stake. To retreat would be a sure sign of weakness – to the Germans, the Luxembourgers and my own troops. A panic would ensue.' The top brass had been blinded by their own success. They had discounted what little Intelligence had been able to obtain on a possible German counter-attack in the West. It had become a matter of dogma to them that the 'Kraut' was on his last legs and even when Intelligence had managed to 'lose' one whole German Army – the 6th SS Panzer Army – (a sure sign that something unpleasant was brewing for the Western Allies), the loss had not shaken their self-delusion. Now they were panicked and confused. It would be up to those young men at the 'sharp end' to get them out of that situation which they did not believe possible. It would cost 6,700 American lives to do so, plus another 52,000 American casualties, 2,500 British and perhaps some 10,000 French.

In the case of Colonel Lanham's Second Battalion, those young men at the 'sharp end' were, as one of them wrote, 'exhausted, on two-third rations [with] no blankets, short on overcoats, no winter boots, short on dry socks'.

At eleven o'clock that morning, while both Hemingway and Bradley were on their way to Luxembourg, they were stopped at every crossroad by anxious soldiers looking for German paras disguised as GIs, and being asked (as a means of checking they were genuine Americans), who Betty Grable was married to and who were 'den bums'. Captain Faulkner led his men of the Second's E Company into the battle at Dickweiler. '[We] moved single file up the road and east to the big woods. Things didn't smell right. Too quiet . . . in the open valley beyond, Osweiler [was] burning in the distance. . . . Suddenly burp gun, MG fire to our rear . . . Jerry MG fire cut across and into my front stopping the lead platoon. . . . We got about 20 to 30 rounds of mortar which chopped up part of the 1st platoon, wounded the only aid man and almost got me. . . . We had arrived at the ambush point and picked up several wounded . . . and a few dead among whom was 1st Sgt Willard. A wonderful man and I grieved in my heart for him. He had been a D-Day man, wounded twice but always said, "It's not *if* you'll get it, but when and how bad". He was right.' Yet another of the few survivors of those halcyon days in Devon (when Salinger's fictional 4th Division sergeant could have high tea with an aristocratic little English girl) had been killed. Willard was not to be alone. That Sunday, Sensfuss's Bavarians were killing veterans and replacements alike with impartiality.

As what was left of Captain Faulkner's E Company began to dig in that afternoon, for it was already growing dark, they faced 'a weird night, with fire coming from all ways, Krauts to our front and flanks, our rear exposed toward Echternach'. By this time Hemingway had arrived at Tubby Barton's command post. It was located at Junglinster, a village which lay astride the main Echternach–Luxembourg road and which housed the Grand Duchy's prize possession, 'Radio Luxembourg', currently being used as a propaganda station by the American Army. A worried Barton told Hemingway and his companion Bill Walton that Bob Chance (the commander of his 8th Regiment) was 'carrying the ball' for the 4th Division. For the time being, Lanham's two remaining battalions were not actively engaged fighting the enemy. He asked Hemingway if he would ensure that 'Bob [Chance] and his outfit' received a 'good publicity play'. The long drive, however, seemed to have made Hemingway ill again and he was in no mood to give anyone a 'publicity play', good or bad.

When Tubby Barton handed the correspondents over to Colonel Lanham, the latter saw that Hemingway was indeed sick. He suggested that the two correspondents should move in with him at his command post just outside the tiny hamlet of Rodenbourg, two kilometres along a winding dirt road from Junglinster. Hemingway did not object, although the command post was so crowded that it meant he would have to share a double bed with Walton. The CP was located in a decaying old mill on the stream at the edge of the rambling little hamlet. It had been built in the early eighteenth century, complete with strong, thick-stone cellars, which had attracted Lanham to it after his experiences in the 'damned château' in Normandy, and belonged to Abbé Nicolas Didier, the local priest. Here, while runners and messengers flew back and forth bearing the latest tale of woe from the Sauer front, Hemingway was seen by Lanham's regimental surgeon.

He confirmed Lanham's suspicions; Hemingway was really ill. Dosing the writer heavily with sulfa pills, usually given to the wounded, he ordered him to bed. Ernest Hemingway tamely obliged, but when the MO had departed, he started to rummage around the place looking for something to drink. According to his own story, Didier★ had been a collaborator (the locals say differently) and had been forced to give up his

---

★   Abbé Didier had, in fact, been sacked from his post at a school in nearby Echternach in 1942 for refusing to work with the Germans and had returned to Rodenbourg. His brother, who was mayor of the village, did collaborate and was tried on that score after the war.

room in the mill so that Hemingway and Walton could have it, so Hemingway felt it was proper and just to drink anything Didier had been foolish enough to leave behind. In fact, Abbé Didier had managed to get out his best wine and what the thirsty, sick author found was the cheap red wine he used for the sacrament. But it was liquid and alcoholic and Hemingway had no other choice. He started to work his way through Didier's cellar, taking a maniacal delight in refilling every bottle with his own urine.

Later he explained that the Abbé's wine bottles served him as a kind of chamberpot (naturally he didn't say chamberpot), since it was well below freezing that third week of December and he didn't want to go down to the latrine below; he wasn't going to risk his life 'with the fever and all'. With an elephantine kind of humour he then took to labelling the bottles filled with urine as 'Schloss Hemingstein 1944'. The prank rebounded upon him when he went into the cellars during the hours of darkness looking for another bottle of wine and found one of his own. He did not approve of the vintage.

While Hemingway sweated it out in the priest's house, the Fourth battled on in the confused fighting of the Grand Duchy's 'Switzerland', as at the top. Bradley's 1st and 9th Armies were taken away from him and given to Montgomery, his detested rival, and Patton arrived post-haste in Luxembourg and attempted to save his boss's reputation by a swift drive into the German flank.

On the morning of 18 December, the men of the Fourth, reinforced by tanks from General Patton's 3rd Army, counter-attacked in thick fog, which ruled out any air support. They pushed into a deep gorge, with sheer cliffs rising on both sides and their path strewn with huge boulders almost as big as their 30-ton Sherman tanks. They didn't get far. The lead tank was knocked out and the infantry started to go to ground, as their ranks came under intense small arms fire from the 'People's

Grenadiers'. It was clear that they were not going to do much in the gorge, so they attempted to go round it, fighting their way through the nearby village, which in happier and pre-war days had been a tourist attraction for wealthy Dutch and Belgians. At the Parc Hotel they fought a pitched battle with the Germans, who tried to blast their way into the place by means of pole charges, while, as the US Official History states, 'morale was . . . bolstered superbly by the company cook, who did his best to emulate the *cuisine soignée* promised by the hotel brochures by preparing hot meals in the basement and serving the men at their firing posts'.

Day after day, the Grenadiers and the 'Ivy League' slogged it out. The rear headquarters of Lanham's 2nd Battalion was surrounded. The hard-pressed Headquarters staff fought their way out. Losses mounted alarmingly. By 20 December, the 2nd Battalion reported that its rifle companies were now down to 60 men, half their official strength. One of the armoured units supporting the Fourth withdrew without orders. Desperately Barton threw in an infantry company to fill the gap. It lost all its officers save a young lieutenant in his teens who had just come up as a replacement.

So it went on, day after grim day, while Hemingway sweated, dosed, drank the Abbé's wine and refilled the empty bottles with his own special vintage – 'Schloss Hemingstein 1944'. (One wonders what a collector's item like that would bring at an auction today?) By now both the attackers and the defenders were weakening; their losses had been too high. So it was that, as that first terrible week of what Winston Churchill was now calling the 'Battle of the Bulge' came to an end, both sides were content to consolidate their positions.

In Echternach, General Sensfuss personally led the attack on the stubborn 132 Americans who had been under siege there since 16 December. He was slightly wounded in the assault down the long narrow street, but he did have the satisfaction of

taking the *Amis'* surrender. Now he controlled the whole of the
limited road network leading from the River Sauer to the
capital of the Grand Duchy. But the possession of the roads had
come too late. Now the defenders, as weary and as weak as they
were, had retired to a fairly strong defensive position on both
sides of the main road leading to Luxembourg City. It had cost
them 2,000 men killed, wounded or reported missing in six
days, but the 4th Division and its comrades from the 9th
Armoured Division had stopped Sensfuss's drive. On Friday
22 December 1944, when Hemingway finally rose from his bed
in Lanham's command post, the Germans halted. Now, in due
course, it would be the task of the Americans to send them
back whence they had come.

On that same Friday, Patton's 3rd Army became operational in
Luxembourg, after the Army had been hastily withdrawn from
the Saar and Alsace area of France to meet the new German
challenge. One of his divisions, the 5th Infantry under the
command of General 'Red' Irwin, was scheduled first to
support the Fourth and then take over the battered division's
positions. Thus it was that on the morning of 22 December
that Hemingway saw what was his last action. Colonel Luckett,
commanding the 12th Infantry Regiment which, together with
Lanham's 2nd Battalion, had borne the brunt of the fighting,
inviting Hemingway to join him on a hilltop and watch the
Fifth's infantry attack.

The plan was that, after an artillery bombardment, the Fifth
would attack in two-battalion strength from the hamlet of
Michelshof in the direction of German-held Echternach. It was
a tough assignment. Not only did the Fifth know little of the
enemy's dispositions, but it was also faced with very rugged
terrain. Everything that could go wrong did so. The advance
party got lost in fog, then came under artillery fire. The main
body following experienced the same kind of difficulty.

Colonel Luckett, the veteran, found 'this magnificent display of force', as he later described it with a certain degree of *Schadenfreude*, all very amusing. 'They [the infantry of the Fifth] were dressed in snow camouflage made from sheets and went across the plateau two or three miles conducting marching fire. What they were shooting at, I don't know. Ernie and I had a pleasant time joking about it.'

The Fifth's attack ended in confusion, with the disorganised infantry unable to reach even the start line for their real attack. Hemingway had seen enough. He returned to Tubby Barton's Headquarters at Junglinster and occupied himself with collecting material on what had happened to the Fourth while he had been sick. At least he said he did. In fact, he was probably preparing for Christmas as everyone else was, for the threat posed by the Germans in that part of Luxembourg had abated. Now the Germans contented themselves with constant artillery and mortar fire and bombarding Luxembourg City itself with long-range shelling, fired from a gun on the other side of the border. Everyone who could was planning parties and Hemingway had already been invited to two – a stag party to be given by Tubby Barton at his schoolhouse-mess in Luxembourg City, to be followed by a champagne affair hosted by the US 70th Tank Battalion in the same place. They were not going to be happy affairs for many of those involved.

About noon on Christmas Eve, Martha Gellhorn, Hemingway's third wife, arrived in Luxembourg City from Holland. She scented a story in Luxembourg–Belgium and was soon to head for the US 101st Airborne Division – 'the battered bastards of Bastogne' – currently surrounded in the Belgian township of that name. In the capital of the Grand Duchy she registered at one of the two hotels which had been taken over for the war correspondents. Here she came to the notice of Colonel Ruggles of the 4th Division, who, unaware of the trouble between her and Hemingway, invited her to spend Christmas Eve and Day with her husband at Lanham's command post in Rodenbourg. 'It was my intention to surprise Ernest pleasantly,' Ruggles stated later, 'but I'm afraid it was otherwise.' How right the unfortunate colonel was, for what was to occur this Christmas Eve was a catastrophe which Hemingway would characterise as Martha's 'big Christmas counter-attack'.

The 54-year-old General Barton had commanded the 4th Infantry Division since it had arrived in Britain in early 1944. Now he was being relieved of his command and was being sent back to the States. Officially, it was stated that he was being transferred on account of ill health. Many of his officers, however, believed he was losing the Fourth because he had handled the Division badly in the 'Death Factory'. (He was not the only divisional commander to be relieved 'on account of ill health' after the Battle of the Huertgen Forest.) Now this Christmas Eve stag party was intended to be a kind of farewell present for the departing General. Buck Lanham had not been invited. Colonel Lanham had quarrelled violently with both Barton and his second-in-command Brigadier General Rodwell during the fight in the 'Death Factory'. As a result he had been ordered to remain on duty. But there were others present that night who also had a bone to pick with the senior commanders because of the latter's handling of the Fourth in the Huertgen.

For the first two hours, the stag party went well. There was turkey, with creamed potatoes and cranberry sauce. (In the line the infantry were on half rations.) On the mess radio, Dinah Shore sang that haunting popular little ditty of that year, *I'll Be Seeing You*. There was plenty to drink, too. Not only champagne and local brandy, but also a ration of whisky and gin obtained somehow or other through the British Army NAAFI – one bottle of each type per officer. The drink loosened the tongues of the flushed officers. They talked of the 'Death Factory' as they always seemed to do when they had been drinking and Colonel Luckett, who had seen his regiment decimated in the Huertgen, became angrily critical of Tubby Barton's handling of the Division there.

Brigadier General Rodwell tried to silence him, reminding him this was in a way of a farewell party for the Divisional Commander. Luckett wouldn't be silent. In the end Barton himself ordered Luckett out. Glowering and flushed, Luckett left, taking Hemingway with him and leaving Barton to party alone with only one of his regimental commanders present.

They drove to the mess of the 70th Tank Battalion of the US 9th Armoured Division, which had recently supported the Fourth on the Sauer, in particular Colonel Luckett's 12th Regiment. Although the tankers, newly arrived in Europe, had suffered heavily on the Sauer, their officers were in good form and the champagne flowed freely and in large quantities.

By now Hemingway was fairly drunk, but he was behaving himself well, as he always did that winter in the presence of his friends in the Fourth, who had accepted him whole-heartedly despite his boastfulness and tendency to monopolise the conversation in his self-appointed role as 'Papa' to these much younger men. Leaving the 70th Battalion party, he went across to the shabby Luxembourg hotel where Martha Gellhorn was staying. There he convinced her to come with him to General Barton's billet in Junglinster for a night-cap and a chat.

Surprisingly enough, after the humiliation of their last meeting in Paris, she agreed to come with him. So, while a dozen miles away in their fox holes the men of the Fourth crouched shivering (and it was recorded 'one of our month-old replacements crept 40 yards and tossed a hand grenade into the nearest Kraut slit trench. *Finis*') the Hemingways and General Barton sat drinking Cognac and chatting around Tubby's Christmas Tree.

Then it was time to turn in. Martha decided she would share a bed with Hemingway and they drove the two kilometres down

the frosty, white-sparkling country road to Rodenbourg. Lanham
was still awake. Three of his men on patrol had been wounded
and one killed and he had just sent over Chaplain Boice to give
them spiritual comfort at the Regimental Aid Post. Although
Lanham knew just how shaky the Hemingway marriage was, he
offered them his bedroom in the house, while he would doss
down in his unheated trailer parked outside the mill.

Lanham took an instant dislike to Martha Gellhorn. He found
her snobbish and could not stand her 'arrogance, her general
snottiness'. But he kept his peace, and as he lay shivering in his
icy caravan, he wondered how the two of them were getting on
in his bedroom. Neither side ever recorded what happened that
last night they ever spent together. Later, Martha Gellhorn
would write about the whole time she lived with him: 'I spent
seven years in Hemingway's orbit . . . I am goddamned if I am
going to be hounded by those seven years.' She would never be
able to understand how Mary Welsh could endure him –
'a slave's life with a brute for a slave owner' – and observed
caustically that Hemingway 'was progressively more insane
every year. And the biggest liar since Munchausen!'

But if nothing is really known of what happened in that
bedroom in Abbé Didier's house that crisp frosty Christmas
Eve, with only a dozen miles away young men still dying by the
score, what was to follow between them in the coming week
was recorded in all its bitterness and acrimony.

It started the next morning when the two of them decided to
accompany Lanham in his Christmas Day tour of his three
battalion command posts. Ernest Hemingway sat up front with
the driver, while Lanham sat at the back, together with Martha
Gellhorn. Hemingway started to show off his importance with
the Fourth and knowledge of the battle they had just fought
with Sensfuss's 'People's Grenadiers', although he had spent
most of the time in bed ill. Martha Gellhorn did not like his

high-handed manner. She began to chide him in French. (Her
first real lover had been a Frenchman and she spoke the
language fairly fluently.)

Lanham sat there in silence, watching the back of
Hemingway's neck growing ever more red with suppressed rage
and embarrassment. Finally, Hemingway could stand it no
longer. He turned round to face his wife and snapped, 'In case
you don't know it, Buck speaks much better French than *you*
do!' That quietened her for a while (according to Lanham, who
naturally took Hemingway's side). A little while later Lanham
ordered the jeep stopped. He had spotted the jagged white trail
of a V-2 in the brilliant blue of the winter sky. It was heading
for either Liège or Antwerp, the Allies' two major supply bases,
now under constant German attack.

Martha Gellhorn, always the newspaperwoman, whipped out
her pencil and notebook and wrote down the time and place of
the sighting, saying, 'Remember this, Ernest, that V-2 is my
story, *not* yours!'

Hemingway waited until the tour of the command posts was
over, then he turned on Martha and told her that she had just
been as close to the frontline as she ever would be. He claimed
that she had made a lot of money writing about the war, but she
had never seen a man killed in action. As Martha Gellhorn had
been reporting the war since 1939 on three different continents,
the accusation wounded her, and it was made even more hurtful
by the fact that her husband publicly used his private nickname
for her in front of Lanham. For her he was 'Mr S', while she was
'Mooky'. It didn't take a great deal of intelligence on Lanham's
part to see the connection between Mooky and the then
commonly used slang word for vagina and sexual intercourse –
'nookie'. Publicly Ernest was calling her a 'cunt'.

On New Year's Eve, a week before the publication of his article
on the Battle of the Huertgen Forest in *Life*, Bill Walton

chanced to be in the correspondents' hotel, the Cravatte. Here he was introduced to Martha Gellhorn for the first time. She had just returned from the fighting front at Bastogne where she had written that, despite the battle raging there, the landscape had an other-worldly beauty – 'scenery for a Christmas card, smooth white snow hills and bands of dark forest and villages that actually nestled'; and it was there that she had thought up a 1945 resolution for the men who ran the world to get to know the people who had to live in it.

Walton thought Martha very attractive and they spent the late afternoon together. It was a beautiful crisp snowy day, with the bombers dragging the white vapour trails behind them through the hard blue sky as they headed for Germany. So they went tobogganing down one of the slopes of the fortress capital in the company of dozens of little red-cheeked, local children.

When he got back to the Cravatte, Walton found Hemingway waiting for him in his room, 'I've just been coasting with your wife,' Walton told Hemingway, 'and I'm going to take her to dinner.'

Hemingway grinned maliciously. 'And me too . . . I'm coming along.'

The dinner was not a success. Hemingway was savage and bitter and berated his wife throughout the meal. In the end, Walton gave up trying to calm the atmosphere, but when they were alone together afterwards, he turned on the writer and told him his conduct had been impossible.

'Willie,' Hemingway lectured, 'you can't hurt an elephant with a bow and arrow.'

Some minutes later, to Walton's astonishment, he started to strip off his war correspondent's uniform to reveal his dirty long johns beneath. While Walton stared at him in amazement, Hemingway went into the corridor, found the cleaner's closet and seized a broom and bucket. He placed the bucket on his head, as if it were a knight's helmet, rested the broom like a lance over his right shoulder and marched off to lay siege to his wife's room.

Wisely, knowing Hemingway's mood, Martha Gellhorn had securely locked her door. Hemingway lost his temper again. He tried to batter it down, while Martha shrieked, 'Go away, you drunk!'

The door was too stout for Hemingway and drunk as he was, he had not too much stamina. In the end he gave in, much to Martha's and Walton's relief. Tamely, he returned to Walton's room.

At the front, every single gun of Patton's 3rd Army burst into angry life. For twenty minutes, at Patton's order, his gunners were to plaster the German positions throughout Belgium and Luxembourg with rapid fire. It was the 3rd Army's flamboyant commander's unique way of wishing the enemy an unhappy New Year.

Alone in her room, listening to the thunder of the cannon only a dozen or so miles away, Martha Gellhorn must have felt equally unhappy. Hemingway's friend Lanham had once said of him: 'When Hem is nasty, he qualifies as the King of All Nasties.' This disastrous New Year's Eve he had proved that all right. Now their marriage was finally and utterly ruined. The two of them had no more common ground; there was no hope for them at all.

Despondent, saddened, overwhelmed by what she had seen at the front this terrible December 1944 and her husband's crazy impossible behaviour, Martha wrote to her editor at *Collier's*, Henry La Cossitt: 'Oh, what a world! To think that Our Lord bothered to die for it.'

GOODBYE TO ALL THAT

Hemingway greeted his brother Leicester effusively when the latter arrived at the Hotel Cravatte that first week of January 1945. Leicester was travelling with William Wyler, the Hollywood director of 'sophisticated movies', currently masquerading as a colonel in the Hollywood Irregulars. It was Wyler's task to get footage on the successful American defence of Bastogne. In the meantime Leicester, who was not particularly liked among the Irregulars because of his noisy enthusiasm and boring attempts to trade on his famous brother's name (Hemingway also thought he was 'a shit'), managed to get himself attached to Ernest for a few days. The latter told Baron with great glee, 'You are in the right place and on time'.

'Is it that bad? Leicester asked, thinking the Germans were still a danger in that part of Luxembourg.

'That's the wrong word,' Ernest corrected. 'Wonderful is more accurate. I'll show you the positions. How long have you got? I'll take you on patrol, and I'll show you point-by-point where the Germans came from and what we did and how everything is now. This has been a time from which to learn if ever men could learn.'

In fact, the 4th Division had gone over to static defence and was waiting to be relieved by the 87th Division. Tubby Barton had already departed for the States and his successor in command of the 4th Division, General H.W. Blakely, was not so keen as Tubby to grant the writer's every wish. The relationship between the Ivy League Division and its most celebrated propagandist was beginning to cool. Probably Lanham, who soon would be moving himself, had been warned not to associate so much with Hemingway. As his promotion in the Regular Army depended upon the 'Efficiency Report' signed by his superior, Lanham had taken the hint.

Still the two brothers 'went on patrols', as Leicester phrased it. Ernest told his younger brother how his health had improved in the last week or so and that Martha Gellhorn had visited him. 'Marty was just up here. Didn't go good. She's a real woman, but . . .' Most of their time together, however, was spent back in 'a fine hotel in Luxembourg'. Here, at the Hotel Cravatte, 'we frequently savoured lovely distillates' and 'wallowed in the warmth of cheerful surroundings late in the day, the drinks like dreams in thin glasses'. According to Leicester, when they returned to the hotel, Hemingway always hid his pistol because he 'had learned a depressing lesson back in Paris. Other correspondents, unless they were genuine friends, were out to get him.'

Up to this time one of the correspondents present in the Hotel Cravatte that January had been an admirer of Hemingway and his work. He was young Cyril Ray, a war correspondent for a British paper, who, like Hemingway, had been in trouble with the military authorities during the campaign in North-West Europe. He had borne arms, too, as a correspondent and civilian, by herding some German prisoners to the rear, armed with an empty sten gun. That had never been found out. But one of his dispatches had angered the American authorities and he had been promptly 'de-accredited', as the ugly official term had it. The British Army had equally promptly re-accredited him and now he was back in Luxembourg reporting on the Battle of the Bulge.

What he saw now of Hemingway, whose pre-war novels he had admired, turned Ray against the famous author. '[Hemingway] was pretty wrecked and drunken in those days,' he recalled long afterwards. '[He] swaggered around in a drunken stupor, waving revolvers. . . . His marital affairs were common gossip. Here, too, though, he made most of them for the sake of his bully boy image.' Ray concluded that 'Hemingway vulgarised the job of war correspondent for the sake of "Flash Alf" publicity. . . . He should have stayed at home and written novels instead of deeming it Papa Hemingway's divine destiny to liberate France single-handed.'

Although Hemingway was to remain in Europe until March, his days, both as a correspondent and as a civilian warrior, were over. When, on 11 January, the relief of the Fourth commenced, Hemingway returned to Paris where Mary was preparing to go to London for a while. The London *Time-Life* bureau was short-staffed and she had been ordered there by her boss, Charles Wertenbaker. So, just after successfully reactivating 'Mr S', Hemingway was condemned to a bachelor existence once again in the Ritz. But he had visitors a-plenty and he was also one to attract cronies and hangers-on – and trouble as well!

Once it came in the burly shape of William Saroyan, one of the Hollywood Irregulars. He was on leave in Paris and had come to the Hotel Scribe, where the war correspondents were billeted. Here at the bar he spotted Hemingway surrounded by other correspondents. One of them waved to Saroyan to come across to meet his fellow writer and said, 'Here's Bill Saroyan'. 'Where's Bill Saroyan?' Hemingway asked. Saroyan, who shared Irwin Shaw's dislike of Leicester Hemingway and was not particularly fond of his elder brother either, sneered: 'In London you had a beard, but even without it, I haven't forgotten you. Did shaving it off make you forget me?' Hemingway, normally only too eager for a brawl, ignored the insult and turned back to the fawning newspapermen, whose sycophancy Saroyan found 'embarrassing to witness.'

A few days later Hemingway had his revenge on the burly young playwright. Peter Wykeham Barnes, with whom

Hemingway had flown back in the summer of 1944, happened to be in Paris on forty-eight hours' leave. The 2nd TAF had by now moved to the Continent and in the latter part of January 1945 had wrought great slaughter on the Germans retreating from the Battle of the Bulge back into their own country. Now Barnes wanted to rest. He was not going to get one, for at the Scribe he too bumped into Hemingway. The two of them took on board quite a load of 'grog' and then adjourned to another of those luxury hotels Hemingway favoured during his sojourn in war-torn Europe – the Hotel Georges V.

Here they ordered dinner and 'everything was ringing like bells when Ernest espied William Saroyan sitting two tables away. . . . This worked on him like a powerful injection. . . . He started by stating, "Well, for God's sake, what's that lousy American son of a bitch doing here?" The more . . . I tried to hush him, the worse he got. . . . Finally Saroyan's companions . . . began to come back at Ernest. I'm not sure how it developed, but shortly afterwards I was in a full-scale brawl, rolling about under the tables and banging the heads of total strangers on the wooden floors. I got the impression that someone bit my ankle. . . . The management arrived, reinforced by gendarmes and the whole lot of us were thrown out *up* the stairs and into the Paris blackout. The two factions separated . . . Ernest was laughing like a hyena!'

In that third week of January, while Mary was in London, Hemingway received some good news from the Swiss branch of the International Red Cross in Geneva. The Swiss Protecting Power, which looked after the welfare of Western Allied prisoners in German hands, confirmed that 'Bumby' (Jack Hemingway) was alive and well and being held as a prisoner in Oflag VII. This was located on the saucer-shaped plateau of a large hill overlooking the little wine town of Hammelburg, where they had grown the vine since the time of Charlemagne, and out to the great wind-blown artillery and rifle ranges where German troops had trained for over fifty years. The camp itself was made up of two compounds. The larger of the two housed some 5,000 Yugoslav officers, including the whole Yugoslavian general staff; the smaller of the two held American prisoners, including Bumby, and many officers recently captured during the Battle of the Bulge, with at least two American generals' sons among them. The week before his receipt of the good news, a 'distraught Ernest' had told Leicester in Luxembourg: 'Bumby's been captured. He was on an OSS mission and got hit and picked up by the Krauts. We may be able to pull a snatch job and get him back. I'm getting more information.'

As Leicester Hemingway pictured him at the Hotel Cravatte, 'he kept pacing the floor and slamming his right fist into his left palm. What had him in his impotent rage was that he didn't know if Bumby would be treated as a prisoner of war or as an enemy agent. Ernest was determined to get his son back, but so far he had not even been able to find out how far to the rear Bumby had been taken.'

Now he knew where his son was located, Hemingway again began talking rather wildly of pulling a heist job, although how and with what he never made clear. Probably it was just drunken talk and when Mary returned at the end of the month, the idea was dropped once more, while Hemingway concentrated on 'Mr S'. But even as he did so, another anxious man (in this case a father-in-law), started to concern himself with the fate of his relative. The son-in-law was Lieutenant-Colonel John Waters, who had been a prisoner of the Germans since early 1943. Currently the young Colonel was part of a terrible death march from Poland, as the German captors herded their ragged, half-starved American prisoners westwards before the advancing Russians, to a destination which would be Hammelburg. The father-in-law in question was General Patton. In due course, 'Ole Blood and Guts' would ensure that

that heist, about which Hemingway had talked so wildly, actually would take place. It would end in disaster.

Meanwhile, just as the Russians were beginning to flood over the German frontier to the East, the Western Allies were starting to do the same in the West. They had recovered from the shock of the surprise German counter-attack in the Ardennes and despite the terrible weather, were striking back or preparing to do so. The final assault on the Siegfried Line, which had held off the Western Allies all winter, was about to commence.

Naturally, Hemingway's 'favourite division', the Fourth, was also going to take part in the great assault on Hitler's Wall. On 1 February 1945, the advance elements of Lanham's 22nd Regiment were assembling near Hautbellain in Luxembourg to prepare for an attack on the Siegfried Line beyond Bleialf, where that Regiment which had been decimated in the 'Death Factory' had attacked before in what now seemed another age. By the time Lanham and his fellow regimental commander Colonel Chance came to Paris to take their first leave since D-Day, the 22nd Regiment were in position near Buchet, whence they would assault 'the Verdun of the Eifel', Brandscheid, in virtually the same manner as they had done back on 14 September 1944.

Lanham and Chance checked in at the Hotel Crillon and then drove over to Hemingway's 'Command Post' at the Ritz, bringing with them a present for the writer: a pair of German machine pistols in a velvet-lined case, complete with ammunition. Mary, as always, was not particularly impressed by the two colonels from the Fourth. Chance reminded her 'of a small-town banker, a bit pudgy and conservative all around'. Lanham 'was sprightly, prickly'. But Hemingway, whose cheeks 'were already pink from excitement and champagne', did not notice his mistress's dislike. He insisted they should all have a drink. One drink led to another and, as Hemingway himself admitted a little later, he went 'a little wild'.

He started walking about the hotel room with one of the loaded guns in his hand. Chance and Lanham protested mildly, but they thought Hemingway knew how to handle weapons and felt he was safe enough. What they didn't realise was just how drunk he already was! As Mary recalled long afterwards: 'The boy from Oak Park, Illinois, decided he must demonstrate his appreciation of the present by shooting at least one of the pistols, if not both, from the hip. . . . Regretting there were no Krauts within range', he aimed through the back window shooting at an imaginary enemy in the back garden of the French Ministry of Justice. Now he turned on the room itself. He decided to shoot at the fireplace. Lanham stopped him just in time while Mary 'hopped around trying to keep out of his direct line of fire, my irritation mounting'.

But Hemingway was not to be restrained. He spied a photograph of Mary and her husband Noel Monks. He told Chance and Lanham that Noel Monks was being 'faintly difficult' about giving Mary a divorce and then ducked into the bathroom. Mary followed him, muttering 'Don't be a bloody fool' and 'watched in feeble, hypnotised revulsion as he set the picture into the bowl of his toilet and shot it with half a dozen bullets'. The toilet shattered, water began to leak out and there was instant confusion and consternation. Lanham grabbed Hemingway's arm and prevented him firing any more. The management appeared. There were curses and protests. The two colonels and Mary tried to mop up the mess with the Ritz's best towels. Hemingway thought it all a great joke and began a long speech in French, presenting Colonel Lanham, 'who will soon be a general' and who was a 'brave soldier of the line, fighting without cease since D-Day', and ending with a request to send him the bill for the damages. '*Nous n'avons plus de temps à perdre,*' he added. '*Il me faut une nouvelle toilette immédiatement, avant le matin.*'

Mary did not think it a great joke at all. Neither did Lanham. He told her he considered what Hemingway had just done was an adolescent trick. Later when they were alone, Mary, who now apparently had doubts about her future with this crazy drunken man, told Hemingway what Lanham had said. 'Hope so,' Hemingway mumbled. 'But a lot of people in grown-up jobs think of this adolescent as Papa.'

Although Lanham had told Hemingway that his 22nd Regiment was soon to start a major attack, this time Hemingway did not drop everything as he had done several times before to hurry to the scene of the fighting. Instead he started to criticise his former friends behind their backs. Although he would continue to address flattering letters to Tubby Barton for another half a decade or more, the General now became for him 'our lost leader' and he composed a nasty little parody about Barton based on a Browning poem, beginning: 'Just for a hooker of Bourbon he left us – For a Ballroom Banana to stick on his coat'. He criticised Bill Walton (also behind his back) for the *Life* article on the fighting in the 'Death Factory'. Even Lanham himself was not exempt for Hemingway's mean-minded maliciousness although the writer supposedly now counted on him as one of his greatest friends.

Having convinced his younger brother, who had always tried to ape everything his adored Ernest did, that he should apply for a transfer from the Hollywood Irregulars to a real fighting organisation, Leicester went off to the 4th Infantry. But Hemingway stubbornly refused to follow, although the 22nd Infantry Regiment was involved in very heavy fighting in the German Eifel. Instead, although he wrote to Lanham that he missed 'the double deuce' (the Twenty-second), and was bored by life behind the front, he continued to enjoy Miss Mary and the delights of Paris. On the same day that the Twenty-second finally took Prüm, the largest town in that part of the Eifel, which had been their objective back in September 1944,

Hemingway and Marlene Dietrich dined with Colonel Charles Codman, General Patton's principal aide, at the Ritz.

The General was in town for a spot of leave. But at the *Folies Bergères* he had been invited by Madame la Directrice, surrounded by her tall, half-naked beautiful girls, to come there any time he needed 'a rest'. Indignantly Patton had snorted, 'Jesus, I am not *that* old!' So he had gone off hunting instead, leaving his aide, who had lived in France before the war, to discuss Hemingway's books with the Master and the 'Kraut'.

Hemingway was pleased they both preferred his *Sun Also Rises*, which had once been so unpopular, and told them one of the real people he had characterised in the novel had challenged him to a duel. 'I sent word for him to come over to the Rotonde and bring his gun,' Hemingway maintained. 'Waited two hours for him but he failed to show.'

'Speaking of guns,' Marlene said, 'my driver was shot in the shoulder yesterday. Not far from Strasbourg. Most annoying.'

'German sniper?' Colonel Codman enquired.

'No, one of our sentries,' the actress replied. 'Very poor memory, my driver, never can remember the password.'

It was all good light stuff, the kind of sophisticated chat that the rich Bostonian, Codman, remembered from cocktail parties before the war. His boss, Patton, on the other hand, was only too eager to leave Paris and get back to the cleaner air of the front. He had contracted a bad case of the runs in the French capital and he growled to Codman that night, as he sat down gingerly in his chair, 'I was right in bypassing Paris in August. I should have had sense enough to let it go at that!'

Later Mary Welsh explained Hemingway's reluctance to go to the front and write about his experiences there thus: 'Ernest felt it futile to attempt stories which might get into print in *Collier's* six weeks after he had cabled them. Although he felt sure the war would be ending with an Allied victory, he could not write a forecasting piece that far in advance. His wounded head was stuffed to its walls with actions, landscapes, people, gestures and conversations, material he felt too important to spend in a weekly-forgotten magazine.'

By now Hemingway had made his decision. He would return to Cuba to write and, as he wrote to Lanham, to take care of his own regiment, which consisted of three sons – and naturally Mary Welsh. Mary Welsh, for her part, had not quite made up her mind that she wished to belong to that particular regiment. On 27 February 1945, she wrote her parents: 'This afternoon I'm going to ask for my travel orders, permission from the army to go home. The War Department in Washington has already granted permission. . . . Apparently there are stories circulating that I am going to marry Ernest Hemingway. . . . Until I get home and we can talk it over, please say nothing about it. . . . *It is not settled yet* [author's italics].'

Hemingway, however, was confident that everything was settled. Three days later on 2 March, the author went 'shopping for transport' back to New York. While Jack Hemingway still languished in Hammelburg, Hemingway's two other sons, Patrick and Gregory, would be beginning their school vacations on 14 March and he wanted to be home in Cuba to entertain them when they did. He found the transport he required that Friday in Paris. A bomber was returning to the States, carrying with it a VIP in the shape of General Orville Anderson, who had commanded an anti-aircraft brigade in England and on the Continent and who, on that December Sunday when Hemingway had ridden through the snow to the Fourth in Luxembourg, had been forced to abandon his Headquarters and his Sunday lunch, in order to escape being captured by the point of the 1st SS Division. Just before he departed on Thursday 6 March, Hemingway scribbled a hasty note to Mary, addressing her as 'Dearest Pickle'. 'I love you always and always will,' he declared. 'Now off to get our life started. Don't let anything bother you. I'm sorry to be so sticky getting off. Will be wonderful when I see you and will be truly faithful to you every minute I am away. In my heart and in my body.' He signed it, 'Your loving husband, Mountain,' and adorned the note with a large heart, complete with arrow through the centre and labelled, 'Cheyenne valentine'. Love and war going hand in hand right to the very end.

There was only one other thing to be taken care of before he left war-torn Europe for good – the question of his divorce.

On that Tuesday, when Hemingway landed in London and hurried off to the Dorch to meet Martha Gellhorn for the last time, the men he had left behind were still fighting. The 22nd Infantry Regiment, under a new commander now, had just assaulted yet another river line. This time it was the River Kyll, fifty miles from the Rhine. They were consolidating their positions on the far bank and waiting for Colonel Chance's 8th Regiment, plus the 70th Tank Battalion whose guest Hemingway had been that Christmas Eve, to pass through them. By now they had been engaged in continuous contact with the enemy for 193 days, and there were still two more months before the conflict would at last be over. By then the 4th Division would have suffered 9,359 battle casualties in killed and wounded.*

The Twenty-second's former commander, now Brigadier-General Lanham, was already on the Rhine. As Assistant Divisional Commander of the 104th Infantry Division, he was engaged in stamping out the last resistance in Cologne, Germany's fourth largest city. It had been cleared up to the western bank of the great river, which was the country's last natural bastion of defence. Now a dramatic little tank battalion was going on in the rubble right in the shadow of the great

---

* This does not take into account non-battle casualties and men taken prisoner. These amounted to a further 10,000. Thus, in eleven months of combat the 4th Division had a 150 per cent turnover in personnel.

Gothic cathedral. But the great Hohenzollern Bridge, which spanned the river to the left of the cathedral, lay in the water in ruins. There would be no easy way across. There'd be plenty of hard fighting to come before the Rhine was finally conquered.

Even London itself, two hundred miles behind the Rhine, was still under fire. On the night of 5–6 March, eighty German fighter-bombers had pulled a new trick on General Pile's gunners who had been defending the island now since 1939. They followed in a stream of RAF bombers returning from a bombing raid on the Reich. Helplessly, the anti-aircraft gunners of Pile's AA Command had to let them pass overhead without a shot being fired. Thereafter the Germans ranged far and wide, attacking not only RAF fields, but moving trains and road transport and naturally the capital, giving the 'Tommies' a taste of the kind of medicine the Reich had been receiving for the last months. And the V-1s and V-2s were still coming across the Channel, nearly nine months after Hemingway had spotted that first one together with Wykeham Barnes. By the time the last one came down on a sewage farm near Hatfield on the morning of 29 March 1945, Hemingway would be long back in his *finca* in Cuba.

No, the war was still not won this Tuesday as Hemingway made his way to the Dorch. Thousands of men and women were still to be killed before the horror ceased. But they were of no concern to Hemingway; his mind was concentrated solely on his personal problems.

Martha Gellhorn was sick in her room with the flu and Hemingway's visit was not long, but decisive. 'Though he had previously refused even to talk of divorce,' she recalled long afterwards, 'he then came to say yes, he would get the divorce in Cuba as I wanted. . . . I was intensely eager for the divorce so I could get my passport changed back to Gellhorn. I wanted above all to be free of him and his name; and step out of the whole picture fast.'

Hemingway stayed long enough to reassure Martha that he would look after her interests during and after the divorce as if they were his own. Then he went. He never saw her again. Soon he would acquire a housemaid in Cuba named Martha and after years of trying to dominate Miss Gellhorn, he took pleasure in giving orders to the Cuban Martha and have them instantly obeyed in a way he had never been able to do with her namesake.

A few hours later he was in the bomber, flying peacefully over the Atlantic, together with the General. It was very uneventful, save for a 'battle-fatigued radio bloke who got the screemies' a couple of times. Hemingway told him that getting over-excited did no good. 'But you can't understand,' the radioman replied, 'I'm going home to be married!'

Hemingway, who hoped that once the formalities were taken care of he would soon be getting married himself, told the man: 'I wasn't figuring on going home to be buried myself.'

That night he was photographed in the New York Stork Club wearing his war correspondent's uniform, complete with medals. It was the last photograph of him taken in uniform. Thereafter it was packed away in mothballs together with the author's other souvenirs of the great struggle. Ernest Hemingway's part in the Second World War in Europe was over.

A TOURIST IN A HELMET

But if Hemingway was finished with the war, the war was not finished with him, even in the Finca Vigia, his farm just outside Havana, Cuba. Naturally, he missed Mary, who was travelling to the States in a slow boat, and although he had promised her that he would shape up, cut down on his drinking and concentrate on writing, while at the same time putting the *finca* in order for her arrival, he was bored and depressed. It was not only because he missed Mary, however. As he wrote to Lanham from Cuba: 'It is a hell of a thing going away from the 22nd tho. It probably sounds wet but I was, and am, absolutely homesick for the regiment and I miss you very badly Buck, I don't give a damn about writing. Will have to get over that. Have gotten over everything else. Certainly have the Black Ass [depression] today. Miss Mary so much it makes me sick. Always before we had our Double Deuce problems and some sort of fight going on when I was away from her and I had your companionship. . . . So I am blackassed and temperamental – and no Grosshau to go to [to] take my mind off things.'

Despite this strange justification for going to battle – combat as a cure for loneliness and boredom – there was a more serious undertone to the letter: Hemingway's concern for his prisoner-of-war son in far-off Germany. As he wrote to Lanham in the letter: 'No new word on Jack.' Hemingway tried to console himself, however, with the remark that 'Have a hunch [he] will be OK.'

In the event, on the day that Hemingway wrote that letter to Lanham, 2 April 1945, Jack Hemingway was definitely not OK. In fact, he and the rest of his fellow prisoners from

Hammelburg were in serious danger and had been for the last seventy-two hours or more. With the end of the war only a month or so off, Jack Hemingway and nearly two thousand other officers of the US Army prisoned in Oflag VII were running the risk, not only of being shot by their German captors, but of being shot by those men who had carried out the daring raid to rescue them: an infantry and an armoured company of General Patton's 4th Armoured Division.

Five days before, at 9 p.m. on the night of 27 March, some 307 American soldiers from Patton's favourite division, the 4th Armoured, assembled in 53 vehicles along the bank of the River Main near the German city of Aschaffenburg and waited for the order to 'roll 'em'. They were under the command of Captain 'Abe' Baum, a big, husky, red-haired ex-pattern-cutter from New York's garment district. His orders were to break through the thinly held German front opposite and drive for 60 miles to Oflag VII and free the prisoners held there. Why, he didn't ask. As he would say later: 'They gave me something to do and I took care of it.'

In fact, his Army Commander General Patton seemed at this stage of the war to have lost contact with reality. The sixty-year-old General appeared now to believe he could conduct a private war without reference to his superiors. Keeping the purpose of the raid secret from General Bradley, he now proposed to break into Hammelburg and rescue his son-in-law, Johnny, for his beloved and only daughter.

The fact that he was risking the lives of 300-odd other young Americans to do so did not concern him one bit. If he succeeded no one would question his motives for having ordered the daring raid. If he failed, he could hush it up. To his chagrin he would discover later that neither eventuality took place. As his superior General Bradley would characterise the abortive raid on Hammelburg later: '[It began] as a wild goose chase and end[ed] as a tragedy.'

For forty-eight hours Baum's force battled its way to the camp, through a whole German division. Then the steam went out of his attack. He halted and contented himself for several hours with bombarding the camp itself. Waters, the man he had come to rescue (although Baum didn't know that then, of course), left the camp in order to arrange for their rescuers to cease firing; they were endangering the lives of their fellow Americans. He was shot in the process and now finally Baum moved. The wire of the Oflag was crushed by his surviving tanks and the POWs rushed out to greet their liberators; among them was Jack Hemingway, whose weight was now down to 160 pounds from the 180 he had weighed when he had been captured.

But liberty did not last long for the newly-freed prisoners. The whole of that part of Germany had been alerted to the sudden *Ami* breakthrough. Baum, his survivors, and those of the liberated POWs who had thrown in their lot with him, were surrounded on a height. The Germans attacked on three sides. Baum ordered his force to break up; it was every man for himself. 'Break up in groups of four and take off,' he commanded, just before he was wounded in the abdomen himself, his fly being ripped off by the impact of the German bullet. 'Goddamnit,' he exploded angrily, 'you son-of-a-bitch, you've shot my nuts off!' Thereupon he was taken prisoner by a German NCO, who obviously understood English for he laughed 'uproariously' at the remark.

Now Jack Hemingway, in company with several hundred of the more adventurous and fitter 'Kriegies' (as they called themselves)* from Oflag VII, plus the survivors of Task Force Baum, went on the run in the hilly Franconian countryside of that part of Southern Germany.

'That night,' Jack Hemingway recalled much later, 'we rode with our rescuers and hid at several road blocks where various vehicles were hit.' Every man's hand was against them and the

---

* From the German word for POW, *Kriegsgefangene*.

3rd Army was still many miles away. Troops, police, German Home Guard (Volkssturm), Hitler Youth, both male and female, were alerted to apprehend the survivors. The Americans, unfamiliar with the countryside and weak from lack of sleep and food, hardly had a chance.

'I was in the lead tank and it was hit in the front by one of these Panzer things [a German panzerfaust missile launcher] and I was knocked off the tank. A couple of friends and I decided it wasn't a healthy place and took off on our own for a week before we were recaptured.'

Together with the rest who had been retaken or evacuated from Hammelburg, as the American threat there loomed ever larger, he was marched, footsore, despondent and very hungry through Nuremberg, the ideological capital of the National Socialist Reich. Shortly after they had passed the main station, the long dreary miserable column of recaptured 'Kriegies' were attacked by their own planes, which killed some sixty POWs before flying away to their 'goddam ham and eggs', as one of the survivors complained bitterly. Fortunately, Jack Hemingway was not one of them. He survived and was placed in Stalag III outside the city.

There he stayed for another week or so before Nuremberg was threatened and he rejoined the long columns of Allied POWs heading slowly for the Bavarian–Austrian Alps, where it was rumoured the Nazis would make a last-ditch stand. During the march, Jack Hemingway and a couple of friends made another escape with the aid of old German guard, who wanted to desert to his native village. Again they were out of luck. They got caught. 'But this time we were caught by kids with submachine-guns who were very frightened. And I tell you, that was very spooky.'

It would be late June before Jack Hemingway arrived home in Cuba. But after the events at Hammelburg, the name Patton – 'an impossible histrionic character and unmitigated liar', as Hemingway described him in a letter to his editor Maxwell Perkins that summer – was mud in the Hemingway household.

Mary Welsh finally arrived in New York. First, however, she had to visit her aged parents and break the news to them that she was going to divorce Noel Monks. So Hemingway had to be content with telephone calls and letters. Again he complained bitterly that he was very lonely and that he was suffering from recurrent nightmares about the war. In one of them, he told her, he was surrounded by Germans, pinned down or killed by a direct hit. The war was still very much with him, whether he liked it or not. Instead of starting the great trilogy on the Second World War, of which he had talked so much in Europe, he tended to brag more about the conflict than write of it. Now in the bars of Havana, the number of 'Krauts' he had killed (122, or so he said) replaced the number of fish caught or game shot of which he had boasted before the war. After it had taken Martha Gellhorn three years to get him to go to Europe in the first place, now he felt he could insult anyone who had not gone to the war. Meeting a former hero and comrade of the Spanish Civil War, Hemingway could turn on him with a cutting, 'Oh, you managed quite well to keep out of the war, didn't you!' His servants were now 'my command' and in a letter written to Lanham he commented: 'I am not armed. However I can scare the shit out of all of them by looking at them.' All the same, he was 'just killing days and wishing I were a soldier instead of a chickenshit writer. Old worthless wish.'

In that same letter, Hemingway related how someone he knew asked: 'Ernesto, you were never actually under fire were you?' He answered, according to his own statement, 'Shit no! Do you think I'm crazy?' Naturally he and Lanham knew just how often he *had* been under fire and these people back home were just idle boasters who did not know the real face of war. 'I haven't met anybody whose [sic] been on less than sixty missions and the ground people have all slain more krauts than we ate K rations. Popular opinion seems to be fighting krauts is in the class with self abuse compared with fighting the terrible

Nipponese. . . . Honestly Buck, I think you had a regiment before Huertgen that could outfight any regt in the world.'

Yes, the war was very much with Hemingway then and even much later. Three years afterwards in December 1948, he would still be writing letters embellishing on his role in the great struggle: 'In the course of 1944, I also ruined my health, smashed my head up badly twice and came home in 1945 stony cold broke! So it would gripe . . . to have to pay extra for those days at sea, hours in the air, more than a hundred days in combat, Normandy, the Rat Race, Schnee-Eifel, Huertgen Forest, the Bulge. Fight smashed-up, sick, going up to the Bulge Fight with a temperature of 104, wearing a sheep-lined coat as underwear to absorb the sweating and another one over it.' And for all that, 'I was decorated with the Bronze Star, which was the highest piece of junk they could give a civilian and an irregular . . .'. But he was proud of his medal all the same, even though Lanham had advised him not to accept it in the first place.

For Ernest Hemingway back in 1936 (in his *Wings Always Over Africa*), 'the only people who ever loved war for long were profiteers, generals, staff officers and whores. They all had the best and finest times of their lives.' By 1945 his attitude had changed radically. He had enjoyed a good war. His war, limited to seven months out of a total conflict of nearly six years, had been short exciting spells at the front before returning to deluxe fox holes in two capitals, together with a new mistress, famous people, other writers and a glamorous Hollywood movie star who claimed she loved him passionately. As he had written to his son at the time, his life at the front in Europe in 1944 had been the happiest and most useful period of his whole life. He had been both participant, acting like a rather elderly infantry officer and indulging himself in his love of lethal violence, and an observer, writing and storing up priceless material for current and future use in his trade as a writer. But what had he made of it all?

According to Leicester Hemingway, brother Ernest thought there had been a purpose to the war. '[He] had had his first-hand view of the war and he said that it made sense. He said that the First World War had made no sense to him at all. Twenty years after the Spanish War, he said, the more he read and remembered about that one, the less he understood any of it. *But the Second World War made sense* [author's italics].'

The 'sense' that Hemingway made of the Second World War appeared in the form of *Across the River and Into the Trees*. It appeared in 1950, five years after the end of the great conflict, when Hemingway had had plenty of time to absorb, digest and interpret his war-time experiences between May 1944 and March 1945. It was his first novel in ten years and the only one he published about the war. It was a literary failure and one wag summed its contents up quite fairly, I think, as *Across the Ribs and Between the Knees*. It was a bitter, subjective, self-indulgent book about a disappointed, dying American infantry officer, Colonel Cantwell, spending his last leave in post-war Italy. Colonel Cantwell had fought in Italy in the First World War, as Hemingway had done, albeit as an ambulance driver. He had gone through the same battles, too, in Europe in the Second World War – D-Day, Normandy, the Schnee Eifel, the Huertgen, and so on – which Hemingway had observed briefly as a war correspondent. We can assume, therefore, that Cantwell's thoughts reflect, to a certain extent, Hemingway's own views and conclusions on those months he spent in Europe during the war.

Cantwell (Hemingway) treats the Italian servants in the Hotel Gritti, Venice, where he is spending his last leave, in the same way as Hemingway had treated the servants in the Dorch and the Ritz. He patronises them as quaint and servile, there solely to cater to his whims and play his absurd game with medals and military societies. Europeans, it appears, are only to be treated as equals if they are female, bedworthy and aristocratic, like Cantwell's highly improbable nineteen-year-old mistress, Contessa Renata.

Europeans are stereotypes and mostly contemptuous: 'Our British cousins, who could not fight their way out of a wet tissue towel.' The French were '*Vive la France et les pommes de terre frites. Liberté, Vénalité et Stupidité.*' The Germans were always 'krauts', as faceless and as uninteresting as that tasteless vegetable of the same name.* The kraut's only role is to die in a grotesque fashion and to be eaten by 'kraut' dogs and 'kraut' cats. Otherwise, the 'krauts were all professionals'. Another cliché of the war.

Individual, named Europeans are contemptible. 'Montgomery was a character who needed 15 to one to move and then moved tardily. . . . I have seen him come into an hotel and change from his proper uniform into a crowd-catching kit to go out in the evening to animate the populace.' Leclerc, the French General, was 'another jerk of third or fourth water whose death I celebrated with a magnum of Perrier Jouet Brut 1942'.

Cantwell/Hemingway's fellow Americans fare hardly better. Hemingway slashes at them left and right. Eisenhower was a 'high pressure salesman' who maintained his headquarters far behind the front so that he could be 'removed from contact with his working people'. The Army Commander 'had never killed in his life except with his mouth over the telephone'. Eisenhower's Chief-of-Staff, General Bedell Smith, was 'not the villain. He only made the promise [on the campaign in the 'Death Factory'] and explained how it would go. There are no villains, I presume, in a Democracy. He was only just as wrong as hell. Period.' Patton was compared to a lobster, 'with protruding eyes'. Unlike Patton, however, who was much given to tears when he was moved, the lobster 'probably never cried in his life'.

Everyone came in for stick from GI to General. 'GIs somebody christened them. God how I hate that word and how it was used. Comic book readers. All from some certain place.'

---

* *Kraut* is the southern German name for the cabbage family.

This was a reference to common newspaper habit of including the GI's home town together with the soldier's name when it appeared in their columns. Cantwell concluded bitterly: 'Most of them [GIs] were unwilling. . . . But they all read a paper called *The Stars and Stripes* and you had to get your unit into it, or you were unsuccessful as a commander.' So much for Tubby Barton and his admonition that black Christmas to Hemingway to give 'Bob and his outfit a good publicity play'.

Hemingway's fellow correspondents naturally were savaged. 'They were draft dodgers, phonies who claimed that they were wounded if a piece of spent metal ever touched them, people who wore the purple heart from jeep accidents, insiders, cowards, liars, thieves and telephone racers. . . . They had women at it though in wonderful uniforms.'

The last reference was undoubtedly to Martha Gellhorn and later in the novel Hemingway delivered a tasteless and transparent attack on her in her disguise as Colonel Cantwell's divorced war correspondent wife. 'She was an ambitious woman and I was away too much,' Cantwell explains to his unbelievably tolerant mistress who has to listen to all this nonsense. 'She had more ambition than Napoleon and about the talent of the average High School Valedictorian . . . she is too conceited ever to be sad, and she married me to advance herself in Army circles and have better contacts for what she considered her profession, or her art. She was a journalist.'

In essence, just as the author had been throughout his months in Europe at the height of the war, Hemingway/Cantwell is concerned almost exclusively with himself. The novel is used as a kind of psychiatrist's couch so that he can unload his hurts, his prejudices, the injustices which he feels have been done to him on the long-suffering reader. There is no sense of the time (1944–45), the place (Europe) and the people (both European and American). Hemingway/Cantwell is a totally self-centred, confused, bitter individual.

General Lanham thought it a 'dreadful book'. He also made fun of the title with a pun, *Across the River and Into the Cat House*. Before publication, Hemingway had asked him to go through a draft of the novel but he refused. Now he hoped 'to Christ I wasn't the model for Colonel Cantwell'. Hemingway had apparently told Leonard Lyons, the columnist and old friend of Hemingway's, that he was. 'From then onwards whenever my name was mentioned in a paper in connection with some damn thing or other, it would always be "the hero of *Across the River and Into the Trees*" and I couldn't abide the book.'

When Hemingway told Lanham that he was the hero of the novel, Lanham replied sourly, 'You damn well know I'm not, Ernesto, you know *you* are the hero of every book you've ever written', which was very true.

Of all the people who had known Hemingway during the war in Europe, Lanham was best placed to disprove the Hemingway legend and what went into the novel, especially about the events in the 'Death Factory'. As he phrased it carefully: 'People have told me what he told them about his wartime adventures, people of the utmost veracity . . . and I know what Hemingway told me, and they are totally different. It may have been the creative juices boiling in him. These things boiled around in his head all the time and then they fermented and eventually a story came out.'

Perhaps the most significant and revelatory aspect of that 'story' is the setting for Cantwell/Hemingway's bitter reminiscences of the war in Europe. It is the first-class Gritti Palace Hotel, filled with the post-war rich, 'fat and hard as only the Milanese can be', complete with their beautiful young mistresses. It was a setting very well known to Cantwell's creator for he had 'fought' his war from similar establishments in London and Paris.

His short stays at the front (18 days was the longest) had been spent at divisional and regimental headquarters, places generally regarded as not very dangerous. Thereafter, he had fled back to the comforts of those grand hotels with plenty of vintage champagne and their obliging, obsequious servants, like the ones who fixed the smashed-up toilet at the Ritz, 'toot-sweet'. What had the real Hemingway really known of the life of the average American GI and the ordinary European men and women among whom they lived and fought? During those months in Europe in the Second World War, Hemingway had associated with the 'feather merchants', civilians masquerading as soldiers, and staff officers at various rear echelon headquarters. The Europeans he came into contact with were either hotel servants; adventurers who attached themselves to his Irregulars when the going had been good, but who disappeared promptly when the winter snows came and the going got tough; or socialites like Lady Cunard and well-educated upper-class socialists like Foot and Malraux.

In May 1944, Hemingway had had an unrivalled opportunity. It was not one granted to his fellow American novelists, such as John Marquand or John Steinbeck, when they had come to Europe the previous year. America's foremost writer, who claimed the war as his own special province, had had the chance to go to the front in five countries in that final climactic phase of the Second World War in Europe. And what had he made of it all? Had he recorded the hopes, the fears, the worries, the sufferings of these 'little people', American and European, all around him? He hadn't. Admittedly, Papa had gone to war – under duress – when he hadn't needed to, and had added to that hairy-chested 'Hemingway legend'. But he had remained what he had always been ever since he had first sprung to fame in the late 1920s: the rich American, cut off by his money, fame and influence from the European world and that of the common soldier. An American staying in a grand hotel.

Yes, Papa had gone to war, but in the final analysis, he had been simply a tourist in a helmet.

ENVOI

'I have never been happier nor had a more useful life ever'.
Ernest Hemingway, Hemmeres, 15 September 1944

For those interested in such things, it is still fairly easy – even in 1999 – to follow what I like to call the 'Hemingway Trail'. Nearly sixty years on, the route Hemingway took across Western Europe in 1944–45, is not particularly difficult to find. The traces of the author's passing are everywhere. The Central London he knew is still pretty much the same as when he was there, although not as shabby as it was at the tail-end of the war. The ruins and the bomb-craters have long vanished. Naturally the Dorch is still there, although it is temporarily shrouded with scaffolding. Undoubtedly, in due course, it will be back in business once more, housing and hosting 'personalities' and 'royals' from Elizabeth Taylor to Elizabeth Regina, just as it once did Papa and Ike.

The National Fire Service's static water tank in Lowdnes Place has vanished of course, but St George's Hospital, where the author made his boozy recovery from his accident, still flourishes, as does the White Tower restaurant in Soho. It has not changed much since Hemingway first met Miss Mary there and although Mr John Stais, that obliging Greek gentleman, died in 1984, his widow still owns the place.

It is only when the searcher leaves London and tries to follow the trail to those one-time operational airfields, from which Hemingway in his innocence believed he flew on 'ops' (or was that, too, part of the Hemingway myth?) that difficulties are encountered. Dunsfold, Surrey, where Hemingway got into trouble with the local police on account of his V-1 souvenirs, has virtually disappeared, although there is still some sort of flying presence there in the shape of British Aerospace. They are as touchy about people taking photos as Embry's 2nd Tactical Air Force's security guards would have been back in 1944.

At Thorney Island, whence Hemingway flew with Wykeham Barnes to fight the 'buzz bombs', the situation is pretty much the same. The field has been submerged in the rebuilding of Portsmouth, which was so cruelly battered in the blitzes of 1940–41. For a while, however, the old base did help in picking up the pieces of 'Waste-More-Land's' involvement in Vietnam. In the 1960s it housed, for a while, the first wave of the 'Vietnamese Boat People'.

It is only, however, when you cross the Channel and head for that remote border area where once 'The 1,000-Year Reich' held sway, that you can delude oneself that this is the real 'Hemingway Trail'. Here, there is something tangible, unchanged since Papa was here in the flesh. It is Papa country. Naturally, just across the water, the places where he stayed are quickly and easily identified. At Madame Poulard's in Mont St Michel, the young cooks still make omelettes 'as thick as cakes' behind plate glass windows for all to see. Just outside Rambouillet, where Hemingway finally fulfilled that old dream of actually fighting as a soldier, there is a lone crossroads. It is adorned by a cairn of rough stones, a plaquet and the tricolour. It is tribute to where that 'jerk Leclerc' set off on his drive to liberate Paris. In Houffalize, Belgium, where Hemingway once told the bewildered natives he had never been promoted beyond the rank of captain because he could not read or write, that lean Panther tank with its iron cross bears witness to the fact that this tranquil square had once known another kind of more lethal tourist from just across the border with West Germany.

Walk along the heights on the Belgian side of that border and there it is, probably very much the same as when Hemingway first saw it back in that fateful September of 1944. The railway bridge over the River Our has never been repaired and most of the old houses near the one where Hemingway and Lanham celebrated their first feast on German soil are still roofed with the rusty tin the villagers put up there, when their slates disappeared in that winter of artillery duels and mortar barrages. *Hemmeres*!

'Schloss Hemingstein' is still there, too, but naturally it no longer bears that grand title. Now it's the plain old Markgraff house once again. Today, Bleialf, where Hemingway watched as Lanham's Twenty-second made its first attack on the Siegfried Line at Brandscheid, is a tourist resort. Where once the Twenty-second bled, there are swimming baths and tepee-like wooden cottages for visitors. What do these tourists, German and Dutch for the most part, make of the rusting pieces of metal still to be found in the woods everywhere thereabouts, or the old men in funny military-style caps with an ivy leaf badge who visit the area annually?

Grosshau, where Hemingway viewed his first 'roast Kraut', has been totally rebuilt. The spot where Pfc Garcia won his Medal of Honor in his last desperate engagement is now a parking lot at the top of the trail that the 22nd Regiment took. Go into the woods on either side and you'll find the foxholes in which they suffered and died, and where Lanham's 'magnificent command' withered away. At such moments, Hemingway's presence is very strong.

But of all the places along the Hemingway Trail, there'd be one, in particular, which Ernest would find especially to his taste. Of course, he'd find it hard to recognise the interior at first – it has been completely revamped. But if he swaggered through the opulent lounge, as he did that day in August when, as legend has it, he ordered '73 martinis' for his bunch of rogues, he'd spot the bust of himself right on the bar and know where he was all right – the Ritz-Hemingway Bar, Paris!

And I suppose he'd find a bar dedicated to him as good a place as any to end the Hemingway Trail. Don't you?

SOURCES

Book One

Chapter 1

Carlos Baker, *Ernest Hemingway: Selected Letters 1917–1961* (Granada 1981)
Carlos Baker, *Ernest Hemingway* (Scribner 1961)
M. Welsh, *How it Was* (Weidenfeld & Nicolson 1977)
J. Steinbeck, *Once There Was a War* (Heinemann 1959)
N. Longmate, *The GIs* (Hutchinson 1982)
Kenneth S. Lynn, *Hemingway* (Cardinal 1989)
R. Ingersoll, *Top Secret* (Partridge Publications 1946)
C. Codman, *Drive* (Little Brown 1957)
The Dorchester – The Renaissance (1989)
L. Hemingway, *My Brother, Ernest Hemingway* (World Publishing 1962)

Chapter 2

C. Baker, *Ernest Hemingway, op cit*
M. Welsh, *How it Was, op cit*
The Times, Obituaries, 1951–1960
J.G. Hughes, *The Greasepaint War* (NEL 1976)
C. Whiting, *1944* (Century 1984)
Hastings and Stevens, *Victory in Europe* (Weidenfeld & Nicolson 1984)
R. Capa, *Slightly Out of Focus* (Holt 1947)

Chapter 3

C. Whiting, *1944, op cit*
C. Baker, *Ernest Hemingway, op cit*
Office of Public Information, *History of the 'Dorothea L. Dix'*
S. Fuller, *The Big Red One* (Corgi 1986)
N. Longmate, *The GIs, op cit*
E. Hemingway, 'Voyage to Victory', *Collier's*, 22 July 1944
C. Baker, *Ernest Hemingway: Selected Letters, op cit*
K. Lynn, *Hemingway, op cit*

Chapter 4

C. Whiting, *Fire over Britain* (Century Hutchinson 1986)

M. Welsh, *How it Was,* op cit

K. Lynn, *Hemingway,* op cit

N. Longmate, *The Doodlebugs* (Hutchinson 1986)

The Dictionary of National Biography

C. Baker, *Hemingway,* op cit

E. Hemingway, 'London Fights the Robots', *Collier's,* 19 August 1944

Chapter 5

K. Lynn, *Hemingway,* op cit

J. Meyers, *Hemingway* (Hamish Hamilton 1986)

Ed. *BBC War Report* (Collins 1945)

E. Hemingway, 'London Fights the Robots', *op cit*

C. Baker, *Hemingway,* op cit

Hastings, *Overlord* (Simon & Schuster 1984)

M. Welsh, *How it Was,* op cit

A. Chisholm, *Nancy Cunard* (Sidgwick & Jackson 1979)

Book Two

Chapter 1

B. Jacobs, *Soldiers* (Norton & Ci 1958)

C. Baker, *Hemingway,* op cit

J. Meyers, *Hemingway,* op cit

C. Baker, *Hemingway: Selected Letters,* op cit

M. Welsh, *How it Was,* op cit

C. Whiting *Poor Bloody Infantry* (Century Hutchinson 1987)

Hastings, *Overlord,* op cit

D. Mason, *Breakout* (Ballantine 1970)

Chapter 2

R. Smith, *OSS* (University of California Press 1972)

Collins and Lapierre, *Is Paris Burning* (Pan 1967)

J. Meyers, *Hemingway,* op cit

K. Lynn, *Hemingway,* op cit

C. Baker *Hemingway,* op cit

D. Brian, *The Faces of Hemingway* (Grafton 1989)

Chapter 3

Collins and Lapierre, *Is Paris Burning, op cit*
C. Baker *Hemingway, op cit*
J. Meyers, *Hemingway, op cit*
K. Lynn, *Hemingway, op cit*
J. Keegan, *Six Armies in Normandy* (Cape 1984)
C. Codman, *Drive, op cit*
C. Whiting, *Operation Northwind* (Leo Cooper 1987)
C. Baker, *Hemingway: Selected Letters, op cit*
R. Smith, *OSS, op cit*
S.L. Marshall, *Bringing up the Rear* (Presidio Press 1979)
D. Brian, *Faces of Hemingway, op cit*

Chapter 4

M. Welsh, *How it Was, op cit*
C. Baker, *Hemingway: Selected Letters, op cit*
I. Hamilton, *In Search of J.D. Salinger* (Minerva 1989)
A.E. Hotchner, *Papa Hemingway* (Bantam 1966)
C. Baker, *Hemingway, op cit*
Nelson and Jones, *Hemingway: Life and Works* (Facts on File 1984)

Chapter 5

C. Baker, *Hemingway: Selected Letters, op cit*
C. Baker, *Hemingway, op cit*
Communication to author from I. Goldstein, New York
W.S. Boice, *History of 22nd Regiment* (Privately published 1959)
C. Whiting, *Siegfried* (Leo Cooper 1985)
K. Fagnoul, *Kriegschichsale* (Doepgen Verlag, St Vith, 1970)
W.S. Boice, *History of 22nd Regiment, op cit*

Book Three

Chapter 1

C. Baker, *Hemingway: Selected Letters, op cit*
M. Welsh, *How it Was, op cit*
Stars and Stripes, 24 September 1944
'War in the Siegfried Line', *Collier's*, 18 November 1944

A. Hotchner, *Papa Hemingway* (Bantam 1966)
Zum bitteren Ende (Kreis Bitburg 1980)
W.S. Boice, *History of 22nd Regiment, op cit*
John Gorth, *Studio Europe* (Vanguard Press 1935)

Chapter 2

J. Meyers, *Hemingway, op cit*
C. Baker, *Hemingway, op cit*
Interview with Cyril Ray
Correspondence with Iz Goldstein, New York
R. Smith, *OSS, op cit*
C. Baker, *Hemingway: Selected Letters, op cit*
C. Whiting, *Siegfried, op cit*
J. Meyers, *Hemingway, op cit*
M. Welsh, *How it Was, op cit*

Chapter 4

K. Lynn, *Hemingway, op cit*
M. Welsh, *How it Was, op cit*
Stars and Stripes, October 1944
M. Morriss, *Yank*, November 1944
C. Whiting, *Battle of the Huertgen Forest* (Crown 1989)
W.S. Boice, *History of 22nd Regiment, op cit*

Chapter 5

K. Lynn, *Hemingway, op cit*
C. Baker, *Hemingway, op cit*
W.S. Boice, *History of 22nd Regiment, op cit*
W. Walton, *Life*, 1 January 1945
Hohenstein and Trees, *Holle im Huertgenwald* (Traingeverlag, Aachen, 1986)

Book Four

Chapter 1

C. Baker, *Hemingway, op cit*
K. Lynn, *Hemingway, op cit*
W.S. Boice, *History of 22nd Regiment, op cit*

N. Hamilton, *Monty* (Hamish Hamilton 1985)

L. Hemingway, *My Brother, Ernest Hemingway, op cit*

M. Welsh, *How it Was, op cit*

C. Whiting, *The Secret War* (Century 1985)

Chapter 2

J. Meyers, *Hemingway, op cit*

C. Baker, *Hemingway, op cit*

W.S. Boice, *History of 22nd Regiment, op cit*

R. Collier, *The Warcos* (Weidenfeld & Nicolson 1989)

Correspondence with M. Milmeister, Luxembourg

H. Cole, *The Ardennes* (The Department of the Army, Washington, 1965)

Chapter 3

L. Hemingway, *My Brother, Ernest Hemingway, op cit*

Correspondence with Cyril Ray

C. Baker, *Hemingway, op cit*

M. Welsh, *How it Was, op cit*

C. Codman, *Drive, op cit*

J. Meyers, *Hemingway, op cit*

Chapter 4

C. Baker, *Hemingway: Selected Letters, op cit*

C. Whiting, *48 Hours to Hammelburg* (Berkeley Books 1982)

Interview with A. Baum

C. Baker, *Hemingway, op cit*

E. Hemingway, *Across the River and Into the Trees* (Cape 1950)

INDEX